"In *Preaching Hope in Darkness*, Scott M. Gibson and Karen Mason give us much-needed resources for how to preach, counsel, and comfort congregations that have been impacted by suicide. They provide preachers with what we need: solid research, practical wisdom, real-life case studies, concrete strategies, and an insistence on the hope of the gospel in the face of despair. Especially in a world like ours at a time like now, this book will be a gift to so many!"

JARED E. ALCÁNTARA, associate professor of preaching,
Truett Theological Seminary

"For those of us called the holy work of walking with others through the grief of suicide and for all of us who want to do whatever we can to prevent such deaths, this book is an invaluable resource. Well-researched, practical and encouraging, it will help you counsel, preach, and teach. The appendices of liturgies, bible study, prayers, and sermons are a gift to the church. Every pastor should have this on the shelf!"

MARY HULST, University Pastor, Calvin University

"Writing a book that integrates the discipline and art of preaching with the discipline and skill of the counselor is a rare entity. The reader will be impressed with the thoughtfulness and significant research that has led to the publication of such an important book for those who care for and minister to lives that are affected by suicide. Dr. Scott Gibson is a gifted teacher and preacher whose life has integrated the work of pastoral ministry with the reflective life of the scholar-teacher. Dr. Karen Mason is a teacher's teacher whose creative classroom teaching is enriched by her profession as a counselor. Both Dr. Gibson and Dr. Mason have their work well integrated with sound biblical and theological understanding. Certainly, every pastor will find this a very profound but readable publication. The case studies, sermons, and worship aids further enhance this helpful book. Definitely a must read for every pastor and counselor."

RAYMOND F. PENDLETON, senior professor of counseling,
Gordon-Conwell Theological Seminary

"This brilliant and practical book will equip and inspire you to preach the most difficult sermons of your ministry. An essential resource, it should be required reading for every pastor. This rare resource will literally enable you to save people for this world and the age to come."

KEN SHIGEMATSU, senior pastor, Tenth Church, Vancouver, BC;
r, *Survival Guide for the Soul*

T0285676

"This book is a gift to the church. Few issues are more pastorally challenging than suicide, and here we find a wealth of insights and resources to enable those shepherding God's people to be agents of prevention and to care well in the face of tragedy. It deals openly and honestly with the difficulties and complexities surrounding this topic. We learn from the wisdom and expertise of the authors, a preacher and a suicide preventionist, including findings from their recent research with clergy and the suicide bereaved. We hear from pastors who share knowledge gained from having to respond in heartbreaking situations. Case studies and discussion questions strengthen the reader's engagement with the issues. Above all, the authors consistently direct us to the hope of the gospel of Jesus Christ, a message that protects against suicide and provides comfort and strength for the bereaved."

KEITH CONDIE, co-director, Mental Health & Pastoral Care Institute,
Mary Andrews College, Sydney, Australia

"The hardest sermon I ever had to preach wasn't hard because of the exegetical complexities of a particularly difficult text nor because of the homiletical challenges of crafting the sermon. What made it hard was that I had to preach it to a congregation reeling with me in the aftermath of a double suicide. How I wish I'd had this resource to guide me then, and how glad I am that I can now share it with the pastors I teach! Having taught with both of the authors, I can attest that I don't know anyone who knows more about preaching than Scott nor more about suicide than Karen. Combining their expertise makes for an invaluable and unparalleled source of wisdom for preachers and pastoral caregivers in responding to the devastation caused by suicide."

DAVID A. CURRIE, professor of pastoral theology,
Gordon-Conwell Theological Seminary

"Karen Mason and Scott Gibson have partnered to produce a volume whose relevance extends beyond the preacher. It needs to be in the hands of every church staff member and seminary student. It is concisely written but offers powerful practical help in understanding suicide, working to prevent it, responding to those struggling with it, and ministering those who have been left behind when a loved one becomes a victim. The opening case studies and questions make the book a natural for a seminary classroom, and the rich footnotes point the way to other resources should one want to go deeper. The appendices provide guidance in addressing the topic in preaching, teaching, and pastoral care, with useful samples of sermons, liturgies, and Bible study outlines. Mason's clinical expertise and Gibson's homiletical/pastoral experience blend perfectly in this work. I am grateful to both of them for this fine effort."

R. ROBERT CREECH, Hubert H. and Gladys S. Raborn Professor
of Pastoral Leadership, Truett Theological Seminary

"Karen Mason and Scott Gibson have filled a void in contemporary pastoral care and preaching literature. This book is a unique resource to comprehend and care for God's people through personal ministry and broadly through the proclamation of God's Word in public ministry. It is more than a basic overview of the issue of suicide in congregations or solely focused on ways to speak about suicide—it is a practical blending of both. As most graduate programs continue to offer, on average, only one pastoral counseling course in master's level ministry preparation programs, this book is a must read for students preparing for ministry. It is also a catalyst for serving leaders who encounter the intense desperation of suicide. Mason and Gibson's format from page one is pastoral, practical, informed by research, and definitely realistic. Sadly, there are too many stories of clergy assuming that training in suicide prevention is not needed in their shepherding role. Because of this, lifesaving opportunities to bring suicide prevention into traditional aspects of church life are missed, and people of faith fall through the cracks in local church safety nets. The specifics found in these chapters can provide a guide for integration and, in doing so, contribute to breaking down the walls of stigma—shame and isolation—that can intensify suicidal thinking or cause people to leave their churches. Congregants assume their leaders possess the helping knowledge and models that this book can provide. We dare not avoid suicide and pretend it doesn't exist in our congregations. All it takes is one courageous step into the topic in a sermon or a conversation, and you as a ministry leader will say, 'It was worth my time to read this book.' People of faith want their leaders to walk with them through their dark valleys. This often begins through the ministry of God's Word. Mason and Gibson will help you to be more confident when suicide is involved, no matter what that ministry context may be."

GLEN BLOOMSTROM, director of faith community engagement, LivingWorks

"Pastors and faith leaders are in a powerful position to be conduits of truth and hope, especially as they message from the pulpit. The rise of suicide has challenged the health of our public and our culture, especially our spiritual and faith lives, in a way that no other public health crisis has. Like most professionals, most clergy have not received training because the translation of the science around suicide, how to understand it, prevent it, and help those who have been impacted by it, is so new and is just being converted into practice. *Preaching Hope in Darkness* provides pastors with direction, blending homilectics and suicide prevention, so they can preach with confidence, hope, and the truth on a topic that has been so misunderstood for too long."

MELINDA MOORE, associate professor, department of psychology, Eastern Kentucky University

"Gibson and Mason's work is both theological and practical. It's biblically grounded and application focused. Their description of building 'fences' through a pastor's preaching and teaching develops a useable framework for suicide prevention and intervention. The sermons, Bible studies, worship outlines, and prayers are valuable resources for postvention pastoral care. A much-needed text for any seminary student or parish pastor."

DENNIS GOFF, The Lutheran Foundation, Fort Wayne, IN

"As one who has done too many suicide funerals in my life, all I can say is that this is an invaluable resource that I wish I had years ago. The weaving together of mental health and pastoral care with worship and preaching is something rarely seen in one place. What a helpful and useful book!"

JIM SINGLETON, associate professor of pastoral leadership and evangelism, Gordon-Conwell Theological Seminary

"Suicide raises so many questions for the believer. There are no fewer questions for the pastor. Among them are the following: How does the pastor preach to a family and a church who have witnessed a suicide? How does a pastor give care in such a situation? These are very practical questions that the pastor must answer in the pastoral office. But he or she cannot approach pastoral practice without also considering the larger theological and sociological issues involved. This book helps the pastor in both respects. The pastor will not be left without resources for practice and theory in dealing with this very difficult issue. This book will be impactful for the modern church, helping the minister to do more effective and holistic ministry. He or she will gain some of the essential tools to preach with the light of hope in the midst of darkness."

RALPH D. WEST, founder, Church Without Walls

"*Preaching Hope in Darkness* integrates insights from homiletics and pastoral care to resource pastors with theological perspectives, pastoral wisdom, and practical aids to prevent and respond to suicide. This volume takes seriously the lived context of people wrestling with suicide and its consequences. It will benefit seminary students and experienced pastors seeking to join the dots between preaching the gospel and embodying the love of Christ in pastoral practice."

JULIAN GOTOBED, director of practical theology and mission, Westcott House, Cambridge

PREACHING HOPE IN DARKNESS

Help for Pastors in Addressing
Suicide from the Pulpit

PREACHING HOPE
IN DARKNESS

Help for Pastors in Addressing
Suicide from the Pulpit

SCOTT M. GIBSON
& KAREN MASON

LEXHAM PRESS

Print ISBN 9781683594116
Digital ISBN 9781683594123
Library of Congress Control Number 2020943018

Lexham Editorial: Elliot Ritzema, Matthew Boffey, Kelsey Matthews
Cover Design: Christine Christophersen
Book Design and Typesetting: Abigail Stocker

To our dear friends, colleagues, and mentors

For Scott: Kenneth L. Swetland
For Karen: Raymond Pendleton

CONTENTS

INTRODUCTION

Pastors are spiritual medics. We take the phone call,
then we grab our jackets and Bibles and head into the crisis.
On the way our hearts ache and pound
at the same time.

Lee Eclov, Pastoral Graces

THIS BOOK IS A CONVERSATION between Scott and Karen, between a preacher and a suicide preventionist, and we invite you, the reader, to join the conversation. We invite you to join because of our conviction that preaching the hope of the gospel is key to protecting against suicide.

The gospel is the hope given by the life, death, burial, and resurrection of Jesus Christ from the dead. This gospel is good news, providing forgiveness of sin and a new, changed, hope-filled life and perspective found in people's turning to Christ from their old way of life. Yet few clergy prioritize preaching the gospel in the face of suicide. In a survey of 258 evangelical clergy and their use of suicide-prevention competencies, preaching or teaching about suicide was one of the competencies they used the least.[1]

Preaching hope in the face of suicide is like finding the Mother Lode of the California Gold Rush. Miners unearthed this sixty-mile-long stretch of gold deposits in the early 1850s, but the gold was there long before anyone found it. Many preachers are like those who lived on this land before the Gold Rush—they sit on wealth without knowing it or not knowing how to access it. The purpose of this book is to point out the Mother Lode (what preaching the hope of the gospel has to do with suicide prevention) and show how to mine it (how to preach to protect against suicide).

This requires a conversation between two colleagues and friends from two fields that don't converse much. We are like Christians from two different countries who have the hope of the gospel in common but speak a different language. While most suicide preventionists acknowledge the importance of clergy and faith communities in preventing suicide, they may not have many conversations with preachers. Preachers may not strike up conversations with suicide preventionists until tragedy strikes in their church. But the prevention of suicide requires all hands on deck. Both fields are crucial to preventing suicide. With this book, we believe we can bridge the differences between them.

Scott is a preacher and homiletician. His theological and academic training equipped him to serve as a pastor and from there move into teaching at a seminary. His research has focused on various aspects of homiletics, including preaching for special occasions. After conversations with Karen, Scott became concerned that preaching was an unexplored area of suicide prevention. He began to ask, "How can a pastor adequately prepare a congregation for a tragedy like suicide? What can pastors do to engender the hope of the gospel in the regular rhythms of congregational life? What does a pastor need to know as he or she prepares to preach to the suicide bereaved?"

Karen is a suicide preventionist. Suicide prevention includes all the efforts of people from all walks of life working together to reduce the risk of suicide and increase protections against it. Her training as a social scientist means that she is immersed in suicide prevention research. Her commitment to Christ means that she is always filtering the research through the grid of faith and reflecting on how Christian faith intersects with what researchers are finding. She has discovered that suicide prevention research has much to offer preachers. For example, preachers need to know that there are suicidal people in their congregations who are listening carefully to their sermons, trying to understand how faith informs their choices. Shouldn't preachers know, then, that some suicides are preventable and that there is sometimes a connection between suicide and mental health conditions like depression? Shouldn't they know that romanticizing suicide in a funeral could foster copycat suicides? Suicide prevention research has a lot to offer preachers so that they are preaching with all the information they need. Ignoring the social science research would be like trying to open a jar with one hand.

While homiletics and suicide prevention come from different countries and speak different languages, both fields travel different paths to arrive at the same destination: the value and dignity of each life and the crucial importance of communicating this clearly. Preachers and suicide preventionists have common goals and commitments. This book will help you understand these.

What Is Unique About This Book

You may have read other books on preaching or on suicide prevention. This book is unique because it integrates the two. This book will help you apply what is known about homiletics *and* suicide prevention to preaching, the activity that is the focus of so much of your time and effort. Protestant clergy spend approximately one-fourth (22 percent or 10 hours/week) of their work week preaching (including preparation) and 13 percent of their work week (4 hours/week) teaching.[2] Preachers and teachers need this book.

Each chapter begins with a case study and discussion questions. We wrote the case studies to help you connect the book to the real world of your ministry. We know that you are engaging suicide in many ways, or will, and we want to reflect together on the intersection of your preaching with suicide prevention. Each chapter is rooted in the case study and will reflect on the case discussion questions. (While the cases are based in our experiences, all identifying information and details have been changed to protect confidentiality.)

In addition, while the book will draw from a great deal of homiletics and social science research, it also includes the research that Scott and Karen (with her colleagues) have done, some for this book specifically. Scott interviewed twenty pastors, suicide bereaved persons, and funeral directors. Karen and her colleagues have interviewed or surveyed over a thousand clergy. For this book, Karen interviewed three survivor congregants and surveyed 258 evangelical clergy and 370 evangelical congregants. This book builds on their latest research to make it accessible to you and to inform your preaching.

We have also included sample sermons, Bible studies, a bibliography, and practical tools. While the book is focused on preaching sermons and provides you with several example sermons, it also includes Bible study teaching ideas for youth pastors ministering to young adults and youth. It includes liturgies for both World Suicide Prevention Day (September 10) and for a suicide funeral. The appendices include many practical tools like a handout for survivors following a suicide, a response protocol following a suicide, resources for parents who want to support their student following a suicide, and a sample letter to youth group parents about a suicide prevention Bible study series. Our hope is to provide you with as many supports as possible in your ministry of preaching and teaching. This book was written for you.

Disclaimer

In this book, we are not suggesting that preaching will eliminate the risk of suicide in your church. Suicide is unpredictable and the result of a delicate mix of risk and protective factors.[3] A young person in your church may have all the benefits of a clear biblical concept of the sanctity of life but kill himself as a result of various other influences on his life. The suggestions in this book are offered with the understanding that they lower the chances of suicide in your church but may not eliminate them.

1

UNDERSTANDING SUICIDE

Everyone who competes in the games goes into strict
training. They do it to get a crown that will not last, but we do
it to get a crown that will last forever.

1 Corinthians 9:25

Case Study

LUCAS[1] IS a thirty-something associate pastor having thoughts
of suicide. These thoughts surprised him. In seminary, Lucas had
some struggles here and there, but he felt a connection to God and
his people. But after seminary, three things happened: first, his congregation put him on a pedestal; second, he lost the sense of being
a regular person connected to other regular persons; and third, he
stopped getting periodic, positive feedback on his performance. No
more "A+ Great Exegesis" on his seminary papers. That led to questioning himself more and more.

With more self-doubt came a kind of paralysis, so that he actually put less time into his sermon preparation (when he occasionally
preached) and, in his estimation, preached more and more poorly.
He didn't share this sense of failure with anyone because the church

had some conflict with the senior pastor and because congregants expected him to know what he was doing. Progressively, he started to lose interest in his ministry, sleep more (he even missed a few early morning meetings), have less energy, feel worthless as a minister of the gospel, and wake up early to rehearse all the ways he was letting the church and God down. Lucas didn't realize it, but he was severely depressed.

One weekend, after a difficult discussion with a congregant, he went home and viewed pornography. He believed that viewing pornography was a sin but felt unable to stop himself. He became convinced that the church and God would be better off without him. Then came the thoughts of suicide. They happened once or twice in a two-week period, then became more frequent, up to three times a week, especially after viewing pornography. As the thoughts became more frequent, they also became stronger and harder to ignore. At this point, Lucas was puzzled and afraid. He had never had thoughts of suicide and didn't know what to do.

In an effort to deal with this, he reached out to Harry, a friend and pastor from a neighboring church, who suggested he see a counselor. When the counselor first asked him if he was having thoughts of suicide, Lucas realized how serious the situation was and that he didn't want to act on these thoughts. With the counselor's help, he began to identify triggers for the suicidal thoughts and how to understand his guilt, as well as his sense of burdensomeness and lack of belonging. With aid over time, he learned how to manage these thoughts so that he would not act on them, until they gradually went away.

Case Study Questions

1. How would you respond to someone who claims that Lucas is "just trying to get attention"?

2. Why could Lucas not just pray or "buck up" and stop being depressed and suicidal?

3. If Lucas killed himself, how would you respond to someone who believed that suicide was either a selfish, vengeful, or angry act?

4. What is your reaction to the counselor asking Lucas about his suicidal thinking?

5. How was Lucas's suicide prevented?

Introduction

Does it surprise you that Lucas is depressed and suicidal? A study of depression among clergy revealed a rate twice as high (11.1 percent) as that within in a sample of US residents (5.5 percent). Clergy depression was related to job stress, life unpredictability, doubting one's call, and social isolation.[2] What is depression? Depression is more than just feeling blue. It is some combination of feeling sad, losing interest in life, experiencing changes in sleeping and appetite, difficulty concentrating, low energy, and feeling worthless or guilty. Lucas fits this profile. In another study, nearly half of a group of US pastors reported struggling with depression.[3] Pastors are not exempt from depression.

People of faith have struggled with some form of depression throughout time. Sufferers in the Bible included Rebekah (Gen 27:46), Rachel (Gen 30:1), Job (Job 3:24), Jeremiah (Jer 20:18), and some psalmists (Ps 88; Ps 102). Both Martin Luther and Charles Haddon Spurgeon struggled with depression.[4] Of course not all depressed people are suicidal, but one of the symptoms of severe depression is having thoughts of suicide.[5] Job (Job 3:20–22), Moses (Num 11:15), Elijah (1 Kings 19:4), and Jonah (Jonah 4:8) all wished for death. John Donne, William Cowper, and Edward J. Carnell were suicidal.[6]

Reaching out to Harry helped to prevent Lucas's suicide. But in order to help Lucas, it was important that Harry understood some facts about suicide and have some skills that allowed him to engage Lucas around this issue.

The following ten facts about suicide will show how complex it is. Alongside these facts are clergy skills that enable them to address this important issue. In a recent study, experienced clergy told us that they use these skills to prevent suicide.[7]

Suicide Facts

Fact 1: Suicide is a top killer

As of 2018, suicide is the tenth leading cause of death in the United States.[8] In 2018,[9] 48,344 Americans died by suicide (many more than the 18,830 Americans who died by homicide—the sixteenth leading cause of death). Among Americans ages 10–34, suicide was the *second* leading cause of death. (The first was unintentional injury like a traffic accident.) This means that suicide is an issue that will likely arise at some point in your congregation, if it hasn't already.

But a suicide death is just the tip of the iceberg. For every fourteen suicide deaths each year, approximately five hundred people attempt suicide, and three thousand people think about suicide.[10] About 8 million Americans have suicidal thoughts each year.[11] That means that many in your congregation and others in the United States have thought about, are thinking about, or will think about suicide.

Clergy skill: attitude. Attitude affects how clergy assess the seriousness of suicide risk and how they intervene.[12] If Harry believed that Lucas had the right to die or was just trying to get attention, he might not have gauged accurately how serious the situation was. But because Harry believed that Lucas needed help, he connected him with a mental health professional.

Fact 2: Suicide should be viewed in the context of mental health

Suicide often happens in the context of mental health conditions. This can include depression, anxiety, PTSD, or impulse-control disorders like substance abuse.[13] In a very large national study, the majority of people who thought about, attempted, and planned to die by suicide had a mental health condition.[14] If a pastor is suicidal, it is likely he struggles with a mental health condition, although not all depressed people become suicidal,[15] and not all suicidal people have a diagnosable mental health condition.[16] Most people with a mental health condition will not die by suicide,[17] although the suicide rate is higher among those with such conditions.[18]

Clergy skill: knowing your pastoral role. Clergy have told us that early in their career, they often saw suicidal thinking as only a spiritual issue. They missed the mental health condition. So they advised the suicidal person to pray more or to not kill themselves because it would be a sin. Clergy have told us that with more experience, they understand that a mental health problem exists *alongside* a spiritual problem. One experienced pastor told us, "You look at it from both sides—spiritual and emotional." Another told us, "We are not ignoring spirituality, but we can't ignore what is going on with the body." At this later point in their understanding, they focus on providing for the needs of the soul while *also* referring the suicidal person for mental health treatment. A military chaplain told us that where mental health and regular pastoral care overlap is "where the gold is." He continued, "Keeping the identity pastoral, that is what is unique. It is in providing for the needs of the soul, the combination together, taking into consideration the mental health issues, where there will be healing." It is important to recognize that Lucas is experiencing a spiritual crisis (guilt, self-doubt, and a sense of letting God down) as well as depression, and Harry can recognize both these needs.

Fact 3: Suicide is an attempt to escape from pain

When some older adults were asked why they attempted suicide, the reason given most often was a desire to escape.[19] Suicide is less about attention seeking, selfishness, vengeance, or anger, and more about escaping from pain. Lucas doesn't want to die as much as he wants to escape from the pain of his accusing thoughts and his depression. Some depressed people have experienced painful circumstances like child maltreatment,[20] chronic pain,[21] discrimination,[22] or divorce.[23] But painful circumstances are neither "good reasons" nor "good-enough reasons" for suicide. Many people endure these painful circumstances and do not kill themselves.

Clergy skill: theological reflection. When many pastors first reflect theologically on suicide, they wonder whether suicide is an unforgivable mortal sin that would damn someone to hell. Clergy also object to suicide on the basis of the sanctity of life and the preservation of the natural course of life.[24] But they need a theology of life to address questions like, What is a good life? What makes life worth living? What should someone like Lucas do if he loses the good life? Why should a person with diminished functioning stay alive? What are the reasons to keep living when an individual is in the midst of painful circumstances?

In addition, clergy need a theology of suffering to address the questions someone like Lucas has: Why doesn't God give me joy? Why do people suffer? Is a life of suffering worth preserving? Is there hope in suffering? They also need a theology of community to answer questions like, What is Christian community? Can someone exclude herself from the faith community? Clergy are crucial participants in suicide prevention because Lucas and others need theological answers to these questions.

Fact 4: Some suicides are preventable

Not every suicidal person reaches out for help. For those like Lucas who do reach out, suicide is preventable for several reasons. First, most people who are suicidal are ambivalent: a part of Lucas wants to die, but another part of him wants to find another way out of the pain and stay alive.[25] Second, not all people who are suicidal go on to attempt or die by suicide,[26] and it can take one to five years to get to the point of making an attempt.[27] The longer Lucas goes without making an attempt, the less likely he will be to attempt. Third, researchers know some of the elements that contribute to suicide risk and other elements that reduce risk and protect against suicide. Religion and spirituality can increase or decrease risk. For example, religious struggles contribute to suicidal behavior. One study of veterans found that struggles with God (e.g., they "felt angry at God") and concerns with ultimate meaning (they "felt confused about [their] religious/spiritual beliefs") helped to explain veterans' risk for suicidal behavior.[28] But religion and spirituality can also protect against suicide.[29] In one study, suicidal persons' faith gave them reasons for living.[30] The counselor helped prevent Lucas's suicide by discussing his faith. One of Lucas's most important reasons to live was his moral objection to suicide.

Effective clergy bring at least four specific skills to minister to a suicidal person:

Clergy skill: listening. Listening is a basic pastoral counseling skill that seems simple on the surface but actually is complicated. Early on you might hope that listening is like learning piano scales—just a step toward more impressive skills. But you use this skill every day, and it is critical to your ministry. Clergy told us that early in their career they didn't listen to people because they thought they had to have all the answers for curing the person, so, instead of listening, they would give advice.[31] One said, "I was rushing to find a solution, rushing to fix a problem before even getting a complete picture of what was going on in the person's life." Over time, they said they "got off the pedestal" of having to have the answers and would instead really listen and try to understand "so the person feels validated, so the person feels heard, the person feels I care." You improve this basic skill the same way you improve every skill in life: through deliberate practice.[32]

Clergy skill: risk assessment. Dreaming about a trip to France is different from making specific plans to go to France, which, furthermore, is different from actually buying the tickets to go to France. This continuum of dreams to plans to buying tickets is similar to the continuum from having thoughts of suicide to planning the action to acquiring the means to kill oneself. Risk assessment is trying to figure out where someone is on that continuum. The only way to assess risk is to ask them. Asking doesn't plant the idea in their mind.[33] Of course, suicidal people don't always tell the truth.[34] Asking is not foolproof, but it's the best way at this point to find out where they are on the continuum. Most clergy that we've interviewed[35] tell us that they developed risk assessment skills by getting trained through LivingWorks, the QPR Institute, the Connect Program, or BeNice.[36]

Clergy skill: referral. Many early career clergy do not refer. One pastor told us, "In the beginning I was a 'quivering mass of availability.'[37] I wouldn't refer. I overextended myself in terms of doing more than my role and exceeding my competencies." More experienced clergy tend to be better about referring because they see that suicidal people need treatment for a mental health condition or help finding solutions to their intractable life problems, and because clergy see themselves as part of a network of complementary providers who put their different expertise areas to work to help people.[38] But in order to refer, Harry needs a list of resources in Lucas's community. One clergy person told us that not having a list "is just about the scariest thing that I face."[39] An important fact to know about referral is that a referral doesn't always mean a follow-through. In a study of twenty-one countries, 45–51 percent of attempt survivors did not enter treatment primarily because they didn't perceive the need or wanted to handle their problem alone.[40] Clergy need to monitor follow-through with a referral.

Clergy skill: Sabbath rest. Experienced clergy know that the command to take a Sabbath rest (Exod 20:8–11) includes them. In the beginning of their career, clergy may feel guilty or selfish taking a Sabbath or saying "no" to a non-emergency on their day off.[41] After more experience, clergy understand there will always be someone in need and that their own needs and their family's needs cannot be sidelined. The reason Sabbath is so important is that caregivers who work with suicidal people report lower health scores than caregivers who don't work with suicidal people.[42] This stress can amplify stress that is already part of the clergy role. Protestant clergy have some of the highest work-related stress and the lowest personal resources,[43] and, as noted above, clergy are vulnerable to depression and anxiety. Sabbath rest is a crucial part of engaging suicide.

Fact 5: Suicide attempts are serious

One of the most important facts about suicide is that practice makes perfect. With each attempt a person develops greater ability to harm herself more seriously using more deadly methods.[44] That's why individuals who have made a previous suicide attempt are at higher risk for suicide.[45] One important fact is that some people require less practice. Among young adults ages 15 to 24 years old, there is one suicide for every 100–200 attempts, but among adults ages 65 years and older, there is one suicide for every four attempts.[46] Men also make fewer attempts before dying by suicide.[47] This fact should make clergy pay attention to suicide attempts. The other reason suicide attempts are serious is that the risk of suicide death is highest right after the attempt[48] and up to five years later.[49]

Clergy skill: take suicide attempts seriously. Following an attempt, it's important to make sure the person who attempted is

seeing a mental health professional or getting help with their intractable life problems and following through on all referrals. If the person
who attempted suicide is hospitalized and regrets not dying, tell the
hospital staff. Pastors at one church were sued (though not found
guilty) for not reporting to hospital staff that a congregant who was
hospitalized for a drug overdose still wanted to die.[50]

Fact 6: Belonging and meaningful contribution reduce the risk of suicide

Only a few effective treatments for suicidal behavior exist,[51] and one of
them can be implemented by a church: sending caring letters. People
in the United States tend to be more and more socially isolated.[52] The
US Surgeon General Vivek Murthy has said, "The most common illness [I treated] was not heart disease or diabetes, but it was isolation
and social disconnection."[53] Lucas was isolated. Isolation is a life-
and-death issue.[54] In one study, patients without a sense of belonging
used more lethal means in a suicide attempt and were more likely to
re-attempt.[55] Stronger social connections help people survive longer.[56]

Dr. Jerome Motto found a way to increase social connection. He
studied 3,006 patients who were discharged following a psychiatric hospital stay for depression or being suicidal. He followed three
groups: those who followed through with post-hospital treatment,
those who refused treatment after having received a non-demanding
letter or phone call on a set schedule, and those who refused treatment
and did not receive calls or letters. The call or letter "was limited to
expressing interest in the person's well-being"[57] and was signed by the
person in charge of the patient's care. A letter might say, "Dear X, It
has been some time since you were here at the hospital and we hope
things are going well for you. If you wish to drop us a note we would
be glad to hear from you."[58] A self-addressed unstamped envelope
was enclosed, and if the person wrote back, their letter was answered.
Those who were not contacted but still received treatment had higher

suicide rates than those who were not contacted and refused treatment. The contact group had the least over the first two years, though results were not maintained over five years.[59] Two ways to lessen risk for suicide are, first, to increase a sense of belonging, and second, to reduce burdensomeness or increase a sense of meaningful contribution (which we will discuss in the next chapter).[60] People who are contemplating suicide need to know that someone cares.

Clergy skill: community building. Silence about suicide reigns in many churches. More experienced clergy try to "change the conversation about suicide."[61] By bringing suicide out in the open, they try to foster a culture of congregants willing to reach out for help and congregants watching over each other. Clergy use the curative power of social connection to lower the stigma of suicide. They work to foster genuine, non-judgmental relationships with congregants in order to see how people are really dealing with life issues.[62] Clergy make sure that, following a suicide, family members receive the same care that family members receive following other kinds of deaths. Suicidal people and those left behind in a suicide need this kind of connected and authentic community so they can reach out for help without fear of judgment.

Fact 7: Suicide grief is more complicated than grief after other deaths

Grief following a suicide is often complicated grief, a kind of prolonged grief that includes distressing intrusive thoughts, inability to accept the death, anger and bitterness related to the death, detachment from others, and feeling that life is empty and meaningless. It can include symptoms of post-traumatic stress disorder[63] and depression with suicidal thinking.[64] Complicated grief occurs most likely when the survivor (the person left behind after a suicide) was closely related to the person who died by suicide.[65] Grief is complicated because suicide is often sudden, unexpected, and violent. What makes suicide grief particularly difficult is the stigma, which makes it hard "to disclose thoughts and feelings in a supportive context."[66]

Clergy skill: ministering to survivors. Clergy tell us that early in their career they didn't know what to do with grief and therefore offered very little follow-up to survivors of suicide.[67] One pastor said, "I would have treated [suicide] like any other death. No follow up, no pastoral care to survivors."

One reason clergy don't do much is that they don't know what to do. One military chaplain said, "I was more worried about saying the wrong thing … I was wondering, 'Do I hug them? Do I touch them?' I was missing what they were going through." Over time, clergy become less focused on themselves and more focused on the survivors. Another military chaplain said, "I am more focused on how the families are feeling. … I'm not worried about what I'm doing or if they'll reject me … I'm laser-focused on them and what they are going through." Such clergy provide the survivors with spiritual and pastoral counseling. They are willing to reflect theologically on suicide and to say, "I don't know," when asked how this could happen or why God allowed it. Such clergy avoid platitudes and instead acknowledge suffering as emphasized in Proverbs 25:20: "Like vinegar on a wound is one who sings songs to a heavy heart." These clergy are able to listen to survivors' guilt and anger and to encourage survivors to talk about their loved one beyond their suicide, because suicide is not the core of the deceased's identity.

Fact 8: It matters how suicide is talked about

In Vienna, Austria, only nine suicides occurred from 1980 to 1984. After the press dramatically reported on a suicide in 1986, thirteen more suicides occurred that year alone, and nine others occurred in the first few months of 1987. After this epidemic of suicides, members of the media consulted with suicide experts and stopped sensation-alizing suicide. Suicides in the metro decreased to three in 1989 and four in 1990.[68] Since then, several agencies have worked together to develop guidelines for how media should report on suicide.[69] These guidelines inform how clergy do religious services and other public memorial observances.[70]

Clergy skill: conducting memorial services. Clergy have told us that early in their career, when conducting memorial services, they were focused on themselves and "doing it right."[71] Later, they came to focus more on the survivors, knowing that survivors will remember this day for the rest of their lives. "There's no ideal or perfect way to do this. It is really just about trying to be the minister of help, respect-ful of [survivors'] right to grieve, a way to allow them to say goodbye, and bring a sense of closure to the person." While these services may never get easy, more experienced clergy use the service to educate the congregation if the family agrees. One pastor said, "It's okay to ask questions because God is big enough to hear all our questions and feelings." However, clergy also avoid (1) detailed descriptions of the suicide, the method, and the location; (2) romanticizing or idealizing the person who died, such that vulnerable people might view suicide as a way to garner recognition in death; (3) oversimplifying the cause of suicide or presenting suicide as the act of a healthy person; and (4) emphasizing that the deceased is now at peace from their problems such that vulnerable people might view suicide as a viable solution. It is recommended instead that clergy say something like, "It's sad that the person wasn't able to reach out for help; no problem is so great that it's not possible to work toward a solution."

Fact 9: Contagion and clusters exist

Suicide contagion is defined as "exposure to suicidal behavior of others through the media, peer group, or family."[72] An example is the publicized suicide of a young woman in 1839 at the Monument to the Great Fire of London, which was followed by a boy's suicide attempt. He explained later, "I wished to be talked of, like the woman who killed herself at the Monument!"[73] Contagion can happen when a church is exposed to suicide. The good news is that you catch a cold only when your immune system is weakened. Contagion happens to vulnerable people: adolescents[74] and young adults[75] with small intense social networks,[76] fringe individuals, or people who are depressed[77] or have attempted suicide or have lost someone to suicide.[78] Much evidence for contagion exists. For example, in Germany, a fictional six-week TV show broadcast in 1981 and again in 1982 depicted a nineteen-year-old male dying by jumping in front of a train. Up to seventy days after the first episode, the number of railway suicides increased most sharply among fifteen- to nineteen-year-old males (up to 175 percent).[79]

A suicide cluster is "a group of suicides or suicide attempts, or both, that occur closer together in time and space than would normally be expected in a given community."[80] There is much evidence for clusters. For example, "Fifteen patients who hung themselves in swift succession in 1772 from the same hook in a dark passage of [a] hospital. Once the hook was removed there was an end of the epidemic."[81] Another example: 19-year old Kiyoko Matsumoto jumped into the Mihara-Yama volcano in Japan in February 1933, and 143 people followed her example that year. A policeman stationed at the crater's edge was credited with stopping 1,208 attempted suicides in the following two years.[82]

Clergy skill: managing contagion and clusters. Clergy begin managing contagion and clusters at the memorial service but continue to monitor vulnerable people (described above). They offer to meet with the more vulnerable, they watch them more closely for suicidal behavior, and they provide them with ways to grieve and get help, if needed.

Fact 10: Faith leaders fill key roles in suicide prevention

The 2012 National Strategy for Suicide Prevention states that faith leaders have key roles in suicide prevention.[83] One important role is preaching. Professor Ferdi Kruger argues that preachers form the attitudes of hearers.[84] While he cautions preachers to preach the word, not their own words, he also asserts that "preachers have the privilege of wrestling with theological and existential issues raised by the congregation's experience in society"[85] in order to "equip hearers to be salt and light in the midst of the reality in society."[86]

Clergy skill: preaching. Through preaching, you can shape your faith community's attitudes to suicide. Jackson Carroll writes that "clergy give shape to a congregation's particular way of being a congregation. ... Through the core work of the pastoral office—preaching, leading worship, teaching, providing pastoral care, and giving leadership in congregational life—a pastor helps to 'produce' or at least decisively shape a congregation's culture."[87] One pastor told us that she preaches on suicide in order "to normalize it, to signal to the congregation that this is a safe place to talk about these types of things."[88] This pastor told us that she offers narratives of hope. From Hagar to Elijah, Mary to Paul, the Bible is filled with stories of people who faced all kinds of adversity, but who didn't kill themselves. Those stories speak of the role of faith and hope, but also the role of the community, in helping people find their way back to life.[89]

In their sermons, clergy are not "doing therapy from the pulpit." But they are aware of who might be in their congregation—they assume they have a suicidal person in their congregation each week. They think, "How would I intentionally address that one person?"

Summary

In this chapter, we opened with a case study of Harry encountering suicidal thinking in his friend and colleague, Lucas. We then reviewed ten facts about suicide and corresponding skills that clergy maintain to prevent suicide in their friends, colleagues, and congregations. We can't escape the fact that clergy deal with suicide on a broad scale. However, the scope of suicide that pastors deal with also suggests how much pastors can do to prevent suicide. In the next chapter, we will look at seven specific ways pastors prevent suicide in their congregations.

PREACHING TO YOUR CULTURE

If the church cannot speak intelligibly to [cultural] issues
and how Scripture informs our understanding of such issues,
then we're making the gospel irrelevant. Instead, people will
look to things like NPR or Fox News or Facebook or their
coworker as their primary source of discipleship.

Tim Chang, Gordon-Conwell Theological Seminary alumnus,
in a focus group on discipleship

Case Study

PASTOR MILES sits at his desk preparing a funeral sermon. This
sermon is especially hard. It is for the funeral of a high school youth
group student, Samantha, who died by suicide. She was popular and
well-liked at youth group and at her high school. She took her life
after her boyfriend broke up with her. Pastor Miles expects that not
only will her grieving family and youth group be there, but several of
her unchurched friends and teachers, too. Pastor Miles is struggling
to find a way to preach the hope of the gospel while acknowledging
the tragedy of suicide.

But what is making this sermon harder is that his state is currently debating a Death with Dignity ballot measure which would legalize Physician Assisted Suicide (PAS) or physician-assisted death. The debate on the radio and television is non-stop. The position in support of the measure claims that people have an inherent right to take their life and to request that their death be assisted by a physician. The argument is that there is no difference between PAS and a person refusing life-saving medical treatment. There is very little air time devoted to the opposing perspective.

But what adds to the complexity of preparing this funeral sermon is that Pastor Miles's mother was diagnosed with Amyotrophic Lateral Sclerosis (ALS) two years ago. He and his brother are helping with the medical bills for her care, but they are running out of money. His mother has begged numerous times to "just let me go." Pastor Miles is sure that the death of a young woman with her life ahead of her is morally wrong but not so sure what he believes about the best way to care for his mother.

Case Study Questions

1. What is the difference between Samantha's suicide and the physician-assisted suicide of a terminally ill person?

2. What does the church have to offer the public discussion?

3. How much should Pastor Miles's own experiences with his mother affect his position on the debate?

4. How does Pastor Miles negotiate cultural messages in his sermon?

5. How does emotionally-charged public debate influence sermon writing?

Introduction

While we were initially working on this book, Netflix released 13 *Reasons Why*, a series about why a high schooler, Hannah, kills herself (more seasons have been released since then). The series presents suicide as a reasonable choice, and it also portrays bullying, teen sex, underage drinking and drug use, fast driving, fist fighting, lying to parents, parental neglect, teen homelessness, a copycat suicide, *graphic* portrayals of a car death, and two rapes. Those are at least thirteen reasons why Christians should object to the series. But we also notice the uproar against the series from many people in our culture, not just from Christians. Voices in our culture are for and against suicide. Cultural voices are blended with our own experiences.

My (Scott's) aunt died by suicide. As a pastor, and now a seminary professor, I cannot ignore the ravages of suicide. In each one of these capacities—family member, pastor, and seminary professor—the specter of suicide has visited my life.

My aunt was a delightful, humorous, lovely woman. Her death by suicide was a dark cloud that hung over the family. No one, even to this day, wants to recognize her death as it was, a horrific taking of her life. I can recall my conversation with the pastor at the funeral. He said heavily, "This family needs help." I knew it, but few others wanted to come to that realization. The family needed not just help; the family needed the Lord.

I encountered suicide in both the pastorate and seminary. One seminary student, a young woman from overseas, was deeply depressed. She came from wealth, receiving money regularly from her family, who rejected her new-found faith in Christ. After her tragic death, large amounts of cash in unopened envelopes were found in the small trash cans in her room. The death cast a thick fog over the seminary community, raising questions about how this happened and what could have been done to prevent it.

In preaching about suicide, it is important to recognize that congregants are members of cultures with perspectives on suicide and that they have their own experiences with suicide. We cannot ignore the ongoing narrative of suicide in cultural conversation. Focus on suicide is not new to the current generation but stretches backward through the generations that have brought us to where we are today. From Saul and Samson in the pages of the Bible to Cleopatra to Arria, wife of Caecina Paetus, who stabbed herself upon the suicide of her husband, to Ernest Hemingway to Robin Williams, deaths by suicide capture the imagination of every age.

Cases of suicide can be found in literature through the ages. For example, Shakespeare writes of suicide in *Hamlet*. His jilted lover Ophelia drowns. *Romeo and Juliet* contains a double suicide. Tolstoy's Anna Karenina dies by throwing herself under a train. Virginia Woolf portrays the suicide death of Septimus Warren Smith in *Mrs. Dalloway*. More currently, in Jan Karon's *To Be Where You Are*, the character Avis Packard remains haunted into his seventies by the suicide death of his mother.[1]

Suicide shows up in popular films. A prime example is the classic film *It's a Wonderful Life*, where the guardian angel Clarence Odbody is summoned to help George Bailey on earth. In heaven when he's about to receive his assignment, Odbody asked the senior angel if George is sick. "No," replies the senior angel, "worse, he's discouraged." The story unfolds to show a hopeless George Bailey about to take his life by jumping off a bridge. But George's guardian angel cuts off George by jumping into the water first—and George saves him. Odbody shows George that he has friends who care for him more than he knows.[2] Other films include *Vertigo* (1958), *Harold and Maude* (1971), *Ordinary People* (1980), *The Big Chill* (1983), *Leaving Las Vegas* (1995), *The Artist* (2011) and *Three Billboards Outside Ebbing, Missouri* (2017).

Suicide and the language of suicide are prevalent in culture, and as pastors we want to sharpen our awareness and become increasingly free to address the matter and more comfortable ministering into it.

One Christian response to culture has been to withdraw from it. However, while our citizenship is in heaven (Phil 3:19–20; Col 3:1–4), we are to be salt and light in our culture (Matt 5:13–16) and to work for the welfare of our cities (Jer 29:7). Christians participate with unbelievers who are blessed by God's common grace to work in the world to curb the destructive power of sin, maintain the moral order of the universe, and help to preserve an orderly life.[3]

So how can we in the church relate to cultural voices about suicide? What do we affirm and what do we reject? How do we stand with unbelievers in our culture who reject suicide? The first step is to understand what culture is saying, and the second is to respond in a way that glorifies God. Regarding how pastors in particular can help shape a congregation's response to culture, Jackson Carroll writes, "The pastor's calling is to use her or his gifts and training to help members discover how biblical teachings and the church's traditions and practices apply to their lives and help them to face the challenges of the social and cultural context in which they live."[4]

Voices in the Culture for Suicide

For the sake of this chapter, we'll focus on three common beliefs about suicide in our culture, though it will be clear that these concepts are related. The three beliefs are: suicide is justified when life is painful; people should be free to live out their truth authentically; and people are valuable if productive and burdensome if not productive.

Suicide is justified when life is painful

The first belief is that suicide is justified when life is painful, either physically or emotionally. This message has been communicated through series like *13 Reasons Why* and whenever a person in pain dies by suicide. As Montaigne writes, "History is full of those who by a thousand ways have exchanged a painful and irksome life for death."[5] Around 1250 BC, Rameses the Great, an Egyptian pharaoh, killed himself because he lost his sight.[6] In 30 BC, Marc Antony and Cleopatra killed themselves when Octavian's forces triumphed.[7] In AD 73, 960 Jews died by suicide at Masada to avoid Roman domination.[8] In 1941, Virginia Woolf killed herself in the context of worsening mental health.[9] Arthur and Cynthia Koestler killed themselves March 1, 1983. Arthur Koestler had been suffering from Parkinson's Disease and "the slow-killing variety of leukemia."[10] He wrote, "After a more or less steady physical decline over the last years, the process has now reached an acute state with added complications which make it advisable to seek self-deliverance now, before I become technically incapable of making the necessary arrangements."[11] Robin Williams, who suffered from Lewy body dementia,[12] died by suicide in 2014. Aaron Hernandez of the New England Patriots killed himself in 2017 while serving life in prison for murder.[13]

The exposure to the suicides of people in pain is endemic: Sophocles' Antigone, Goethe's Werther (*The Sorrows of Young Werther*), Flaubert's Emma Bovary (*Madame Bovary*), Tolstoy's Anna Karenina, Dostoyevsky's Smerdyakov (*The Brothers Karamazov*) and Svidrigailov (*Crime and Punishment*), Shakespeare's Romeo and Juliet, Othello, Portia (*Julius Caesar*), and Lady Macbeth, opera's Floria (*Tosca*), Brünnhilde (*Götterdämmerung*), Gilda (*Rigoletto*) and Aida, and film's Thelma and Louise, Russell Casse in *Independence Day*, Maggie in *Million Dollar Baby*, and Will Traynor in *Me before You*. We read in history that hari-kiri among the warrior class in Japan provided an honorable way of escaping the painful shame of wrong-doing,[14] similar to the suicide of Judas (Matt 27:5).

This widespread exposure might convey the message that suicide is justifiable when people are in pain. Related to this perspective is that suicide is justifiable philosophically and, in the name of tolerance for diverse perspectives, people should be free to live out their truth authentically.

People should be free to live out their truth authentically

Suicide has been justified for as long as people have been writing about it. The Babylonian *Dialogue of Pessimism,* written around 2500 BC, concludes that the meaninglessness of life must logically result in suicide:

> Now then what is good?
> To break my neck and thy neck,
> To fall into the river is good.[15]

In the fifth to third centuries BC, Greek Cynic, Stoic, and Epicurean philosophies upheld the right to suicide if a person was unable to live by their principles (or in the case of severe pain or disease).[16] For example, a Stoic saying was, *"Mori licet cui vivere non placet"* (He is at liberty to die who does not wish to live). [17] During the Renaissance, Greek and Roman philosophy was recovered,[18] and some Renaissance philosophers argued for the rational right to suicide on the basis of human liberty.[19] For example, Montaigne wrote, "Living is slavery if the liberty of dying be wanting."[20] David Hume wrote, "That suicide may often be consistent with interest and with our duty to ourselves, no one can question."[21] In the nineteenth century, Schopenhauer wrote, "It is perfectly clear that no one has such indisputable right over anything in the world as over his own person and life."[22] The existential poet Williams Carlos Williams writes, "The perfect type of the man of action is the suicide."[23] Jérôme Paturot wrote, "A suicide establishes a man. Alive one is nothing; dead one becomes a hero. ... I must decidedly make my preparations."[24] Albert Camus wrote, "There is but one truly serious philosophical problem, and that is suicide. Judging whether life is or is not worth living amounts to answering the fundamental question of philosophy."[25] Certain cultures have sanctioned suicide. Schopenhauer reminds us of the practice of *sati* by Hindu widows or the practice of giving oneself to the crocodiles in the Ganges.[26]

Some use suicide to communicate a point. In the eighteenth century, the "Lovers of Lyons" were not allowed to marry, so they shot each other simultaneously.[27] Jan Palach burned himself to death in Prague in 1969 to protest the Soviet invasion of Czechoslovakia.[28] Thích Quảng Đức, a Vietnamese Mahayana Buddhist monk, burned himself to death in Saigon in 1963 to protest the persecution of Buddhists by South Vietnam's government. Jim Jones said of the 914 adherents to Jim Jones' People's Temple who killed themselves in 1978,[29] "We are not committing suicide; we are committing a revolutionary act."[30] Modern suicide bombers act out their community's "unceasing despair,"[31] their community's inability to go on the offensive in any other way.

This cultural voice has conveyed the message that suicide is justifiable philosophically and that we ought to tolerantly support divergent perspectives. Another concerning cultural message is that people are of value only if they are productive.

People are valuable if productive and burdensome if not productive

"Death with dignity" movements suggest that suffering people lose their dignity when they lose physical and mental capacities and become a burden to others. The underlying belief is that people who are unable to contribute in productive ways lose something human. The loss of dignity is so painful that it justifies suicide. The argument is that these people deserve to have the legal option to die with the help of a doctor. These movements might support physician-assisted suicide (PAS), which is defined as a doctor assisting a patient to take his or her life, or euthanasia, which is defined as the active, intentional termination of a patient's life by a doctor who thinks that death is a benefit to that patient. It includes either acts of commission (lethally injecting a patient), or omission (withdrawing tube feeding).[32]

Five states now allow PAS (or have Death with Dignity Acts): Oregon (1994/1997), Washington (2008), Vermont (2013), California (2016), and Colorado (2016).

Voices in the Culture Against Suicide

Though there is widespread consent for suicide among culture, there are also voices in culture that condemn it. In response to each of the above common beliefs, here are some dissenting views.

Suicide is justified when life is painful

Many well-known people throughout history, both Christian and not, lived with painful limitations yet did not kill themselves: Beethoven (deafness), Abraham Lincoln (depression), Franklin D. Roosevelt (paralysis), Helen Keller (deafness and blindness), John Nash (schizophrenia), Marlee Matlin (deafness), and Temple Grandin (autism), to name a few. Philosophers who argued for suicide (e.g., Montaigne, Hume, and Schopenhauer) didn't kill themselves despite their own physical suffering. Shakespeare's Hamlet contemplates suicide ("to be, or not to be") but does not kill himself. In Mozart's opera *The Magic Flute*, Pamina and Papageno do not kill themselves but find other solutions to their problems. The response to the Netflix series *13 Reasons Why* has been a "sizeable uproar," with "warning emails from schools, complaints from mental health professionals and concerns from parents."[33] Film characters like Conrad in *Ordinary People*, Ron in *Born on the Fourth of July*, Lieutenant Dan in *Forrest Gump*, Grace in *The Horse Whisperer*, and King George VI in *The King's Speech* choose life despite their suffering.

Chesley B. "Sully" Sullenberger, who became famous for landing a plane on the Hudson River after both engines were disabled, has spoken out about his family's pain since his father's suicide. Sully has made public service announcements where he recommends reaching out to the National Suicide Prevention Lifeline, so that "others can be spared the pain that suicide inflicts on victims and those they leave behind."[34] He wants to share his story because "it's time to bring the discussion about this crisis facing so many families into the open."

Other voices in our culture are raised against suicide. Signs on bridges urge people in crisis to call hotlines. People have gathered into suicide prevention coalitions. States have funded suicide prevention offices (e.g., the Office of Suicide Prevention in Colorado, which began in August 2000) or suicide prevention plans. Many voices are raised against the social ills that create vulnerability to suicide such as bullying, hazing, and stigma against mental illness. Preventing suicide and these other ills have become part of the social discourse. These cultural voices are against suicide for people in pain, but there are also philosophical voices against suicide.

People should be free to live out their truth authentically

Not all philosophers have supported suicide. In the seventeenth century, Thomas Hobbes claimed in *Leviathan* that natural law forbids a person from doing "that which is destructive of his life, or taketh away the means of preserving the same."[35] In the eighteenth century, Immanuel Kant argued against suicide in *Grounding for The Metaphysics of Morals*: "The one who has suicide in mind will ask himself whether his action could subsist together with the idea of humanity *as an end in itself*."[36] In the nineteenth century, John Stuart Mill in *On Liberty* argued that suicide prevents further free choices: "The principle of freedom cannot require that he should be free not to be free. It is not freedom, to be allowed to alienate his freedom."[37] In the twentieth century, existentialists Jean-Paul Sartre and Albert Camus expressed personal disagreement with suicide.[38]

Emiko Ohnuki-Tierney refutes the perspective that kamikaze pilots were voluntarily making a political point. She uncovered their journal writings, "in the hope that such a colossal tragedy would not happen again in Japan or elsewhere."[39] She refutes the perspective of Onishi Takijiro, a navy vice-admiral, who alleged that "the Japanese soul ... was believed to uniquely possess the strength to face death without hesitation"[40] by testifying to the soldiers' agony over their impending death. For example, Hayashi Tadao wrote on November 26, 1940, "I do not want to die! ... I want to live!"[41]

Cultural voices can also be found against Death with Dignity movements, as we will see below.

People are of value only if productive and are burdensome if not productive

Research has shown that while the focus of PAS movements is on dignity, it is often the case that people who seek PAS or euthanasia suffer from deteriorating mental health. Mark Williams has noted that Koestler, journalist and author of *Darkness at Noon*, suffered from depression, mania, and hallucinations at the time of his death.[42] Herbert Hendin, a physician and suicide prevention expert, has argued that people who request PAS experience panic, which is treatable:

> When that panic is addressed it usually subsides, and the request for death disappears. When the panic is not addressed but rather hidden by both doctor and patient behind the slogan of "death with dignity" or when the request is rationalized as the "autonomous" desire of an individual, the patient dies in a state of unrecognized terror.[43]

Jack Kevorkian gained infamy in the 1990s as an advocate for and performer of PAS. Kalman Kaplan and Matthew Schwartz conducted interviews with family and friends of the deceased of ninety-three of Kevorkian's physician-assisted suicides. They found that more than one-third (37 percent) of the decedents for whom depression data was available (the first 47 cases) were described as depressed. This percentage was higher for women (40 percent) than for men (30 percent).[44] Other researchers have found that patients who requested PAS had higher levels of depression, hopelessness, and dismissive attachment, and lower levels of spirituality.[45]

Still other researchers have found that people who request PAS are not depressed but fear becoming a burden.[46] Kaplan and Schwartz, for example, found that 90 percent of Kevorkian's initial cases declared that "they had a high fear of dependence on others in their disabled condition."[47] Linda Ganzini and colleagues studied patients with ALS who were interested in PAS and found that they had greater distress at being a burden than ALS patients not interested in PAS.[48] In another study among hospice patients who refused food and fluids to hasten death, pointlessness and meaningless in life were the main motivations.[49] In another study, patients who requested physician-assisted suicide valued control, dreaded dependence on others, were ready to die, and assessed their quality of life as poor.[50] E. D. Pellegrino found that much of the suffering of dying patients comes from "being subtly treated as nonpersons."[51]

This research suggests that making a decision to kill oneself is not a rational decision related to maintaining one's dignity. It is also important to note that only five states have enacted Death with Dignity acts; many others have not. Fewer countries support Death with Dignity legislation than do not. Even apart from distinctly Christian arguments for human dignity, this is not a settled issue.

Christian Voices Against Suicide

Karl Barth is supposed to have said that Christians should "do theology with the Bible in one hand and the newspaper in the other." Preaching does just that. It articulates God's truth and how it intersects with the culture. Preaching is vitally important to your congregants because they may not know the Bible and may be so immersed in culture that they aren't aware of how culture influences them.

Pastors articulate the intersection between the Bible and culture in their sermons by helping their flock understand the framework of the passage (the exegetical idea) and by articulating how it applies to their day-to-day day living (the homiletical idea).

Sermons are mined from the Bible, drawing an idea from the text (the exegetical idea) and then communicating that idea in a way listeners will understand (homiletical idea). The homiletical idea doesn't veer from the biblical, exegetical idea, but rather is anchored to it. Below are some biblical texts from which homiletical ideas are suggested in italics.

Suicide is never justified even when life is painful. The Bible is full of people in pain who don't kill themselves. The prime example is Job, who was afflicted with painful sores all over his body. His wife says to him, "Curse God and die!" (Job 2:9), but Job responds, "Shall we accept good from God, and not trouble?" (v. 10). In addition, we find Hagar and Ishmael expelled from their home (Gen 21:8–20), Jacob afflicted with a limp (Gen 32:32), Tamar being unjustly treated (Gen 38:12), Joseph imprisoned (Gen 39:20), Moses struggling with speech difficulty (Exod 4:10) and overwhelmed by leadership (Num 11:10–15), Hannah unable to conceive (1 Sam 1), Elijah despondent (1 Kgs 17–19, see especially 19:4), and Jonah vengeful (4:3). None of these chose suicide despite their pain.

Other people in the Bible did choose suicide: Abimelech (Judg 9:52–54), Samson (Judg 16:30), Saul (1 Sam 31:4), Ahithophel (2 Sam 17:23), Zimri (1 Kgs 16:18), and Judas (Matt 27:5; Acts 1:18). The Bible doesn't shy away from this issue, but the Bible never recommends suicide, not even in the midst of suffering. And it does not recommend suicide from a philosophical perspective, either.

Fear God and keep his commandments. Ecclesiastes is the same kind of literature as the Babylonian *Dialogue of Pessimism*, but it comes to a very different conclusion. While the Teacher recognizes that "everything is meaningless" (Eccl 1:2), he does not recommend suicide. The writer concludes that humankind should "fear God and keep his commandments" (Eccl 12:13). Suicide is not justified even when people are in pain because "God will bring every deed into judgment" (Eccl 12:14).

The Bible in fact lays out moral objections to suicide. God commands his people, "do not murder" (Exod 20:13; Deut 5:17). Life is a gift from God, and the natural course of life should be preserved (Deut 32:39; Job 1:21; 1 Cor 6:19–20; Eph 5:29; Phil 1:20–26). In addition, using suicide to make a point does not fit with Christ's injunction to love enemies (Matt 5:43–44) and the apostle Paul's injunction to "overcome evil with good" (Rom 12:17–21). Christians' freedom (1 Cor 10:23) ought to be oriented toward life (Deut. 30:19).

People never lose their value even if unproductive. The Bible makes the strong point that people never lose their dignity. Because *all* people are created in the image of God (Gen 1:28–29), they have worth and dignity regardless of their situation. People cannot earn their worth by being productive or lose it by being unproductive. *All* people deserve to be treated with dignity: women and girls (Luke 8:40–54), children (Matt 19:14), the sick (John 5:1–9), Samaritans (John 4:4–42), tax collectors (Luke 19:1–10), and a Philippian jailer (Acts 16:25–40). C. S. Lewis sums up the Christian stance on human dignity:

> There are no ordinary people. You have never talked to a mere mortal. Nations, cultures, arts, civilizations—these are mortal,

and their life is to ours as the life of a gnat. But it is immortals whom we joke with, work with, marry, snub and exploit—immortal horrors or everlasting splendors.[52]

Some people might argue for Death with Dignity acts because prolonging life is a burden on society economically. But Christians preserve the natural course of life, neither cutting it short and nor taking extraordinary measures to prolong it. However, it is also important to acknowledge that caring for people can be burdensome for one person. That is where the church should come in to provide tangible supports for suffering individuals *and* for their caregivers.

Pastoral Voices Against Suicide

Pastors want to help their congregations with suicide prevention through their preaching. Through the research for this book, pastors emphasized that they understood the importance of preaching to prevent suicide. They wanted to develop sermons that inspire, encourage, and provide hope for their listeners. A LifeWay Research study on suicide noted:

> Most Protestant pastors believe their church is taking a proactive role in preventing suicide and ministering to those affected by mental illness, according to LifeWay Research.
>
> A number of pastors also say they've been proactive in preparing to minister to those at risk of suicide. Forty-one percent say they have received formal training in suicide prevention, while 46 percent have a procedure to follow when they learn someone is at risk. Fifty percent say they have posted the National Suicide Prevention Lifeline number, 1-800-273-8255, where staff can find it.[53]

The challenge for pastors was how to do it, how to craft their sermons with hope in mind. The statistics from LifeWay demonstrate that although pastors think that they are addressing the issue of suicide prevention in the pulpit, listeners do not appear to have heard what was communicated in the same way:

> Fewer (22%) say the church has used sermons in the past year to discuss issues that increase the risk of suicide. Meanwhile, 13 percent say their church has taught what the church believes about suicide; 14 percent say the church trained leaders to identify suicide risk factors; and 13 percent say their church shared reminders about national resources for suicide prevention.[54]

These statistics show that few churchgoers are hearing sermons about suicide or suicide prevention. More needs to be done (and hopefully, resources like this book will help) to help pastors become intentional about addressing suicide and about developing sermons with the hope of the gospel in view.

Thinking back to our case study, pastors in a position like Miles's can speak directly to their disappointment in Samantha's choice and can reinforce to their flock that their lives matter. The Bible speaks plainly about the value of human life. In a culture of confusion, preachers are in the position to be clear about the biblical teachings on suicide, enabling listeners to develop a theology of personhood that is based on Scripture. Congregants need to hear clearly the biblical value for all human life.

Summary

While Christians reject the cultural voices for suicide, Christians can join the cultural voices that are against suicide. For example, Christians might get involved in suicide prevention at the national and local levels. The National Action Alliance for Suicide Prevention has a campaign called *Faith. Hope. Life.*[55] States have suicide prevention plans.[56] National and local efforts are often eager for participation from clergy and faith communities. In addition, pastors preach the hope of the Gospel. In the next chapter, we lay out seven "fences" preachers can put up through their preaching to help prevent suicide.

PREVENTING SUICIDE

An ounce of prevention is worth a pound of cure.

Benjamin Franklin

The prudent see danger and take refuge,
but the simple keep going and pay the penalty.

Proverbs 22:3

Case Study

RIVERTON IS A SMALL RURAL TOWN. The backbone of
the region's economy is farming, ranching, and small businesses. One
of the challenges faced by the community is that parents work long
hours in the summer. Every few years, without adult supervision, an
elementary-aged child drowns in the local swimming hole. Mia, the
principal of the elementary school, wants to implement year-round
school. The community, especially Mayor Oliver and Dr. Will, the
local pediatrician, have been vocal against her proposal. Mayor Oliver
would like to station a lifeguard at the swimming hole, and Dr. Will

would like to teach all elementary-aged children CPR. Principal Mia, Mayor Oliver, and Dr. Will all attend Pastor Joe's church, which fosters lively conversations at fellowship hour.

One morning Samuel and Philomena call Pastor Joe sobbing because their ten-year old son, Alex, drowned when an underwater current at the swimming hole pulled him under. They ask Pastor Joe to do the funeral. Pastor Joe visits with the grieving parents and then performs the funeral. Pastor Joe continues to meet with Samuel for follow-up pastoral care because Samuel seems to be taking his son's death hardest and has stopped coming to church.

After the funeral, Mayor Oliver calls a town hall meeting to address the drowning. The parents choose not to attend, but many from the community are present. All proposals are discussed: year-long school, posting a lifeguard, and training all the children in CPR. Then Principal Mia suggests building a fence at the place where Alex was swimming to prevent other children from swimming in the same area where he and other children have drowned. The community agrees on the fence.

A few weeks later, Samuel calls Pastor Joe to tell him that he feels he is to blame for Alex's death and wants to kill himself. He tells Pastor Joe that he recently lost his job because he couldn't make himself get out of bed in the morning anymore, and he is in constant conflict with Philomena. Pastor Joe wonders how to build a fence for Samuel to help protect him from suicide.

Case Study Questions

1. Prevention addresses the problem *before* it exists. Intervention addresses the problem *after* it exists. Which of the ideas (year-round school, lifeguard, CPR training, fence) are prevention ideas? Which are intervention ideas?[1]

2. When would you focus on prevention, and when on intervention?

3. What are some advantages of prevention measures as opposed to intervention measures?

4. Given the information in chapter one, how might Pastor Joe help to protect Samuel from suicide?

5. What theological "fences" does Samuel need?

Fences of Prevention

Pastors can build fences through their preaching and teaching. Following are seven of the fences that a pastor can build (prevention). The same principles and messages are also important to bring up when speaking with people who are already suicidal (intervention). Intervention ideas follow after each prevention fence.

Fence 1: Preach and teach on connection to others

One of the most hopeless situations for suicidal Christians is that they have lost a sense of having strong bonds with others. Samuel feels lonely and disconnected from others. He is arguing with Philomena and he has stopped going to church. He doesn't feel that he has anyone apart from Pastor Joe to turn to. Suicidal Christians might feel this way because they are depressed and looking through the distorted lens of depression.

To build a fence against isolation, a pastor can preach and teach on connectedness to one another based on the following key Christian beliefs. First, Christians can know that we are connected to God because he is present at all times (Ps 139:7–12; Jer 23:23–24; Matt 28:20; 1 Cor 3:16), especially in times of suffering (Deut 31:8; Ps 34:18; Ps 56:8; Isa 43:2) and when we call to him (Ps 145:18).

Second, Christians are members of God's family; we are members of one another (Rom 12:5; Eph 4:25). Like a family, we bear each other's burdens (Gal 6:2). We love one another (1 Thess 3:12) and encourage one another (1 Thess 5:11). But suicidal Christians also need to understand that the rest of the family depends on them and needs them. Their suicide would hurt their Christian family (not to mention their biological family). Meaningful relationships make life worth living.

Third, it is naïve to assume that Christians are just one big happy family with no conflict. All close relationships have conflict, whether marriages or families or friendships or church families. Pastors need to teach Christians the skills to maintain stable relationships, because broken relationships open the door to feelings of being alone and becoming suicidal. Some of these skills include working out problem areas truthfully and lovingly (Eph 4:15), forgiving others (Matt 6:15), and reconciling with people who repent and setting boundaries with people don't (Matt 18:15–18). These theological truths are powerful fences that help prevent suicide. Pastor Joe could preach on connectedness, reminding Samuel that he is not alone and helping him re-connect with his wife through pastoral counseling.

PRACTICAL INTERVENTIONS

Pastors in a situation like Joe's could do a number of things to help people like Samuel connect to others. They could arrange for Samuel to be evaluated at the local hospital's emergency department or call the National Suicide Prevention Lifeline (1-800-273-TALK). Once sure of his safety, they could send Samuel a "caring letter" that says something like the following: "I'm praying for you at this difficult time. I'm looking forward to seeing you on Thursday." Or they could have someone from the men's group invite Samuel to attend the men's group at church. Men have a tendency to lose their early friendships and not replenish them, such that when their relationships with their wives aren't going well, they have nowhere to turn.[2]

Develop a hope kit with Samuel.[3] A hope kit contains Samuel's reasons to live, which he'll turn to when the suicidal thoughts get strong. Include verses that remind him of God's loving presence. Put in pictures of all the people Samuel is connected to, including a picture of the church family, who would be devastated if he killed himself. Include an index card reminding him of steps for resolving conflict with Philomena. Hope kit apps can be downloaded to his phone.[4]

Fence 2: Preach and teach on the worth and dignity of every person

Another seemingly hopeless situation for suicidal Christians is their enduring self-hatred, sense of being a burden, or sense that their significant others would be better off without them. Again, Samuel feels this way because he looking through the distorted lens of depression. He blames himself for his son's death and for losing his job. Other Christians might feel this way because of an illness (like ALS) or an ongoing mental health condition (like PTSD) or incarceration. An adolescent might feel this way because of a big fight with her parents. A pastor can preach and teach on the worth and dignity of each person based on the following key Christian beliefs.

First, because people are made in the image of God, they have worth and dignity regardless of their situation. Many people erroneously believe that they need to earn their worth by being productive. When they see themselves as unable to contribute productively, it confirms that they are a burden to society or to their significant others. But all people are created in the image of God (Gen 1:28–29). Jesus treated all people with respect and care: women and girls (Luke 8:40–54), children (Matt 19:14), the sick (John 5:1–9), Samaritans (John 4:4–42), tax collectors (Luke 19:1–10), and the sexually broken

(John 8:1–11). Although Christians are sinners who struggle with sin (Rom 7:15; 1 John 1:8), they are uniquely created by God (Gen 1:27–28; Ps 8; Ps 139:14), loved by God (Zeph 3:17; John 3:16), called into a covenant relationship with him (1 Cor 11:23–26; 1 Pet 2:9), and interceded for by God (Rom 8:26–27, 34; Heb 7:25). We are commanded to care for ourselves (Exod 20:8–11; Eph 5:29–30). We need to keep human depravity and God's love in proper tension so that we can help suicidal people have a proper view of themselves.

Second, all people have the God-given purpose of taking care of creation (Gen 1:28). In addition, Christians are gifted by God (1 Cor 12; Rom 12:3–10; Eph 4:7–13; 1 Pet 4:8–11) to build the church, to fulfill their God-given purpose (Eph 2:10). Though some Christians are unable to contribute in conspicuous, public ways, they build the church in many ways, perhaps through a ministry of prayer, or by showing the church how to persist through suffering, or how to accept the care of others. William James said that religion made life worth living in the face of contemplated suicide because of the belief that we are needed to redeem "something really wild in the universe."[5] Meaningful work makes life worth living.

Suicidal people need more reasons for living. Pastors should marinate their congregants in reasons to live *before* they become suicidal,[6] from a young age. Some of these reasons could include having future goals, while committing them to the Lord (Prov 16:3); enjoying the work God has given to do (Eccl 2:24; 3:13; 5:18; 9:10); working at it wholeheartedly as for the Lord (Col 3:17, 23–24); and supporting oneself (2 Thess 3:6–13). People need life goals, like finishing school, getting married, having children, and doing meaningful work. Another reason to live might be understanding that killing oneself won't really accomplish or solve anything. Another reason to live might be the challenge to have the courage to face a difficult life. A suicidal person needs to trust that with God's help he can solve the excruciating problem of coping with life. Samuel will always grieve the profoundly devastating loss of his son, but with the help of many others, he will be able to work out what his new life will look like.

A last important truth is that Christians can forgive themselves for their mistakes because God knows we are limited by our humanity (Gen 2:7; Ps 103:14) and forgives us our sins (1 John 1:9). Samuel is experiencing "moral injury."[7] He transgressed one of his deeply held moral beliefs (being responsible for his son's life), resulting in cavernous emotional shame.[8] Veterans may experience moral injury when they witness or perpetrate what they perceive to be unnecessary acts of violence in a war zone. Samuel is experiencing shame for something he could not control as a limited human being. Pastor Joe questions if Samuel truly sinned. But if he did, Samuel needs to learn to forgive himself because God forgives sinners (Ps 103:12; Matt 21:31; John 3:17; 1 Cor 6:11; Heb 9:14; 1 John 1:7). These theological truths are powerful fences that help prevent suicide. Pastors can preach on the dignity of all persons, reasons to live, and forgiveness.

PRACTICAL INTERVENTIONS

A pastor can write a suicidal person's favorite verse about God's love on an index card and place it in a hope kit. One verse might be Zephaniah 3:17: "The LORD your God is with you, the Mighty Warrior who saves. He will take great delight in you; in his love he will no longer rebuke you, but will rejoice over you with singing." A pastor might add a verse about forgiveness such as Psalm 103:10 "[God] does not treat us as our sins deserve."

A pastor might list a suicidal person's reasons to live on index cards, and add them to the hope kit. Some reasons to live could be "I can rebuild a life worth living." "I want to advocate for policy changes at the municipal and state levels." "I still want to take my daughter to Disneyland." "Killing myself will leave my family more bereft than they already are." "I will courageously face life one day at a time (1 Cor 16:13)." "The brokenness in the world does not negate the beauty of the world."

A pastor might offer to meet regularly with a suicidal person when ready about what his or her new purposes in life may be.

Fence 3: Preach and teach on hope

Pastors cannot help but soak their congregants in hope because the Bible is full of narratives of hope.[9] In the Bible, when everything looks hopeless, God repeatedly intervenes mightily and redeems the bad into something good (Prov 16:4). In Genesis 50:20, Joseph tells his brothers that though what they did was evil, God used it to produce a great good, the salvation of Israel from famine. In Ruth 1:20, Naomi calls herself Mara (bitter) because she lost her husband and two sons. Though Naomi is hopeless, she's confronted by ongoing unexpected surprises: her daughter-in-law Ruth refuses to leave Naomi; after the two women come back to Bethlehem during the barley harvest, Boaz generously helps Ruth in her gleaning; Boaz later agrees to redeem Elimelech's land and to marry Ruth; and Ruth conceives and bears a son who is in the ancestry of Jesus. And of course, the ultimate example of a redeeming intervention is the awful death of Jesus on an instrument of torture through which he atoned for our sins.

The pervasive message of the Bible is that there is always hope. But two caveats: one, just because a pastor tells a suicidal congregant that he should find hope in his situation doesn't mean that he will do so. Two, hope does not always mean getting what we want. Samuel won't get back Alex. Joseph didn't get back all those years in prison, and Naomi didn't get back her husband and two sons. A lot of people of faith lived difficult lives and died horrible deaths (Heb 11:36–38) without seeing God's salvation (Heb 11:39). Hope is believing that God will bring good from what is bad.

A pastor can preach and teach about hope based on the following key Christian beliefs. One, many people in the Bible struggled just like congregants today do. Elijah was on the top of his game when he killed the prophets of Baal (1 Kgs 18:19-40), but he started thinking about suicide when Queen Jezebel threatened his life (1 Kgs 19:4). As one pastor said, "[Elijah] did all the right things and yet finds himself depressed and suicidal."[10] Congregants might recognize their own despair in Elijah's. They might also gain hope in God's compassionate treatment of Elijah (vv. 5-12) and gain hope in the midst of their own difficulties. Narratives of hope are throughout the Bible and include those of Hagar (Gen 16:6-16; Gen 21:8-20); Moses (Num 11:10-15); Hannah (1 Sam 1); Tamar, Rahab, and Ruth (Matt 1:1-17); Elijah (1 Kgs 17-19, especially 19:4); and Jonah (especially 4:3).

Two, we have reason to hope. The Christian virtue of hope (along with faith and love; 1 Cor 13:13) is based in our faithful certainty of a God who is present (Ps 34:18), loving (1 John 4:8), sovereign (Ps 31:15), and almighty (Job 42:2; Matt 19:26; 1 Cor 6:14), who brings us back to the promised land (Jer 29:11), who redeems our suffering (Gen 50:20; Joel 2:25-32; Rom 5:3-5; Rev 17:17), and who ultimately will create a new heaven and a new earth (Rev 21:4). Hope is knowing that Jesus holds our world together (Col 1:17; Heb 1:3). It's knowing that the Holy Spirit is with us forever (John 14:16) to teach us (John 14:26), convict us when we sin (John 16:8), and guide us (John 16:13). Both Jesus and the Spirit intercede for us before God (Rom 8:26-27, 34). Because of Jesus' and the Spirit's ongoing ministry, we have faith that we will find solutions to our problems.

Three, seasons change. We know that God created the world with rhythms (Eccl 3:1-8): crying and laughing come and go; mourning and dancing come and go. This rhythm to life makes us understand that however bad we are feeling, it will not last forever. By God's grace, we will find solutions to our problems and eventually will adjust to the new normal.[11]

Fourth, we can lament. As psychologist Gay Hubbard has pointed out, "When we can find no words to carry our suffering and confusion to God, it is encouraging to find that God himself has provided words for us."[12] In difficult times, the psalms of lament give us the words we need. They allow us to express our hurts to the one person who is powerful enough to change or work through our circumstances: God. Take Psalm 13, for example. We start with a protest: "How long, God, am I going to have to put up with these intolerable circumstances? How long, God, are you going to not intervene?" (Ps 13:1–2). In the middle of our lament, we petition God (Ps 13:3–4): "Look at me and answer me!" The real test of faith is seeking God in the absence of the evidence of his presence and intervention. At the end of our lament, we lean into our covenant relationship with God and his character of love (Ps 13:5–6; 2 Tim 2:13) and trust that he will intervene. Even in the face of no evidence, when everything feels hopeless, believers call out to God because he is in a covenant relationship with us and is a God of love.

PRACTICAL INTERVENTIONS

A pastor can add a suicidal person's favorite verses or narratives of hope on an index card and put it into a hope kit. A pastor can suggest that the suicidal person write a lament psalm about their specific life situation. Giving words to our suffering helps us understand that God loves us and has heard us.

Fence 4: Preach and teach on moral objections to suicide and reasons to live

Most pastors believe that suicide is morally wrong.[13] Suicidal people need their own moral objections to suicide. A moral objection to suicide is a conviction that suicide is forbidden by God. But where will Samuel get that conviction? While the Bible acknowledges the reality of suicide—Abimelech (Judg 9:52–54), Samson (Judg 16:30), Saul (1 Sam 31:4), Ahithophel (2 Sam 17:23), Zimri (1 Kgs 16:18), and Judas (Matt 27:5; Acts 1:18) all took their own lives—we have to look at other passages to discover biblical and moral objections to suicide.

Christian objections to suicide include God's command "do not murder" (Exod 20:13; Deut 5:17) and the convictions that life is a gift from God and that the natural course of life should be preserved (Deut 32:39; Job 1:21; Ps 49:7; 1 Cor 6:19–20; Eph 5:29; Phil 1:20–26). The core aspect of this conviction is that God *alone* decides when life begins and ends, and so no human person should cut that life short. It is related to the conviction that Christians ought to be oriented toward life. Paul writes that he is torn between life and death but chooses life for the benefit of the Philippians (Phil 1:21-26). We also know that every person has dignity and worth (Gen 1:27–28) completely apart from who they are.[14] For example, Paul prevents the suicide of the Philippian jailer (Acts 16:25–40). In verse 28, Paul shouts, "Do not harm yourself!" even though it was that jailer who had imprisoned Paul and Silas. Death is the enemy even for a jailer (1 Cor 15:25–26).

While clear moral objections are important and have been found to prevent suicide,[15] they may not be enough. What if suicidal people are experiencing such hopeless despair that they are willing to destroy the life God has given them? While suicidal people need moral objections to suicide, they also need moral reasons to live. That is, they need to know what *not* to do as well as what *to* do. Think of these as opposite-facing fences: one fence that says it is wrong to take one's own life, the other saying it is right to live it. Why live? Because God provides each of us with a faith community that supports us when we are suffering, because he lovingly created each of us with worth and dignity, and because we have the hope of redemption because he himself suffered. God himself is present with each of us in our suffering, and he provides us with steps to take in the midst of our suffering. These are just some of the reasons for living. A suicidal person may already know the moral objections to suicide but not all the steps to building a life worth living. If pastors communicate only the moral objections to suicide without giving reasons to live, the suicidal person may become even more despairing. The suicidal person may say to herself, "This commandment condemns me to a wretched life of hell on earth. I've tried everything and nothing has worked. There is nothing more I can do, so I am condemned to a dreadful life of suicidal despair until I die." Pastors should listen to William James on this point: "God alone is master of life and death, they say, and it is a blasphemous act to anticipate his absolving hand. But can we find nothing richer or more positive than this, no reflections to urge whereby the suicide may actually see, and in all sad seriousness feel, that in spite of adverse appearances even for him life is worth living still?"[16] Moral objection to suicide is an important fence, but it is certainly not the only one.

PRACTICAL INTERVENTION

A pastor might ask a suicidal person to state in his own words a moral objection to suicide and write it on an index card to put in his hope kit.

Fence 5: Preach and teach on self-control to develop the habit of choosing life

Self-control is a fruit of the Spirit (Gal 5:22; 2 Tim 1:7) that keeps us from impulsivity (Gal 5:16–17). It is related to prudence (Prov 14:8, 15) and patience (Prov 16:32). Social science research has found that self-control is related to better health, less substance use, better academic performance, less violence, less risky sex, and *less attempted suicide*—and therefore longer life.[17] Self-control slows down impulsive decision-making by modifying the tendency to respond in a certain way. Congregants use self-control to regulate or adjust their behavior to match a standard of behavior.[18] In the case of suicide, the standard is to choose life. A suicidal person may hear you preach on the Christian value of all life and on the work of the Spirit in giving self-control, and may develop the motivation needed to regulate her urges to die because she evaluates suicide as not being consistent with Christian beliefs. The suicidal person may then seek out the strategies needed to regulate these urges. The good news is that self-control improves over time just as a muscle is strengthened through use.[19] However, resisting urges to die can be difficult. Augustine makes clear that controlling one's impulse is not easy:

> The enemy held fast my will, and had made of it a chain, and had bound me tight with it. For out of the perverse will came lust, and the service of lust ended in habit, and habit, not resisted, became necessity. By these links, as it were, forged together—which is why I called it "a chain"—a hard bondage held me in slavery. But that new will which had begun to spring up in me freely to worship thee and to enjoy thee, O my God, the only certain Joy, was not able as yet to overcome my former willfulness, made strong by long indulgence. Thus my two wills—the old and the new, the carnal and the spiritual—were in conflict within me; and by their discord they tore my soul apart.[20]

So what do people do when their self-control is low? Habits compensate for low self-control because they are automatic.[21] We don't have to think about habits. A habit can automatically cue a suicidal person to choose life in the midst of suicide crisis.

This mechanism is not yet understood, but the habit of choosing life may be reinforced in the faith community. Just as when people want to stop smoking they enlist their friends to help, social influence can build other good habits, which keep people on track when their willpower is low. Congregants have said that one of the reasons they join a faith community is to "live a life of faith together."[22] They join to get help with adhering to their beliefs. What helps them is the social influence and behavioral guidance of belonging.[23] They want to be formed spiritually into a particular set of beliefs and to be held to these beliefs through positive peer influence. Pastors can make it a goal to build the fence of self-control in their community to help develop the habit of choosing life in order to prevent suicide.

PRACTICAL INTERVENTIONS

To help slow down and prevent people from acting on suicidal think-ing, develop a safety plan with them by constructing a list of things they'll do when the suicidal thoughts intensify. These might include getting out their hope kit, calling you, calling their counselor, going for a walk, taking a shower, or calling the National Suicide Prevention Lifeline (1-800-273-TALK)—anything that hits the pause button.

Fence 6: Preach and teach on grief and suffering

It is difficult to avoid preaching and teaching on suffering because suf-fering is all over the Bible—God's people have never been immune to suffering (2 Cor 1:8; 1 Pet 4:12). Jesus was himself "a man of suffer-ing and familiar with pain" (Isa 53:3). A pastor can preach and teach on managing suffering based on the following key Christian beliefs.

First, suffering is not good in itself. Suffering won't exist in God's new heaven and new earth (Rev 21:4). It is painful. The Bible cap-tures a breadth of emotions experienced by suffering people: anger (Ps 7:11; Mark 3:5; John 2:15–16; Eph 4:26), anguish and bitterness (1 Sam 1:10), anxiety (Ps 6:7; 2 Cor 7:7; Phil 2:26–28), despondency (Ps 42:5, 11; Ps 43:5; Ps 88), distress (1 Sam 22:2; 2 Sam 22:7; 2 Kings 4:27), fear (Matt 14:26–30), grief (2 Sam 19:4), guilt (Matt 27:3), indig-nation (Ps 137), longing (Ps 38:9; Prov 13:12), and sorrow (Ps 6:7, Jer 20:18), to name a few.

Second, Christians take steps to manage their suffering. They practice the presence of God (Ps 23:4) and remain open to joy (Hab 3:17–18), because while we often don't deserve suffering, we also don't deserve the good gifts of God. Christians nurture hope (Gen 50:20; Job 13:15; Jer 29:11; Lam 3:19–26; Rom 5:3–5; 8:28; 1 Cor 13:13; Heb 11:1; Rev 21:4). They pray and do not give up (Luke 18:1–8). They wait for God (Gen 50:20; Ps 33:20; 37:7; 130:5) when it seems God is hiding himself (Isa 45:15). They pray psalms of lament (e.g., Ps 13;

88; 119:84) with protest, petition, and praise.[24] They pray imprecatory psalms when angry at injustice (Deut 32:35; Ps 56:8; 94:1; 137; Isa 61:8; Luke 18:7–8; Rom 12:19–20).[25] Christians also manage suffering by taking care of themselves (Exod 20:8–11), changing the situation when possible (Mark 7:24–30), and getting support (Eccl 4:9–12), though not everyone will be helpful.[26] Christians also forgive others (Matt 6:12) but do not reconcile with those who don't repent (Matt 18:15–17).[27] Christians avoid taking revenge (Matt 5:44; 1 Pet 3:9).[28]

Just as important, Christians take steps to come alongside others in the midst of suffering. They mourn with those who mourn (Rom 12:15), avoiding platitudes, the easy answers that ignore the pain and mystery of suffering. Ravi Zacharias and Vince Vitale write, "To some questions there are answers; to other questions there are no sufficient propositional answers. Both dissolve in the reality of God's presence, and the answers we do have about Him carry us through the questions for which we still don't have the answers."[29] God said to Eliphaz, Bildad, and Zophar, the friends of Job who spoke platitudes, "I am angry with you and your two friends, because you have not spoken of me what is right, as my servant Job has" (Job 42:7). Chrisitans also carry each other's burdens (Gal 6:2) and help others (Matt 25:31–46). Because grieving takes time, Christians minister to survivors long-term.

Preaching and teaching on suffering can help suicidal people make sense out of their suffering. It can help a suicidal person develop strategies for going through times of suffering. Such preaching and teaching can help instill hope in a suicidal person that there is a way through the suffering, and in this way can help prevent suicide.

PRACTICAL INTERVENTIONS

A pastor might ask a suicidal person to pick one way to manage suffering from a menu of options. Once the suicidal crisis has passed, a pastor might ask a lay minister to come alongside a suicidal person. A pastor will carefully consider how to talk about a suicide were it to happen.

Fence 7: Encourage congregants to reach out for help

Pastors tell us that their most important suicide prevention fence is to reduce the stigma of reaching out for help. They try to foster a culture where people "don't have to hide," a "deep community" where pastors model vulnerability, transparency, and non-judgment.[30] Pastors reason that people don't reach out because they fear judgment because of the stigma of suicide. Fearing judgment results in superficial relationships where congregants feel alone with their brokenness and don't reach out when they need help.

When President Eisenhower suffered his first heart attack in 1955, the scientific community did not understand what caused heart attacks. As a result, heart attacks were shrouded in fear and stigma.[31] Ignorance feeds stigma. The same is true for suicides. Even if scientists don't know everything about suicide, they understand more and more. Our Christian perspective tells us that Christian people can experience brokenness because of an interplay between their own sin, our general state of brokenness (Rom 8:22–23), being sinned against (e.g., being abused), and the consequences of all of the above.[32] In short, there is almost always a complex web of reasons behind suicidal thinking; it is not a sign of weakness.

Christians need to know that it is good and right to alleviate suffering. We established in our last point that suffering, including psychological suffering, is not good in and of itself. We are groaning and waiting eagerly for the redemption of our bodies (Rom 8:23) and for heaven (Rev 21:4). Until then, Christians focus on alleviating human suffering. We follow the model of Jesus who preached *and* healed the sick (Matt 9:35–36), and who told us to care for the weak

(Matt 25:31–46). We imitate the early church who helped the needy (Acts 2:44–45), cared for each other (Rom 12:13), and comforted and encouraged each other (Rom 1:12; 2 Cor 1:4; Col 4:11).

Church history is replete with stories of Christians alleviating suffering. Early Christians cared for the sick during epidemics[33] and used their freewill offerings to feed the poor, bury the dead, provide for orphans, and bring relief to prisoners and the aged.[34] Medieval monasteries cared for the sick and the poor.[35] William Tuke, a devout Quaker, started the York retreat in England for the mentally ill and treated patients "like human beings."[36] William Wilberforce worked relentlessly to abolish societal evils, including slavery.[37] Elizabeth Fry, a Quaker, brought the gospel and reformation to women's prisons and insane asylums in Europe because she believed that these women and their children should hear the gospel and be treated humanely.[38] Josephine Baker advocated for legal protections for prostitutes.[39] Missionaries in the nineteenth and twentieth centuries brought the gospel *and* medical care, education, and orphanages, then trained local nurses, doctors, and teachers because they believed that all people had "a sacred right to life temporal and life eternal, and to conditions of life, if not little lower than those of angels, at least a little higher than those of beasts of the field."[40] Their aim was "not only to restore the wholeness violated by sin or disease, but to preserve it, ensuring that, so far as human science can assist the action of the grace of God, preventable ills shall be prevented."[41] Taking steps to alleviate psychological suffering finds itself in this long Christian tradition.

Mental health conditions are highly treatable, and recovery is possible. (This is why people should not be labeled by a diagnosis. People aren't "schizophrenics," but people with schizophrenia.) For example, Jim Stout, a Presbyterian minister, has written about his recovery from bipolar disorder.[42] When suicidal people reach out for help, suicide is preventable. There are real solutions.

Pastors can build this fence in their pastoral counseling meetings by letting congregants know they are willing to talk about suicidal thoughts. They can be transparent to their congregation about their own struggles with suicidal thinking in the past. They can pray publically without judgment for "those who struggle with suicidal thoughts." They can model seeking counseling for themselves.

PRACTICAL INTERVENTIONS

Pastors signal their willingness to talk to suicidal people about what is really going on by asking about suicidal thinking. They might refer the suicidal person to a mental health professional but stay involved as a pastor. They might pray publically for suicidal people (if given permission), not just for congregants suffering physical health conditions (James 5:16). They might seek counseling for themselves if life's stressors overwhelm their personal resources.

Summary

In this chapter, we reviewed seven fences that pastors can build to help protect against suicide in their congregation: preaching and teaching on connectedness, the worth and dignity of every human, hope, moral objections to suicide, self-control, grief and suffering, and reaching out for help. We also suggested ways to intervene with a suicidal congregant using these same seven fences. In the next chapter, we'll explore how a pastor can craft expository sermons to help protect against suicide.

4

PREACHING TO PROTECT AGAINST SUICIDE

Some preachers and counselors seem to think that
the main part of a pastor's job is telling people to behave.
I think it is telling Christians how rich they are.

Lee Eclov, Pastoral Graces: Reflections on the Care of Souls

Case Study

DANNY WAS an average high school senior. He took classes and did well in them. He enjoyed sports. His family was involved in the local Assemblies of God church. He loved and was loved by his family. Danny had a sister, Karen, and a mother, Connie. His father died when he was in the sixth grade. Danny saw himself as the man of the family.

But Danny was a loner. It wasn't that he chose to be a loner. No one sat with him on the bus. He wasn't able to get a date to the prom. Danny was constantly teased for his prominent nose. "Hose nose!" the kids taunted. "Does your mother use your nose to clean the carpets at home?" they jabbed. The name calling was relentless, which made Danny feel even more isolated.

Sure, he was encouraged by his family, but he'd argue, "You don't have my nose." He even was teased by the youth group kids at church. His mother encouraged him to talk with the pastor. "What can he say to me?" Danny asked. "He doesn't understand what I'm going through. Besides, when Pastor Barnes preaches, all he talks about is the long ago and far away. He doesn't understand me."

As his final year in high school was coming to a close, Danny couldn't see beyond graduation, let alone beyond today. His mother noticed him becoming more withdrawn, distant, more quiet than usual. "He's trying to figure out what comes next," his mother Connie mused to Karen. But Danny had given up.

One sunny April day, Danny came home after school. Connie and Karen were gone grocery shopping. Danny wrote a note to them, then killed himself using one of his dad's shotguns.

When Connie and Karen got home, they searched for Danny and found his bloodied body in the tool shed.

After the police were called, Connie telephoned Pastor Barnes. As he hung up after their conversation, he asked himself, "What could I have done to prevent Danny from doing this?"

Case Study Questions

1. What difference can preaching make in the lives of those who are experiencing depression?

2. What can a pastor do to plant seeds of hope in one's preaching?

3. How can a pastor take stock of his or her sensitivity to preaching to the various listeners who may be contemplating suicide?

4. What does suicide prevention look like in one's sermons?

5. Are there biblical themes of which the preacher can be aware as he or she prepares to preach each week?

Introduction

Pastors have the incredible opportunity and responsibility to preach through the seasons of life of their congregation. Pastors invest in the lives of those under their care by getting to know them in their homes, at work, in small gatherings, in larger settings, at ballgames, at school concerts—where people live their lives. The pastor knows the sheep, and when the sheep hear the pastor's voice in the sermon, they know their shepherd cares for them. When the congregation is gathered for worship, the pastor's sermons have the potential for life-changing impact. G. Lee Ramsey, Jr. affirms, "The sermons of a particular pastor in a specific congregation help to build up a pastoral community as the congregation forms and re-forms around the preached word of God."[1]

This chapter explores ways in which pastors can provide protections against suicides like Danny's through their preaching. This means pastors must be intentional about what they say in their sermons and how they say it.

We begin with the task of preaching and the impact preaching can have on listeners who sit regularly under preaching. They may struggle with signs—known or unknown to them—of suicide. Next, we will explore a couple preliminary considerations for pastorally sensitive preaching. Finally, we will consider the characteristics of pastorally sensitive sermons that provide encouragement and support for listeners.

The Impact of Preaching

Edgar J. Jackson wrote over half a century ago that the way a pastor can be effective in preaching and connecting with listeners is to maintain "a constant awareness of their interests."[2] Jackson elaborates, "In every congregation there are people who are battling a bad conscience, or are frustrated by home situations that are unhappy, or have jobs they want to escape. They are in need of the guidance, perspective and new attitude that their minister can give."[3]

If Jackson is correct, and we think he is, instead of making it a goal to preach through every book of the Bible, a pastor first has the responsibility to understand the people to whom he or she is preaching—what their needs are, where they are in terms of spiritual maturity, how preaching can move them on to greater maturity, what they personally are wrestling with, even being able to preach in such a way that will encourage those like Danny who struggle with thoughts of suicide to consider the hope of the gospel.[4]

Preaching is integral to well-rounded pastoral ministry. "Preaching cannot be separated from pastoral care," urges Paul Tauteges. "On the contrary," he says, "it is a vital part of our care."[5] Arthur L. Teikmanis agrees:

> Dynamic preaching is basically pastoral care in the context of worship. The preacher who has done his pastoral work diligently knows that his congregation is not a fellowship of saints. They are sinners called to be saints. ... The preacher is fully aware that there are members of his congregation who have come to the service of worship with a sense of guilt, anger, frustration, loneliness, and despair, while others have come with inquiring and growing minds and are concerned with the problems of life, of culture, and human existence.[6]

Haddon Robinson wanted preachers to consider the impact of God's Word on people's lives, on their fear, needs, hopes, and growth in Christ. He writes, "Life-changing preaching does not talk to people about the Bible. Instead, it talks to people about themselves—their questions, hurts, fears, and struggles—from the Bible." He continues, "When we approach the sermon with that philosophy, flint strikes steel. The flint of someone's problem strikes the steel of the Word of God, and a spark emerges that can set that person on fire for God."[7] The Bible provides the strength people need. When it addresses men and women where they are, by the work of the Spirit something happens. Preaching is targeted from the Bible to people. Teikmanis agrees, "True preaching is not a generalization nor is it a monologue; it is always directed to the needs of the worshipers."[8]

In well-rounded pastoral ministry, we don't want to avoid preaching on death, yet we want to be pastorally sensitive about how we approach it. Rick McKinniss notes: "I began to see that taking the wrecking ball to people's theologies [about death] would tear down not only their ideas but their feelings and hopes as well. ... Through teaching and preaching, I was going to have to build patiently for them a new theological framework, one that would join faith and reality."[9] Developing a biblical foundation is key for Christians in understanding death.

If you've begun to build a biblical foundation concerning death, then you're better able to address suicide directly from the pulpit. Preach on it. Show the biblical teachings on it. Many in our congregations may have either contemplated suicide or even have a family member who has died by suicide; an open assessment of biblical texts that speak to suicide would lessen the awkwardness associated with this touchy subject. James T. Clemons observes:

> In the midst of almost relentless media attention focused on a topic of suffering affecting millions of people, it is strange indeed that so little has been said about suicide from the pulpit. I have often put the question to lay people: "Have you ever heard a sermon on suicide?" And, to preachers: "Have you ever preached on the subject, apart from a funeral service?"

Almost always, the answer has been a simple no. Occasionally a preacher has added reflectively, "But you know, I really should."[10]

There are reasons why we don't preach on suicide. We may be reluctant to bring it up. It's an uncomfortable, messy, awkward topic. Perspectives on suicide may vary, even in one's congregation, from "a person who dies by suicide is headed to hell" to "suicide is like any other death." We may think that raising the topic of suicide may risk encouraging someone to go through with it. There may be concern about copycat deaths. Additionally, we have limited biblical information on suicide, but we do have a rich, textured understanding of the value of the person. Sometimes we're not sure about the ethical elements to suicide and its ramifications. We don't want to offend anyone, either. So, we don't talk about it. We don't preach about it. We remain silent. "When preachers don't address significant issues in some way, regardless of how controversial or difficult they may be," says Clemons, "one of two messages comes thundering through the silence: Either preachers don't care or they don't know what to say."[11]

We cannot let our fears silence us. Pastor and author Zack Eswine writes, "Be careful that your fears do not keep you from listening as a caregiver or your certainties keep you from talking as a sufferer."[12] Through preaching God's words, in spite of our weaknesses, something happens. We preach with sensitivity and care and watch God work. Edgar Jackson affirms the helpful place of preaching in bringing about life change. He writes:

> More than we dare believe, preaching is a vital force, affecting life and creating response. Often the response is more significant than would be measured by a few words uttered by listeners after a service. Something important can take place in preaching. It is tragic when such a rich opportunity is wasted. It is rewarding when life-changing forces are set in motion.[13]

Listeners are hungry for applying what you say to their lives and with each other, even in the dark places. Ian MacLaren, a Scottish preacher, told preachers to remember this about their listeners: "everyone is having a difficult time."[14] Brian Croft encourages, "As you preach the Bible, look for points of application that serve as exhortations to love, care, and serve the sick and afflicted in your church."[15] Here, the preacher plays an important role in meeting the needs of those who struggle. As Paul Tautges notes, "We provide pastoral care through sensitive preaching, and nothing accomplishes that more than regular preaching on this two-fold reality: God's absolute sovereignty *and* his tender care for his own."[16]

When you preach this way, you know you're connecting with your listeners. They engage with what you're saying. You can see it. "When preaching is directed to personal needs, worshipers in the congregation respond, sometimes with smiles and then again with tears, sometimes with excitement and then again with deep reverence, sometimes with quiet thoughtfulness and then again with a challenging disturbance," observes Arthur L. Teikmanis.[17] They want to meet with you to gain your counsel. Church attenders' lives will be changed. Some change you will see outwardly in the way they live, while other change takes place in the hidden recesses of their thoughts and attitudes, all because they heard you preach.

There is something powerful about the preached word. It can bring great hope to those who contemplate suicide and to those whose lives have been affected by it.

Considerations for the Preacher

There are two precautionary considerations that would be helpful for us to reflect on as we begin to recalibrate our approach to preaching. One precaution concerns our words, the other how we say them. Both are important in preaching and, in particular, preaching to prevent suicide.

Watch your words

If we want to preach with passion and conviction, sometimes (if we are not careful) we will take an indicative sentence from Scripture and make it an imperative. All of our sermons have a yellow highlighter over each sentence. Every sentence is said with an exclamation mark. We want to be heard, and we think that the only way our listeners hear us is by cranking up the volume and the imperatival rhetoric.

The words we tend to use are: "must," "ought," "need to," "should," and "have to." When we preach on prayer, we tell our listeners that they "need to pray." When we preach on giving, we tell our listeners that they "ought to give." When we address the topic of hope, we exclaim, "You should have hope in your life!" Or worse, "You don't have hope, do you?" This is guilt-driven preaching—and sometimes we don't even recognize it.

Watch your words when you preach biblical imperatives or turn indicatives into imperatives. Our words can crush our listeners in ways that we may not be aware. "A man's spirit sustains him in sickness," says the writer of Proverbs, "but a crushed spirit who can bear?" By what we say and how we say it, we may be harming our listeners. Lee Eclov reflects:

> Some of the best pastoral advice I ever heard, outside of Scripture, is, "Be kind, for every person you meet is fighting a great battle." No one knows who said that first, but blessed is the congregation whose pastor believes it. Kindness in a worship service, or anywhere else for that matter, seems to help people let their guard down so grace can do its work.[18]

Take a listen to some of your recent sermons. Make a list of the guilt-driven words you use. When you thoughtfully and prayerfully assess your sermons, you will be able to see the ways to make adjustments in what you say. Sure, you may want to retain the force of the imperative by inviting listeners to think with you. Instead of "You need to give," we might say, "We want to give, don't we?" Or, "You should have hope in your life," can be reworded, "We all want hope. You want hope, don't you?" We want to use our words to preach the gospel of grace, not guilt.

Watch your way with words

When referring to the subject of suicide, we want to watch our way of speaking about it. To say that someone "committed suicide," suggests that the act of suicide is a crime, on the same level as someone who "committed murder." Suicide is not a crime. By adjusting our wording, we demonstrate to our listeners compassion and understanding.

What are ways we can refer to suicide? "He died by suicide," or, "She killed herself," or, "He was a victim of suicide." When talking about those left after a suicide you might consider, "survivors of suicide," "suicide survivors," or "the suicide bereaved."

Being intentional about our vocabulary in simple ways like those mentioned above—the words we say and the way we say them—will ultimately build bridges to our listeners so that they can better hear the gospel we preach.

Characteristics of Pastorally Sensitive Preaching

Preaching that protects against suicide centers on the hope of the gospel. When we preach, what are the ways we can advance hope and offer grace to our listeners, cultivating a manner of preaching that moves listeners from discouragement to gospel hope? We'll consider five ways.

1. Preach the gospel

The gospel means "good news." Our credibility in offering hope is deepened when we remember that we preach the good news of the gospel for non-believers and believers, including ourselves.

Non-believers are shown in the gospel the forgiveness of sin through the life, death, burial, resurrection, and promised return of Jesus Christ. They have come to terms with their sinfulness and turn away from that which displeases God by taking on a new direction, a new life in Christ (Rom 3:19–26). Yet, the gospel is for believers, too— for growth toward maturity in Christ. Believers continue to claim forgiveness in Christ every day, for we sin every day. Believers are deepening in faith, holiness, knowledge of the Scriptures, and overall discipleship.

Not only do we want to preach the gospel to those who have yet to come to faith in Christ, but also we don't want to forget to preach the gospel to believers. We want to help Christians preach the gospel to themselves and each other. Doing so makes a difference. When we articulate the gospel from the pulpit, we help listeners understand it for themselves and enable them to speak it to each other. Jerry Bridges observes, "Christians are not instructed in the gospel. And because they do not fully understand the riches and glory of the gospel, they cannot preach it to themselves, nor live by it in their daily lives."[19] Our task as preachers is to define the gospel, speak it, and model it.

Further, we don't want to get in the way of helping our listeners understand it and live it. We are not the savior; Jesus is. As Zack Eswine warns, "When Jesus and the larger story of the gospel are eclipsed," we may "unwittingly exalt ourselves to a high place of knowledge and importance," shrouding people from hearing the gospel.[20]

The gospel—and preaching it to non-believers and believers (and to yourself)—is key for everyone to have confidence in the present and the future.

2. Emphasize the hope of the gospel

We preachers are experts at pointing out the sins of others. But we don't want to forget that the gospel brings incredible hope to those who are struggling with sin, doubts, fears, or despair. Roland Leavell advises, "Preaching should do more than denounce the sinfulness of sin; it must also declare the eternal hope which is promised through Christ."[21] The hope to face today and tomorrow resides in the promise of abundant life now and forever.

The Old Testament prophets are sometimes thought of as doom-and-gloom preachers. However, their message was not simply condemning; they also offered hope: turn to God from depression, from despondency, from a life that displeases him. As Roland Leavell notes, "The ever-brightening hope which the Old Testament prophets preached was but the foregleam of the sunrise of the blessed hope which was revealed from God through Christ."[22] He continues, "The gospel of Christ offers such heavenly gifts as forgiveness of sin, cleansing of the conscience, power over temptation, joy in service, happiness in Christian fellowship, growth in Christlikeness, a triumphant victory over death, and eternal blessedness in heaven."

New Testament preachers preached fulfillment in Christ, who is the hope for every believer. They gave hope to listeners struggling in sin and tangled up in life's questions. Peter prompts his readers to their struggles with hope: "Through him you believe in God, who raised him from the dead and glorified him, and so your faith and hope are in God" (1 Pet 1:21). Paul underscores this hope when he reminds the Colossian Christians of their hope in Christ:

Once you were alienated from God and were enemies in your minds because of your evil behavior. But now he has reconciled you by Christ's physical body through death to present you holy in his sight, without blemish and free from accusation—if you continue in your faith, established and firm, and do not move from the hope held out in the gospel. This is the gospel that you heard and that has been proclaimed to every creature under heaven, and of which I, Paul, have become a servant. (Col 1:21–23)

Listeners need hope, no matter what challenge they face. The gospel is a gospel of hope—and that is what we preach. Paul's benediction to the Roman Christians inspires us to preach to those who may not think they have hope but need to hear it: "May the God of hope fill you with all joy and peace as you trust in him, so that you may overflow with hope by the power of the Holy Spirit" (Rom 15:13).

The hope that we provide our listeners is seen in the promise of the gospel. Hearing sermons of this hope-filled gospel and helping our listeners preach the gospel to themselves daily can be transforming. "Preaching the gospel to myself every day is a great way to keep myself established in 'the hope of the gospel,' so that I might experience the practical benefits that such hope is intended to bring me here on earth," says Milton Vincent. He continues, "Preaching the gospel to myself each day keeps before me the startling advocacy of God for my fullness, and it also serves as a means by which I feast anew on the fullness of provision that God has given to me in Christ."[23]

When our listeners are challenged with overwhelming depression, doubts, or fears, hope can be what they need to make it through the darkness. Vincent writes, "Hope of eternity with Christ in heaven also enables my heart to thrive during the most difficult and lengthy of trials here on earth."[24]

3. Help believers to remember

We can remind listeners who they are in Christ. Help them to remember in the sermon who God has called them to be—those who have been given his grace (2 Thess 2:16), transformed into his likeness (2 Cor 3:18), made children of God (1 John 3:1), sanctified (Rom 15:16), loved (John 3:16), given the fruit of the Spirit (Rom 8:23; Gal 5:22), the gifts of the Spirit (1 Cor 12), and the Spirit himself (Luke 11:13), and so much more! These demarcations of the Christian life are powerful, encouraging, hopeful reminders of what God has done, is doing, and will continue to do in them.

Remembering is part of what it means to be a follower of Jesus Christ. We remember his sacrifice and love for us as expressed in the Lord's Supper, wherein we gather with other believers around the table. There we eat the bread and drink the cup "in remembrance of him." We remember with gratitude and praise the life, death, burial, resurrection, ascension, and promised return of Christ.

Pastor Lee Eclov shares, "One of my favorite pastoral duties is to make people homesick."[25] The local church celebrates the hope of heaven through the testimony of believers in their midst, and the deep-down confidence in Christ celebrated in funerals of believers in Christ. Even music can remind believers about Christ's return and of heaven. This homesickness is filled with gospel hope. Roland Leavell agrees:

> Within every heart there is an unquenchable thirst for assurance of a better life to come. The human heart is weary of spiritual wanderings and it wants an eternal home. It despairs under continual disappointments. It is restive under the frailties of the flesh and with the illnesses that plague the body. There is an irrepressible faith that springs up continuously in the human heart, believing that there awaits a heaven where no sin abounds and no sorrow comes, a heaven of bliss in the presence of Deity and all his redeemed.[26]

When we preach about heaven, we want to be clear about what we're communicating. Brian Croft and Phil Newton observe, "The gospel is frequently obscured when a pastor offers comfort about heaven when *how* heaven is received is not made clear."[27] A clear articulation that the way to eternal life is only in Christ is essential for remembering the gospel and finding hope in it.

Milton Vincent affirms, "The more I experience the riches of Christ in the gospel, the more there develops within me a yearning to be with Christ in heaven where I will experience His grace in unhindered fullness."[28] Says Albert Hsu, "Remembrance as a spiritual discipline gives us strength to live in the present and direction to move forward."[29] We help our listeners remember as we preach. We remind them who we are in Christ, what Christ has done for us, and the promise of eternity with him. The power of the gospel we preach can be an encouragement to those affected by suicide and hope for those contemplating it.

4. Cultivate the power of worship

The gathering of believers in Jesus Christ is a compelling reason for hope and encouragement for those who may be struggling. "Worship can bring to life a healing perspective," observes Edgar N. Jackson. He continues, "Worship can also bring a healing quality of appreciation to life."[30] The pastor who intentionally develops worship that is restorative, biblical, and gospel-oriented will cultivate hope in the congregation. Jackson elaborates:

> The act of giving thanks helps to bring life back into balance by weighing the blessings against misfortunes. Though no life is free of its disturbances, there are multitudes of things and people and happenings for which one can truly be thankful. We need the reality to see life as it is and not as it may seem to be. That person who finds not opportunity for thankfulness is neither fair to himself nor to life in general when he begins to count his misfortunes. That person who has learned the art of thankfulness learns life's quiet satisfactions, and finds a balance that tends to discount anything that would destroy right relations with his Creator.[31]

Acts of worship—like giving thanks in word, expressing praise in song, praying to the Lord, listening to the preached Word—encourages the deepening of faith, bolstering believers to face the challenges of life with renewed strength. Worship engenders an appreciation of life and hope. Thoughtful, prayerful worship planning is key to inspiring hope in the prevention of suicide.

5. Ask questions of your listeners

Finally, asking questions in a sermon can move listeners to a new place of growth or reveal those who contemplate suicide. Reflecting on the death of a pastor friend who died by suicide, Marty Thurber says that, although he is not an expert on suicide, he knows what he would do differently: "I *would not be afraid to ask someone about their future.* What are their dreams? Their hopes and plans?"[32] Pastors are on the front lines of helping people cope. The sermon is an obvious time during which good, thoughtful questions can be asked for listeners to consider—you don't need to answer them, but only articulate them. Listeners will see themselves in your questions and will be challenged by them.

Be aware of other avenues of help. Pastors are not alone in this important ministry. They can be catalysts of hope against suicide by providing avenues for training lay pastors, counselors, home visitors, etc., to aid in creating a hopeful and hope-filled community of faith. In addition, pastors can lift undue burden from themselves by enlisting other pastoral staff (such as associate pastors and elders) in addressing suicide prevention, as well as making connections with community leaders and agencies in the field.

Summary

Preaching that protects against suicide is intentional, integrative, insightful, prayerful, and pastoral preaching that assesses and appreciates the needs of the congregation. "A sermon that grows out of understanding of people, and a firm sense of reality can help men to grow from experience to experience with an increase of maturity and emotional health," says Edgar Jackson. "It is a weekly challenge to growth, and a persistent stimulus to creative choice."[33]

The impact of change in our listeners through preaching is more like being fed over a long period of time than having one life-changing meal. Lee Eclov reflects on the reality of one-by-one, step-by-step, week-by-week preaching to the needs of the congregation. He writes:

> Pastors go into the ministry hoping to see lives changed through Christ. And we do. But like the clock on my wall says, "Things take time." Take preaching, for example. Twice now, in two different churches, I have preached well over five hundred sermons. I don't know if any single one of those sermons was life changing for someone, but I am certain that the accumulated effect of many sermons sanctifies people. I heard somewhere that tug boats move huge ships by bumping them. Bump. Bump. Bump. And slowly the great vessel turns. Preaching, and all pastoring, is like that. We bump lives with pastoral graces—sermons, services, meals, conversations, touches of kindness and discipline, even our waiting—and over time we help people become more like Jesus. Miraculously, we become more like Him in the process as well. Grace occasionally works in a burst of glory, but most of the time it is as slow as summer.[34]

In other words, the word does its work.

Ray was a police officer before he became a pastor. One day when answering a domestic dispute, Ray spoke with Jim, an anxious, depressed husband, and noticed a Bible sitting on a nearby shelf. The officer took his finger and glided it across the Bible, picking up dust. The husband said, "Yes sir, I haven't read it for a while." Ray replied, "That book changes lives." The distraught man paused and then told Ray, "Officer, I was planning on killing myself but because of what you said today about that book, I'm not going through with it." The Word gave him hope. This is the hope we preach. Preaching the Bible changes the lives of people even like Jim and Danny.

What is the main characteristic of preaching that protects against suicide? It is preaching that considers the hope of the gospel and keeps it always in view. This is good, regular, hopeful gospel preaching.

5

PASTORAL CARE AFTER A SUICIDE CRISIS

Preach the gospel at all times. Use words if necessary.

Attributed to Francis of Assisi

Case Study

PASTOR ALEX is a solo pastor and is looking forward to some time away with his wife starting next Monday. He knows he needs this Sabbath rest, but first he has a sermon to prepare and some pastoral counseling appointments. The first appointment is with Aiden, who is going through a divorce. Throughout the first part of the meeting, Aiden looks at the floor. He sounds hopeless. When Pastor Alex asks if he is thinking about suicide, Aiden says, "Yes, but I would never kill myself because it would destroy my children, who need me right now." Pastor Alex develops a safety plan with him that includes going to the emergency department or calling 1-800-273-TALK if the thoughts get stronger, looking at the pictures of his children on his phone, and seeing a counselor. Pastor Alex wonders if Aiden is going to be okay while he's away next week.

On Wednesday night, Pastor Alex gets a call from Emma's mother. Emma is a fifteen-year-old who has attended church on occasion, who participates in the local Young Life group. When Emma's boyfriend broke up with her, she skipped school and swallowed her mom's anti-anxiety pills. Her mom found her and took her to the emergency room. Emma is now in the hospital. Pastor Alex goes to visit Emma. She says she wishes she had died. Pastor Alex tells the nurse on duty that Emma regrets not having died. As he leaves the hospital, he wonders if Emma will be okay when he's away next week.

Thursday morning, Pastor Alex gets a call from Olivia's brother. Olivia, an active member of the choir, killed herself, and her body was just discovered this morning. Olivia had been dealing with another relapse of her eating disorder and depression. The family wants to have the funeral next Wednesday. Pastor Alex expresses his sadness to Olivia's brother and also discusses his upcoming trip and asks if the funeral could be on Monday or if he can recommend another minister for the funeral.

Case Study Questions

1. How might you care pastorally for someone like Aiden?

2. How might you care pastorally for someone like Emma and her family?

3. How might you care pastorally for Olivia's family?

4. Pastors engage the gamut of suicidal behavior from suicidal thoughts to attempts to death. What might be the impact on the pastor?

5. If you were Pastor Alex, what elements of each case would you consider to help you decide to cancel your time away?

Introduction

Contrary to the saying commonly attributed to Francis of Assisi (and it is unclear if he ever actually said it), actions cannot replace the preaching of the gospel. But actions are important, and in fact Francis did say, "All the Friars ... should preach by their deeds."[1] This chapter will take a brief detour from preaching into pastoral care that supports your preaching. Let's listen in on how other clergy have answered some of the questions about how to care pastorally for people with suicidal thoughts, people who have attempted suicide, and survivors following a suicide.[2]

Caring for a Person with Suicidal Thoughts

In the counseling session

The first step in pastoral care should always be to listen. One pastor we interviewed said, "I am looking forward to getting a deeper understanding of what this person is trying to communicate ... so the person feels validated, so the person feels heard, the person feels I care."[3]

This means that it is not usually a good idea to start with theology. According to another pastor, "It's not like you start out [with theological conviction]. 'Don't you know you're seriously breaking a commandment? God says, "Thou shall not kill."' That's not the route to go. Always [begin] with the person and then [apply] the convictions as they can be applicable to the particular person or the situation."[4] Prioritizing listening takes the pressure off the pastor to have all the answers.

The second step is to focus on the safety of the person with suicidal thoughts by referring to the local hospital for an evaluation or calling the National Suicide Prevention Lifeline (1-800-273-TALK). A pastor might refer the person with suicidal thoughts to a counselor.

One important reason for referral is that pastors don't see counseling as their primary role. One pastor said, "I don't consider myself a counselor," and instead "consider myself giving pastoral care to someone."[5] Another reason for referral is sharing the burden of care with other professionals. For this reason, many pastors develop a list of community resources for referral when they first arrive in a new community. See chapter 2 for other safety interventions like developing a safety plan and hope kit.

Most pastors don't bring in the theology of suicide in this second step. One pastor said, "I don't think [discussing theology is] gonna help the conversation. ... My issue right now is trying to keep them alive, and if I thought [theology] would help, then I would interject it, but at that stage, I'm just trying to keep them from jumping."[6] Another pastor said, "I'm not sure that telling the person it is a sin is supposed to stop them from doing it. ... It won't solve the problem."[7] A pastor can avoid the theology of suicide (i.e., "It is a sin to kill yourself") but focus on other theology. Chapter 2 lays out Christian beliefs or "fences" for suicidal people. It can be helpful for suicidal Christians to remember that Christians are never alone, they never lose their worth and dignity, God values their lives and strengthens them, he is present in their suffering, and the church is a loving community which will be non-judgmental when they reach out for help.

Even though theology is not generally the first subject to discuss with a person with suicidal thoughts, it is important to be ready to help with theological questions if they come up. These questions can be complex, and many pastors feel unprepared by their seminary training to address them. One pastor said, "Formal theological training addressing [suicide] that did more than battle over whether or not suicide is a sin (how helpful is that going to be in that moment?) would have been of great value the first time someone walked into my office and asked if their mom was in hell because of her suicide."[8]

Most pastors focus theologically on the sanctity of life, that God alone decides when life begins and ends, and that nothing can separate us from his love (Rom 8:31–39). Reflection should also include theologies of connectedness, the worth and dignity of each person, that God values each life, and that he also strengthens Christians to face their challenges. It is also important to reflect theologically on why Christians can reach out for help without judgment and the reasons for living, even when all seems hopeless.

When meeting with a person who is having suicidal thoughts, it is important to try to shift them toward a more hopeful narrative, to seeing that they have options, that there are other solutions besides killing themselves. Hope is part of what makes suicide morally objectionable. One pastor said, "I have moral objections because I think that [the suicidal person] has problems that are not insurmountable. That he has the possibility of life ahead of him. And that it would be wrong ethically for him to do this."[9] Part of a hopeful narrative is helping them get in touch with their trust in God and their reasons for living.

In the case study, Pastor Alex would agree with Aiden that his suicide would devastate his children. Members of the clergy emphasize that suicide doesn't occur in a vacuum. One pastor said, "[Suicide is] really, really hurting everybody you love."[10] Another said, "Every decision that we make as people affects everybody else."[11] A rabbi emphasized that suicide has a negative impact on society because it "does something to lessen the unshakable value of life."[12]

Long-term pastoral care

After the counseling session, pastoral care occurs over the long term. Pastors should want to increase the person's sense of connection to others. It is a good idea to carve out ten minutes in your week to send a caring letter. For example, Alex might write:

Dear Aiden,

I'm sorry I can't meet with you this week. I want to remind you of my prayers as you go through this difficult time. I also want to remind you of reasons to live: your beautiful children, Abby and Liam. I'm looking forward to meeting with you in two weeks.

—Pastor Alex

If you don't have an associate pastor who could visit, you could make a call to a layperson and ask them to check in next week and throughout the crisis. One pastor said, "It isn't just me trying to help this person, it is the church's ministry."[13] Another pastor said, "We are a community that takes care of each other."[14]

When Pastor Alex gets back from his week off, he checks in with Aiden to see if Aiden followed up on the referral to the counselor and if the counselor needs to collaborate with him. Pastor Alex does not equate a referral to a handoff. He sees himself as an essential member of a team. He sees his role as providing spiritual leadership in partnership with other resources.

In the long term, you will want to increase opportunities for meaningful contribution to the church. Once the crisis passes, explore how someone like Aiden would like to get involved. One pastor said the suicidal person "is going to feel like he's a waste of space, and I'd really want to react against that and let him know that there are a lot of needs in our church ... and you have a lot of gifts to use ... and we'd love to use you in any way possible, whatever that may be."[15]

Caring for the family

Pastors understand that the suicidal thinking of one person affects the family. A parent's depression affects their ability to parent well, and their children may begin to exhibit mental health symptoms.[16] So be particularly vigilant to monitor how children are doing. Ask a family in the church to come around the family during this time.

"Abby and Liam need me" is on Aiden's safety plan, and pictures of them are in his hope kit. It would be inappropriate for his children to know about or help Aiden with his safety plan or hope kit at their age. But Aiden may be willing to confide in Carol, his sister. Pastor Alex might help Aiden contact Carol and minister to her needs as she grapples with her fears for Aiden. Carol also might need Pastor Alex's help in removing Aiden's gun from the house. Pastor Alex might go with Carol to the local police department for temporary safekeeping of Aiden's gun.

Caring for the church

Pastors build and rely on the church as a ministering community. Some churches train lay ministers who can be involved in caring through programs like Stephen Ministries.[17] Even if you don't have this in place, you can still call on your deacons and mature congregants when needed. Lay ministers will ensure that you do not carry the burden of ministry alone and will allow all suffering congregants to be ministered to.

A church provides venues for people to connect and to contribute. Men especially need these venues because their friendship networks dwindle over time, such that in middle age they have few or none to turn to in challenging times.[18]

Caring for the pastor

Many pastors do not learn how to care for a suicidal person in seminary; they learn on the job. For example, one pastor said, "Within the *first* week of my being [at my first church], a woman called me, said she was sitting at her home and she had a razor blade beside her, and she didn't see any reason to live anymore, and that was like day two or three on the job."[19] Another pastor said, "[Suicide] is the biggest area that I was sort of clueless on when I went into the ministry."[20] In light of this gap, you may want to pursue suicide prevention training to ease the burden on yourself and begin to have confidence in how to handle a situation.

Know also that you need regular Sabbath rest. As our colleague Dr. David Currie says, pastors are not exempt from the fourth commandment. One pastor talked about the risk of burnout: "How do you regroup … when you engage a lot of suffering? And particularly when you don't feel like you're making much progress against the suffering?"[21] Pastors said that early in their career they might have felt guilty or selfish taking time off but later in their career sought balance in caring for others, self, and family.[22] Besides regular Sabbaths, pastors mentioned the following self-care commitments: faith practices, supportive relationships, recreation, setting boundaries, reflection, and seeing their own counselor.[23]

One reason to refer a suicidal person to a counselor is "burden reduction," which can be defined as "reducing the caregiving burdens of clergy and clinicians through consultation and collaboration."[24]

Caring for a Person Who Has Attempted Suicide

Immediate pastoral care

The first step for a pastor after a congregant has attempted suicide is to go to the hospital. Don't let the stigma of suicide keep you away. Even though you may object morally to a suicide attempt, you must first be present. In this moment, the ministry of presence is what is called for.

Take the attempt seriously and make sure hospital staff know if the person still wants to die.[25] They may not be lucid if there are drugs in their system, but if they are, ask if they have a safety plan or hope kit. You might point them toward a more hopeful narrative, saying something like, "I want to do what I can to help you choose life." You may also help them to imagine other alternatives. One pastor said, "My advice to [the one who attempted suicide] is, there's all kinds of help."[26] At some point, Pastor Alex can gently remind Emma that suicide would devastate her family. One clergy said, "It wouldn't just be about affecting [the suicidal person], but it would also affect her family, her friends, so just trying to help her understand: have you already gathered and thought through the implications of the decision you're trying to make?"[27]

Long-term pastoral care

Experienced pastors are present long-term. They make sure that the person who attempted follows up with mental health treatment. One pastor said, "My job is sort of triage. Get in there, figure out what's going on, and connect them with the right people. … And then my role as pastor is to monitor that."[28] They connect the attempt survivor to other resources that foster hope. One pastor said, "It seems to me part of my job is helping the person get the supportive resources they need and helping them imagine an alternate and better future."[29] Pastors could suggest these resources:

1. "Survivor stories," "Tried and true self-care tips," and "100 ways to get through the next five minutes"[30]

2. Voices of Hope, a series of unscripted interviews with people who have struggled with suicide[31]

3. *A Journey Toward Health and Hope: Your Handbook for Recovery After a Suicide Attempt*[32]

4. The Beyond Blue Way Back Support Services provides support after a suicide attempt[33]

Caring for the family

Understand that a suicide attempt affects the whole family. Experienced pastors care for the family. The mother of a seventeen-year-old young woman who attempted suicide said that though her pastor came to the hospital to pray, he "never followed up again."[34] The young woman's karate teacher brought a meal, but their church did not. The mother said, "We went through this alone." Whatever the church does for other hospitalizations (like meals or childcare) should be done for the family of someone who has attempted suicide; otherwise the family will feel isolated by the stigma of a suicide attempt. Take the team approach and arrange for the church family to bring meals and other practical supports.

Visit with the family and listen for (misplaced) guilt that they missed the cues and for fears that the person will attempt again. You may help them to understand that they did not fail the person, or you may encourage them to forgive themselves. An experienced pastor might refer a family member to a counselor to deal with nightmares of finding a loved one after an attempt. Help the family connect to resources like the brochures "A Guide for Taking Care of Your Family Member After Treatment in the Emergency Department" and "Guiding their Way Back: Information for People who are Supporting Someone after a Suicide Attempt,"[35] and the book *Valley of the Shadow*.[36]

Family members may also need this advice from *After Suicide Loss: Coping with your Grief* by Jack Jordan and Bob Braugher:

> Protect yourself from the people who are downright judgmental and hurtful, and be patient and direct with those who are trying their best to help. Most people want to support you, but do not know how—and you will sometimes have to be their teacher about what you need from them.[37]

Help the family contact people who can journey with them through this difficult time. Also encourage the family to let you know what they need.

Caring for the church

Use this opportunity to address the stigma of a suicide attempt by praying for the person in church (if the attempt survivor or family agrees). Try to treat the person and their family the same as any other person who was hospitalized. Decreasing stigma in the church will help protect against suicide.

Pastors should be ready to process congregants' memories of previous suicide attempts, the youth group's (misplaced) guilt that they missed suicide attempt cues, and other parents' fears that their children might attempt suicide.

To prevent copycat or future attempts, build the fences from chapter 2 and vigilantly monitor the friends of the attempt survivor.

Caring for the pastor

Most pastors learn on the job about how to respond to suicide attempts. One pastor said that he learned from talking to a suicidal woman. He said, "I worked very closely with a woman ... who had attempted suicide nine times. ... She was very open about her mental issues, and I learned a lot from her because she came to talk to me for spiritual counsel."[38] Foster an openness to learn from congregants.

Experienced pastors know about the need for ongoing Sabbath rest and for burden reduction by collaborating with mental health professionals and sharing the burden of ministry with the church.

Caring for the Bereaved
After a Suicide

Immediate pastoral care

If a family is out of town, you may be asked to contact them. If the family is local, the first step is to visit them and offer the ministry of presence. One pastor emphasized the impossibility of saying anything: "It's not what you say; it's being there, the compassionate presence, the ministry of presence."[39] Another pastor cautioned,

> [The first need] is the need to vent. And the need to have their emotions accepted unconditionally. ... I don't rush in with theology. In the initial shock of it, that's not the time to start providing lessons learned, or trying to say, 'Let's look at it from a biblical or spiritual perspective.' It's really a time to simply grieve with those who grieve.

Usually the family's immediate concern is not how to plan the funeral; it's wondering how to deal with this situation. The family may ask, "How could this happen?" or "Why did God allow this?"[40] Experienced pastors are willing to say, "I don't know." They know that the family will retain very little of what they say. One pastor said, "During the time of death there is numbness, denial, anger, and little of what's said is really retained at that point." Another pastor added, "I will often give handouts to people [because] ... they're not gonna hear what I'm saying. Maybe at some point they'll read this and it may provide some comfort." A possible handout is in Appendix C. If you want to develop your own handout, see the example at the American Foundation for Suicide Prevention.[41] Other pastors provide people with a general handout on loss.

An experienced pastor might set up a home visit from survivors, people who have lost a loved one to suicide and who can help the family navigate this devastating loss. To find out if your state has this service, contact the suicide prevention leadership in your state.[42]

The funeral (body present) or memorial service (body absent) will be discussed in the next chapter.

Long-term pastoral care

One pastor noted, "I think what occurs down the road after the suicide is probably just as important if not more important than what happens at the time of the death." Long-term pastoral care is important because grief following suicide is long-term.

Experienced pastors care pastorally for families the same way they would for a family who has suffered any type of death. Jordan and Braugher explain why:

> There is still a tremendous amount of ignorance and stigma associated with suicide in our society—and this stigma spills over to the survivors. Many studies have shown that survivors of suicide loss are often treated differently than survivors of other types of losses. ... All of this is to note that suicide survivors can be shunned by some people in their communities. ... Suicide creates what we call "social ambiguity." Human beings usually follow unwritten, but nonetheless powerful rules of interaction in their dealings with one another. When the norms for appropriate behavior in a given social situation are unclear, it creates an awkward and uncomfortable feeling for everyone. Supporting someone who is bereaved by suicide is one of these ambiguous situations. Most of your friends and colleagues will be sympathetic to you and will want to help; but they will be at a loss as to what is the "correct" thing to say or do for you. Even though the obvious answer is that people should do the same things they would do if your loved one had died of any other cause, your friends may feel that the

taboo around suicide makes the "rules" of proper interaction somehow different—so they avoid you, or avoid the subject of suicide when they are with you. They hold back on offering the crucial social support that is vitally necessary for you at this time in your life. Likewise, you may feel uncertain yourself about how to act and what to share with others.[43]

Experienced pastors address stigma by making sure a family is not shunned. One pastor said, "An important aspect in ministering to survivors is to make sure that the community reaches out."[44] Experienced pastors will make sure that the church cares for the family immediately and over the long term both practically and pastorally (prayer, cards, meals, babysitting, laundry, grocery shopping, invitations to return to church when ready).

A pastor sets the non-judgmental tone for the church. One pastor emphasized the importance of "fixing the condemning theology."[45] One way to address the stigma of suicide is to talk about suicide as much as the family allows. It will be more challenging for survivors to get the care they need if the conversation about suicide doesn't happen.

Experienced pastors reflect theologically with the family if requested. Jordan and Baugher write, "For some, suicide produces a crisis of faith: 'How could God let this happen?' For others, it raises profound questions about life, death, and the purpose of living: 'What do I believe about life after death?' 'What is the point of my life?' "[46] One pastor explains to the family,

[The] person that committed suicide was in a tremendous, tremendous amount of pain and anguish, and unfortunately saw no other solution or any other line of hope. So I talk about how no matter how devastating the situation is, there is always hope, that Jesus loves us, that we have that unconditional love.

And in this particular case, I don't know what else the family could have done, and so I just reassure them that it's not their fault—that he was an adult, that he had decisions to make, that he did what he thought was in everybody's best interest, and it's still hard.

Experienced pastors help the family process (misplaced) guilt.[47] One pastor said, "[The family] are bound to say, 'If only I had done this or said that.' " Other family members ask, "What didn't I see? How could I have prevented it? What else could I have done?" Pastors help families forgive themselves if needed.

An experienced pastor might refer family members to a survivor support group. Jordan and Baugher write that

> for many people, contact with other survivors is the most helpful form of social support they can receive after the death. Perhaps the most common form of survivor-to-survivor contact involves bereavement support groups. … In most cases, we recommend loss-specific groups—for example, a group just for suicide survivors.[48]

An experienced pastor might refer family members to counseling if they show symptoms of a mental health condition. For example, people with depression will feel profoundly unworthy and have very low self-esteem.[49] While grieving survivors may have thoughts like "I don't care if I live anymore" and "I don't know if I can go on," depressed people may display active suicidal ideation—not only a loss of interest in life, but also an active wish to be dead.[50] Another referral might be required for the person who discovered the deceased, because discovering a body can be traumatic.[51] One pastor explained, "Every time you walk into that room, you have that flashback of what that person looked like."

Be ready to pastor family members through the roller coaster of grief, including anger. Survivors are going through intense grief and profound personal change, and each survivor will go through it differently. One pastor gave the example of a husband staying at the church while the wife attended another church. The wife told the pastor, "I see you up in front of the congregation in those robes and I go back to that [memorial] service. I can't help it and I go there and it's just too painful." This pastor made sure that this survivor was in another church where she could be supported. He said, "I knew that the best way for me to pastor her was not to be her pastor. That I needed to see that she was pastored." If pastors can't pastor survivors, they should find another pastor who can. One survivor couple got caught in church politics and did not receive their pastor's care and ended up leaving the church because "the support wasn't there anymore."[52] Leaving church is not a necessity, but it is not unusual among survivors.[53] A survivor explained that survivors "aren't the same people anymore" following a suicide, and changing necessitates different friends. She explained that she didn't want to remain friends with people who couldn't grieve with her because "it's burdensome for [the friends]." Another survivor pointed out, "Your long-term friends are different from the friends who were there with you in the moment." He explained, "You get the opportunity to find out who your true friends are. And some people are not your true friends." Some family members might not leave the church but may be reluctant to return to church. It's important to call and invite survivors back to church when they are ready. One survivor advised, "Don't stop trying. ... Keep inviting them. Don't lose sight of them."

Over the long term, an experienced pastor might help a family to think about how to remember their loved one. One pastor suggested, "Give some money to groups like the Samaritans, to bring some good out of this." Another pastor said, "In some cases they may even want to volunteer their time [to a cause]. ... There is a need for some people to try to bring some good out of an awful situation." The advice of a psychiatrist to a survivor was, "Don't waste your grief."[54] Jordan and Baugher suggest, "Despite this tragedy, there is an opportunity to make something redemptive come out of it—something that honors the life of your loved one and makes you a better person."[55] One way is to return to joy. They write:

> We encourage you to allow the return of joy and delight into your life. The return of happiness is *not* a measure of whether you loved this person, or continue to grieve their death. In fact, if your loved one was able to come back and have a conversation with you, isn't it likely that they would say something like "I don't want you to suffer any longer. This was not your fault, and I do not want my death to burden you for the rest of your life. Please find happiness again, and do this to honor me."[56]

Add a reminder to your calendar to contact the family on anniversary dates and holidays. You might send a note or visit the family. One pastor met with the family every few months and whenever a death happened at the church. She said, "Each new suicide brings up the last one, and even each new death brings up the last one. ... When all the teen suicides were in the news this fall, [a survivor] was right back in my office." Another pastor said:

> Long term, it's realizing for them that he will never be a part of the family again, so when special holidays or events come up, that's always a time of remembering. And I think it's also important for pastors to remember, to acknowledge the special dates. So if you know that person's birthday, if you know an anniversary, if you think of them at Christmas, just acknowledge and help them to remember. And to celebrate. I think it's important to celebrate the person's life, and to give thanks to

God for the many ways, in this particular case, this person had touched the lives of so many people in so many different ways.

Jordan and Baugher advise loved ones to plan for anniversaries, and they provide suggestions for how to do this.[57] They also advise remembering the loved one's life, not just the suicide. "It is important to remember that your loved one had a life before the suicide (and before they were depressed) that deserves to be remembered."[58]

Caring for the church

Following a suicide, pastors should make sure each congregant hears about the suicide from a caring leader. A pastor might follow a response protocol (see Appendix D). In Olivia's case, Pastor Alex needed to notify the choir director and the choir members first.

Pastors should also expect that interest in suicide will surge among congregants. They will begin to talk about suicides they've encountered previously. They may need to process how they heard about the suicide. In one church, after a congregant took her life, several of her friends reached out to their pastor. They were dismayed that their friend had planned her suicide so carefully that they could not have prevented it. These congregants were distraught and needed their pastor's support. They may need to process that suicide has happened in their church. As one pastor said, suicide is the "shattering of the illusion that it could never happen." Also, expect that some non-family congregants might feel left out of the grieving because they are not expected to grieve. Jordan and Baugher call this "disenfranchised grief … as if there was a 'hierarchy' of who is entitled to grieve the most and receive the most attention and support."[59] Everyone will be affected by the suicide of a fellow congregant.

Congregants may also feel guilt, asking themselves, "What did I miss? What could I have done to prevent this suicide?" Pastors will sometimes arrange forums, caring groups, or listening circles. At these meetings, a pastor needs to be ready to process, "How did we fail here?" One pastor reminded her congregation, "If you could have done something to prevent it, you would have." These meetings may or may not be well attended; sometimes it is actually the one-on-one meetings that help people most.

In light of this, pastors should invite congregants to talk with them. One pastor lets people know that "it's okay to talk about [suicide] ... because when we stop talking about it, that's when it goes underground and gets dangerous." Each Sunday, one pastor invited congregants to talk with him, saying, "Those of you who are still dealing with issues from [the suicide] and you want to talk about this, please call." He would set up meetings with individuals he was concerned about, to tell them that "suicide is not an appropriate way to deal, that there are many ways, to build on their faith, to get them to understand that no matter what they've done, God still loves them."

Pastors should also work to increase a sense of connection in the church. One pastor said, "The thing I would emphasize the most is the need for people to be together and not be isolated after this experience." The sense of connection extends to community life: "Sometimes life stinks, but there's help available in the Christian community. That's what we kept stressing. This is why we're a church; we're not alone. We cry. We acknowledge what happens. We suffer. We hurt. And we do that together."

Experienced pastors will also monitor vulnerable people (adolescents and young adults with small intense social networks, fringe individuals or people who are depressed or have attempted suicide or have lost someone to suicide, oppressed groups who experience prejudice and discrimination). One pastor said the whole church would look out for other vulnerable people, asking, "Who else in our midst might be feeling this way? Who else should we have an eye on now?" Another pastor encouraged congregants to minister to each other: "What does this [suicide] tell us about the people around us?

What more could we be doing? What else do I need to say? ... We need to speak of our love for one another."

Pastors should also help the church reflect on a theology of suicide. One pastor gave this example of congregants asking him a lot about suicide:

> "Pastor, ... are you telling me that if I kill myself, and I love Jesus, I'm going to heaven?" ... There was one person after the other who said, "If that's the case, then I'm ready to go now." ... And the next few days my phone just rang off the hook. And people said, "I am so tired of this life."

This pastoral staff preached carefully the following Sunday, "There's only one unforgivable sin, suicide's not it. ... But that doesn't mean that it's okay. Think of what you all are suffering as a result of what [she] did. Think of the pain that brings to everybody else. And think of the hope that you can offer to one another."

In addressing suicide from the pulpit, you might preach on all seven fences: the importance of connectedness, the worth and dignity of every person, hope, moral objections to suicide and reasons to live, self-control to develop the habit of choosing life, grief and suffering and the need to reach out for help. Pastors may also want to preach about suicide (if families permit) to help congregants grieve and process their (misplaced) guilt. In addition to preaching, continue to have numerous individual conversations with people.

Expect that some survivors will leave the church. This can be difficult for pastors, but do your best to not take this personally. One pastor said, "When you help somebody through pretty severe trauma, even if you genuinely help them, they find it very difficult to be with you because you represent so much pain. And don't take it personally if they go to another church." Speaking of a family who left following a suicide, one pastor said, "Okay, Lord, I've really got to trust you to let them go." You may also find that you need to encourage other congregants to have compassion on survivors who leave. One pastor said, "You have nice people who sometimes feel more outrage for you than you feel yourself."

Caring for the pastor

Experienced pastors understand that they, too, have survived a suicide and need care. Pastors are not exempt from the impact of suicide, especially if the pastor was practically involved. One pastor remembers, "A minister went in and cleaned up, and I can remember that it had a significant impact on him after he cleaned up all the blood and everything."

As a pastor, you need to process your own (misplaced) guilt. A wise mentor told one pastor, "You can't take responsibility for people. You can only be responsible *to* them." Experienced pastors are aware that the person who took their life may not have felt that suicide was a choice as much as the only option in the midst of their intense pain. You may need to reach out and talk through your feelings of guilt with others.[60] One pastor recommends, "Every pastor should have a pastor." Some pastors process with a clergy group.

You should also expect other emotions besides guilt. You may feel anger. One pastor said, "I walked in the funeral home, I saw his body lying there, and my first thought was, 'I want to go over there and slap him.' " It can be a relief to know that other pastors experience a strong mix of emotions.

The challenging aspect of experiencing these emotions is juggling the dual roles of being a community member affected by suicide and being the leader of the community and responsible to provide that leadership. One pastor said, "I think and feel like everybody else. You know there's really nothing different. Except that I also have to lead and think and feel for the larger community." This pastor reached out to colleagues. "I might ask someone to help me come do memorial services or just sit with me while I do them."

Self-care is not optional. It is crucial to longevity in ministry. Ultimately, one pastor left the pastorate a year after a suicide. "[The church wasn't] ready to have me leave, and I wasn't really ready to leave, but after a year of [monitoring vulnerable people], I was burned out."

In addition to self-care, pastors seek out educational opportunities to learn more about suicide. A pastor may want to invite someone to the church to present on suicide prevention. SoulShop provides training and support to faith community leaders about suicide.[61]

Summary

In this chapter, we reviewed how to care pastorally for a suicidal individual, a person who attempted suicide, and survivors following a suicide death. This review showed us that pastoral care in the context of suicide can be complex because people's short-term and long-term needs are different, and the needs of individuals, family members, and the church are different. While balancing these needs, the pastor should maintain a strong focus on self-care in order to prevent burnout because pastors have a clear role in caring in the context of suicide. In the appendices, you'll find a handout for survivors following a suicide (Appendix C) and a response protocol following a suicide (Appendix D).

In the next chapter, we'll describe how pastors craft a sermon for the funeral or memorial service.

THE FUNERAL SERMON
AND POST-SUICIDE CARE

The funeral service is an opportunity to demonstrate
biblically how the gospel is an anchor for us
in the worst storms of life.

Brian Croft and Phil Newton, Conduct Gospel-Centered Funerals

Case Study

PASTOR PAUL sat in his office, his Bible and books piled in front
of him as a massive heap on the top of his desk. He was preparing
once again for a funeral, but this one was different: a death by suicide.
He hung his head and prayed for God's guidance as he readied words
of comfort and hope for yet another stunned and grieving family.

Betsy was a woman in her late fifties who had succumbed to
depression and despair. Her marriage to Charles had crumbled
around her. She didn't quite know why. Perhaps it was the immense
sadness that had still lingered in her heart from the unexpected death
of her mother. Betsy had been with her mother when she died. They
were in the waiting room of her mother's physician. Her mom was
not feeling well after having exerted herself that morning mowing

the grass. As they sat in the waiting room, she seemed to wilt and collapsed onto the floor. The nurse and doctor attended her but she was gone—dead. Betsy had been devastated.

Then there was her marriage. Her relationship with Charles seemed to have grown increasingly distant over the last several years. Betsy even suspected that Charles was having an affair. To cope with the stress, Betsy began taking prescription medication to help her with depression. She became listless. She lost interest in most every-thing—even in her faith. Soon Betsy and Charles were separated—Charles living in their home of thirty-five years and Betsy renting a small apartment. Life couldn't have gotten worse.

In desperation, Betsy ingested all her prescription pills at once. She was found the next morning by her daughter, Denise. Through her sobs, Denise telephoned Pastor Paul. The funeral would be in three days.

But Paul wondered, "What could I have done to help Betsy? Is there a strategy that I can adopt in my sermon preparation or overall pastoral approach that would help those like Betsy who've lost hope? What can I do differently?"

Case Study Questions

1. What would you have done to help Betsy if you were Pastor Paul?

2. What might he need to be aware of as he prepares for this funeral?

3. What strategy for sermon preparation should he use?

4. How can he address the issue of suicide and the hope of the gospel?

5. How is this sermon different from other funerals he has conducted and will conduct in the future?

Introduction

It often falls on pastors to walk with wisdom alongside people through their most difficult problems. Melinda Moore advises pastors, "Often, addressing suicide lies in your hands as an informed spiritual leader. … You will be modeling a grief journey through counseling the suicide bereaved and conducting the funeral. Your leadership will influence how the suicide bereaved are treated by other clergy, congregants, lay ministers, funeral directors, and others in the days, weeks, months following the death."[1]

Few ministerial duties are as challenging or present a greater opportunity as the funeral of a suicide. For many family members, a suicide death is an embarrassment, an inconvenience, certainly unconventional. Grieving families deal with suicide in numerous ways. Novelist Frederick Buechner reflects in one of his memoirs about his father's suicide:

> One November morning in 1936 when I was ten years old, my father got up early, put on a pair of gray slacks and a maroon sweater, opened the door to look in briefly on my younger brother and me, who were playing a game in our room, and then went down into the garage where he turned on the engine of the family Chevy and sat down on the running board to wait for the exhaust to kill him. Except for a memorial service for his Princeton class the next spring, by which time we had moved away to another part of the world altogether, there was no funeral because on both my mother's side and my father's there was no church connection of any kind and funerals were simply not part of the tradition. He was cremated, his ashes buried in a cemetery in Brooklyn, and I have no idea who if anybody was present. I knew only that my mother, brother and I were not.[2]

Buechner continues, "There was no funeral to mark his death and put a period at the end of the sentence that had been his life, and as far as I can remember, once he had died my mother, brother, and I rarely talked about him much ever again, either to each other or to anybody else."[3] But as pastors, we do not have the option to ignore family tragedies like death by suicide. We are called to pastor people through crises, even the death of a family member by suicide. We mark the death and we proclaim the hope of the gospel.

In this chapter, our focus will be on preaching the funeral sermon for a death by suicide—to provide that needed period of which Buechner writes. We will also explore avenues for post-suicide care.

Developing the Funeral Sermon: The Suicide Bereaved

Constructing a funeral sermon for the suicide bereaved takes on different considerations than the typical funeral sermon. Some of the suggestions below are certainly part of preparing any funeral sermon, but they are made in light of the immense distinctiveness of the sermon for occasions of suicides.[4]

Any funeral is difficult. There are emotions that arise from family members, friends, the community of faith, and even the pastor. Upon learning what happened, pastors should first pause. Pray. Ask the Lord for wisdom, insight, grace, tenderness, and guidance. Andrew Blackwood writes, "Long since [a pastor] should have learned that it is possible to [pray] while hastening to the home of sorrow. If he goes in faith, as the servant of the Lord, the Spirit will guide. At such a time the rule is, 'A minister has no more religion than he displays in an emergency.' "[5]

The hope of the gospel

A pastor who preached at a funeral for someone who died by suicide asked, "How do you have an honest but hopeful funeral?"[6] The situation demands both honesty and hope. This hope is found in the person and work of Jesus Christ. This means that the sermon is immersed in the gospel: the life, death, burial, and resurrection of Christ, the believer's hope. The gospel is front and center in the sermon. The hope found in the forgiving grace of Christ is the only pure hope that the bereaved need—and may not know that they want.

The promises of the gospel are a great comfort to the bereaved. Pastors William R. Baird, Sr., and John E. Baird, write in their book *Funeral Meditations*:

> Let attention be centered on the precious promises of the gospel. These bring comfort to the sorrowing. They turn attention from the loss that has been suffered to the eternal truths of our Christian faith. They deliver the preacher from the necessity of passing judgment, whether favorable or unfavorable, upon the dead. They deepen the understanding of even the most casual visitor to the service.[7]

The centerpiece of the gospel provides listeners with a touchstone, a grip of hope in the middle of a storm. Croft and Newton state, "The service is really about how the gospel applies in such settings, not a time for answering unanswerable questions about suicide or the state of the deceased."[8]

The importance of naming

In an earlier time and perhaps in some contexts, the mention of suicide was avoided. For example, in his 1942 book on conducting funerals, Andrew W. Blackwood states, "In the funeral services, whether they be private or public, there should be no allusion to suicide."[9] But advice has since shifted. Emily Askew and O. Wesley Allen suggest, "As at any funeral of a suicide victim, it is important that preachers name the deceased as just that: a victim."[10] One pastor advises, "My principle is that we talk about it in proportion to how publicly known the situation is. ... But if we know what happened, to ignore that I think is to deny people the opportunity to process their own pain, anger, anguish."[11] However, another pastor advises, "Let the family determine how much is said about the cause of death. In [my] case, I never used the word 'suicide' in the service."

Name also the fears that swirl around in the listeners' minds and hearts. They are real. They may conflict with each other. Bryan Chapell suggests that preachers "name the obvious questions that suicide raises about the spiritual status of the deceased and answer with declarations of the sufficiency of God's grace."[12]

Pastors struggle with the question of addressing suicide and sin. What does one say at the funeral? What does one communicate to the family? Chapell advises, "Because we do not believe that suicide is an unforgivable sin, we should not imply that suicide is no sin. The damage such an act does to one's body (the temple of the Holy Spirit), family, friends, church, and testimony is incalculable."

Developing the Funeral Sermon: Learning from Others

Attempting to gain a well-rounded perspective on creating funeral sermons for the suicide bereaved, we consulted three different groups: pastors who have preached these kinds of funeral sermons; family members who have listened to pastors preach to them as they grieve a suicide; and funeral directors who serve both pastors and families. This section is our attempt to learn from these various groups how pastors might be better equipped to preach at funerals for the suicide bereaved.[13]

Pastors

It may be the first time you've conducted a funeral for a suicide death, or it might be one of many. Yet, most pastors may not feel prepared to deal with a suicide or to preach at a funeral for a person who died by suicide. Most often, pastors enter into ministry to the suicide bereaved without any experience, instruction, or concept of what to do or how to do it. Seminary has not, does not, and will not be able to prepare pastors for every aspect of ministry, and certainly not the emotional and spiritual climate of a suicide funeral. Although the pastors surveyed may not have been taught how to engage in ministry associated with suicide, they learned through the experience itself, coming out on the other side strengthened and deepened as a pastor and as a person.

One of the most important qualities of any funeral service is that it be conducted with genuineness. One pastor we interviewed noted that presence is more important in that moment than theological acumen: "Don't try to answer the big questions in a homily. Rather, be a grieving, faithful presence, offering words of comfort and some hope, celebrating the good while not ignoring the trauma." Gentle honesty with one's listeners helps. Another one of our pastors encouraged, "Enter into the real contours of the loss, both in the counseling and in the sermon. Don't sugarcoat what's happened; don't use theological platitudes." Genuineness is a critical feature of preaching in sensitive moments like that of a suicide. One of the pastors who preached at the funeral for a Vietnam veteran who died by suicide after having lost his financial empire advised, "You want no sense of glossing over the reality of the event, the devastation to family and friends, the anger being felt, and public and private shame."

The preacher also wants to be sensitive not to assign the eternity of the deceased. A newly minted pastor remembered reading chapters in *The Baker Funeral Handbook* on suicide and death by accident.[14] He reflected on words he read in the handbook to the effect of neither "damning to hell" nor "preaching into heaven" the deceased person. "This was an important lesson to hear—not just for this situation but for many funerals." As preachers, our responsibility is to be text-based, gospel-focused, and personal.

However, it's that personal factor that can trouble us as preachers—often we know the deceased, which makes leading a funeral a particular challenge. In light of this, one pastor noted, "Conducting a funeral service for a suicide victim that you know is quite different from a victim you don't know." Particularly for the former, "It is important to process your own emotions and sense of grief throughout the funeral proceedings."

Family members

Pastors should think of their sermon as a ministry directly to the family, and indirectly to others. One husband whose wife died by suicide told us, "I would suggest to the pastor that the bereaved are unlikely to pay attention to the funeral sermon, but that in case they and others do, the sermon should avoid personal references and should focus on our hope in Christ." A father whose daughter-in-law died by suicide agreed: "He [the pastor] preached the funeral sermon on a Sunday afternoon in a little cemetery chapel. I can't remember anything he said, but I recall it was a very comforting sermon."

One spouse whose husband died by suicide commented on how the funeral service recording continues to comfort her:

> I've learned in the months that have passed that my husband was both what people saw and what they did not. It's not an either-or thing. It's not as black and white as we seem to think. But at the time, all I could see was the depression and hiddenness that led to his death. Everything else seemed like a lie. I'm glad that I can go back and watch the service, because I hear it differently now. I'm glad now that they spoke of his humor, his servanthood, his kindness and generosity. Those are the things that people knew about him. And somehow, they are both true, even as the dark side is true.

A family member whose cousin died by suicide warned, "It's very important to avoid clichés and 'quick-fix' answers [in sermons], because pain is very real and not easily addressed." She continued, "I think the best approach to ministering and preaching to the suicide bereaved is to feel their pain with them instead of trying to fix it." A suicide bereaved father-in-law advised, "One of the best things a pastor can do is look at what the Bible says." The sermon is best heard by family members when the pastor is present—aware of the layers of emotion and pain as demonstrated in the sermon, which directs the listeners to the hope of the Scripture.

Funeral directors

Funeral directors are in a unique position, since they both serve with pastors who preach the funeral sermon as well as help families who grieve. Their best advice boils down to one point: connect with the family of the deceased.

When asked about what pastors have done well, one funeral director mentioned "sitting with the family, meeting with the family. ... Listening is better than talking. ... Providing helpful suggestions of things that would make the funeral special." Another funeral director agreed: "Listening is a big tool—before, during, and after." He also advised, "Don't make the service too long. Music, some speaking. If at a church, forty-five minutes to an hour. At the funeral home, thirty minutes." Another funeral director emphasized, "Tailor the service and comments to the individual family situations." "An error," said another, "would be to walk in and do the service without getting a connection with the family."

The funeral directors' industry has produced helpful material on suicide prevention and funerals for suicide deaths. The directors who were part of this study expressed special sensitivity to the needs of the suicide-bereaved family. They also were aware of the balance required for conducting a funeral for a suicide death. They seemed to ratchet up the sensitivity when it came to these kinds of funerals.[15]

When We Preach

What do we want to keep in mind as we prepare to preach at funerals for those who died by suicide? Below are matters to consider as you prepare to preach a sermon for the suicide bereaved.

Proclaim hope

Even though this is the darkest of situations, there remains the eternal hope that is found in Jesus Christ. Proclaim it. Reflecting on the suicide death of a pastoral colleague, Douglas D. Webster urges, "Wisdom encourages us to trust in the sovereign care of God, even though our world seems to be falling into chaos and we join Job on the ash heap."[16] One pastor in our study who has preached funerals for the suicide bereaved added, "Sharing the hope we have in Christ is the most loving thing we can do in the face of suicide."

Give words of grace

We want to remind listeners that God is with them. Roger F. Miller emphasizes, "Even though grieving people may be angry at God to the point of rage, God's love is still important to them." He adds, "The effective pastor is the one who can help the bereaved through Scripture, prayer, and message to know that God is present, not as the oppressor but as the comforter on the side of the oppressed."[17]

Provide an atmosphere of forgiveness and healing

Attendees of a funeral after a death by suicide are likely to be experiencing anger, guilt, and second-guessing. Expressing these feelings in hymns or worship songs, words of confession, psalms and prayers of lament, and fitting words in the sermon are ways pastors can help listeners articulate their own responses to this tragic death and offer them to God.[18] Pastors we surveyed about developing the funeral service encouraged other pastors to use the service to educate listeners about suicide and position survivors for the healing process.[19]

Be aware of what families are hearing

Michael Rogness insightfully observes that at times of tragedy, listeners want comfort and pastors want to give it. However, as he notes, "They try to think of something positive, but say things that aren't very helpful at all." Some common unhelpful comments are, "It must be God's will," "God must have wanted another angel," or, "Isn't it fortunate that you have other children?"[20] Paul Tautges warns, "Christ-centered comfort is the only true comfort. ... Any comfort we give to people that lies outside the hope of the gospel is temporary at best and deceptive at worst."[21]

Families are sensitive to what the preacher says. Pastors told us that listeners expect honesty, not empty words. One listener warned, "Don't tell her [the grieving spouse] how much he loved her. You don't know that that is true." She continued, "When in doubt, speak Scripture. It always holds true." In addition, like any overwhelming experience, the words preached may not necessarily be remembered by those listening, especially the mourning family members. They are overcome with their grief. They are muffled from the capacity to hear well without distraction. What does this reality say to the pastor preparing sermons for suicide funerals? Stay focused. Stay on target.

Preach contextually

Mary Hulst reminds us, "To preach contextually means preaching a sermon for these people, in this place, on this day. ... To preach contextually is to connect the preached word with the deep needs of these people at this time."[22] That is why canned sermons are poor homiletical offerings, and regurgitated sermons from past funerals border on violating one's relationship with the bereaved. One pastor noted, "There is no such thing as a 'cookie-cutter' suicide (or funeral for that matter). … The specific circumstances must drive the contextualization of the preaching." The preacher's responsibility is to know the listeners and meet them where they are at that time and in that place.

Pastoral Follow-Up

As noted above, listeners will most likely not remember what is said, but be more in tune with the tone, the affect, the manner in which the sermon was communicated. Since grieving listeners are in an emotional fog following suicide, you may want to give a copy of your sermon to the suicide bereaved. Providing them with a copy of the sermon will allow them to reflect on the words at a time of their convenience. This is just one of many ways in which a pastor can follow up after the service. Here are a few more.

Do pastoral visits

A pastor's duties are far from over once the funeral service has ended. A pastor reflected, "I learned about the importance and power of quiet pastoral presence." Another observed, "Suicide is among the most tender of the pastoral challenges; the family must have a deep sense of non-judgmental presence." He continued, "It's important to stay in close touch, especially after the crowd of mourners slips away, and the bereaved are left alone in their grief. Regular, frequent contact is important in the days, weeks, and months ahead."

Family members are also likely to have theological questions in the weeks and months after a suicide, and these questions can be discussed during pastoral visits. Following the suicide death of a sixteen-year-old girl, one pastor met with her younger brothers for a period of about six weeks. He spent these meetings "explaining the gospel message to them, making sure they knew what happens to people after they die, and how they can make sure their sins are forgiven and their salvation secure." He continued, "I received a message from one of the boys years later after he was in college, telling me how helpful those meetings were to him, and how it strengthened his faith." Another pastor wisely encouraged, "Be ready and willing to engage in biblical/theological questions and conversation about suicide outside the funeral service."

Recommend reading

Providing reading resources for grieving family members may also help in the processing of personal and collective grief. Numerous books and booklets are available that can be of immense comfort to families after a death. Haddon W. Robinson's short book *Grief: Comfort for Those Who Grieve and Those Who Want to Help* addresses grief broadly. Harold Ivan Smith's *The Long Shadow of Grief: Suicide and Its Aftermath* honestly wrestles with the realities of life and faith. Additionally, *Grieving a Suicide: A Loved One's Search for Comfort, Answers & Hope* by Albert Y. Hsu chronicles Hsu's journey as he worked through the death of his father by suicide. These sources—and many more—can be one avenue of help for the suicide bereaved.

Write notes

In an age of electronic media, which has its place in ministry, a personal, hand-written note may provide a level of emotional and spiritual comfort that cannot be done through electronic means. Paul Tautges suggests that these notes may need to continue for some time following the death of a loved one.[23] After my father died in 1991, I (Scott) wrote a note to my mother weekly until she died in 2010. As a son, it was my way of letting her know that she was loved by me, and by the Lord.

Help them to remember

We help families to remember when we suggest tactile and other types of ceremonies that they can employ as a way of remembering the life of a loved one lost to suicide. Below are several examples.

Encourage the family to visit their loved one's gravestone to honor and celebrate that person's life. Pastors can assist in helping the family prepare the gravestone, and they may offer to visit with the family. Gravestones can now be designed online and confirmed in person at the gravestone studio.

Suggest that the family establish a memorial project in the name of the deceased at the local church or in the community as another way to remember. For example, you can help coordinate funding for a local crisis line or needed equipment for the fire department.

Depending on the family as they work through their grief, the pastor may suggest that they assemble a scrapbook of significant events in the loved one's life, a photo collection or a video montage, helping them to remember well.

The anniversary of the death or the birthday of the deceased can be an occasion for the pastor to be present as the family remembers. A memorial observation marking the first year of death can be a fitting expression arranged in conjunction with the family and pastor.

Another option, less common in Protestant spheres, is a "Month's Mind Mass"—a Catholic tradition of honoring someone who died for a month following the death. "The traditions associated with this Mass go back to medieval England," writes Larry Peterson. "The Mass was the standard requiem Mass with several prayers added specifically for those who had passed away during the previous month."[24] Gerry Moloney and George Wadding observe, "The pain of loss is not quite as intense now, and the Memorial Mass helps us to move forward into the future."[25]

Congregational Follow-Up

Preach on suicide prevention

Culture ebbs and flows with suicide awareness. The common reasons for suicide in one era will return in another in a different form. Listeners read the news, blogs, books, articles, and listen to streamed media or radio and are confronted on the television with the realities of suicide—and they try to make sense of it all as they face the realities of suicide in their family or social circles. How much more, then, is it the pastor's prerogative to shape disciples' thinking about suicide? Preach on it. Plan to preach on it. Develop a sermon series on death or one addressing suicide, among other tough issues. The more information that is given to our listeners, the more potential transformation will take place in their thinking, souls, lives, and practices. Preach the hope of the gospel. Preaching on suicide prevention is an aspect of pastoral follow up.

Evaluate your preaching

Take time to examine your preaching by observing your tone. Select ten sermons that you have preached over the last year or so, and ask of these sermons, "Are they guilt-driven or grace-driven?". Look for words of guilt: should, must, ought, need to, or, have to. Assess whether the tone of the text matches the tone of the preached sermon. Cultivating hope in the weekly sermon will find its way into special-occasion sermons like those preached to the suicide bereaved.

Small groups

Pastors are not the only members of the church community who can and should follow up with the bereaved after a suicide. One avenue for this is small groups. There are at least two approaches for small group follow-up. First, as counselors Andrew Weaver and John Preston suggest, "Clergy can also invite bereaved parents to get together from time to time simply to talk and share feelings. Pastors can mobilize other caring people to surround survivors with supportive, loving relationships."[26] Second, churches can establish grief support groups for bereaved family members. These grief groups can be formal or informal.

Grief teams (deacons/lay pastors)

Grief teams of deacons or lay pastors are an invaluable way to extend the reach of pastoral ministry and preaching. Brian Croft reminds us, "Regardless of how you teach your congregation to visit the sick—whether through a short sermon series or through regular application in your expositional sermons—never forget that the preaching of God's word is what gives life to the church, and it is the setting for us to exhort with authority the matters that are most important to the spiritual health of the entire body. Teach your church that the care of the sick and afflicted is a priority for God's people by exhorting them through public preaching."[27]

The interviews for this study with the suicide bereaved indicated that there was an appreciation for the care that pastors provided during the aftermath of a family member's suicide. A LifeWay research study on suicide noted the following:

> About half of churchgoers affected by suicide (49%) say their church prayed with the family afterward; 43 percent say church members attended their loved one's visitation or funeral; 41 percent say someone from the church visited their

family; and 32 percent received a card. Churches also provide financial help (11%), referral to a counselor (11%) and help with logistics like cleaning and childcare (10%) or planning for the funeral (22%).[28]

Pastoral care is immensely important following any death and is a key element toward healing for the suicide bereaved. Preaching on suicide prevention, exploring the tone of your preaching, encouraging small grief groups, and establishing grief teams contribute to a textured approach to healthy pastoral care. By engaging in at least some of these practices, pastors will engage in follow-up that will make a long-term difference in the lives of their congregation.

Summary

This chapter provided pastors with tools for preaching at funerals of the suicide bereaved, whose worlds are torn apart. A mourning spouse observed, "I've heard that every person who commits suicide is essentially a suicide bomber. Those nearest the explosion are torn to shreds by the explosion—and the impact continues in waves to the person furthest from the center." Pastors want to preach sermons and conduct care with the skill of an insightful first responder to those near and far.

We want to serve our congregations and community well by preparing well. Roger Miller comments:

> For all the good things we can do for families in the hard cases, however, we can do just as many bad—and avoiding the bad is the challenge. Poorly given, ministry can have a definite counterproductive effect on those in grief, actually damaging the emotions and spirit. The bereaved may feel estranged from God and the church family just when closeness and nurture is needed most.[29]

To help you prepare well, we have included a sample suicide funeral liturgy in appendix F.

The principles developed in this chapter will serve preachers well as they prepare themselves for the surprises of ministry, even the suicide of those in our flock or in the local community, after which we are called on to lead and love, like the case study that opened this chapter.

We pray God's wisdom and grace be upon you as you serve in these challenging moments of ministry.

YOUNG ADULT AND YOUTH GROUP PREACHING AND TEACHING

Mental health is the mission field of this generation.

Karen Mason et al.,
"How Faith Communities Help Build Lives Worth Living"

Case Study

PASTOR SALLY got a call from Janet, a college sophomore who is hospitalized after swallowing some pills. Sally knows that Janet's father recently filed for divorce and that her distraught mother has been calling Janet nonstop. When Sally meets with Janet at the hospital, in tears, Janet explains she failed a test and lost her perfect grade point average. Janet repeats, "I'm so stupid," "I'm such a failure," and "It's hopeless." Janet is sure she won't get into medical school now. She also feels like a failure as a daughter because she can't help her mom. In fact, her mother has said she is worried about how to pay Janet's tuition. Janet said, "My dad and mom will be better off without me." Pastor Sally prays with Janet and talks with Janet about other options for her problems besides suicide.

Case Study Questions

1. How could Pastor Sally increase Janet's sense of connection with others?

2. How could Pastor Sally increase Janet's sense of worth and dignity as an imperfect human?

3. If Janet cannot get into medical school, what other hope can Pastor Sally offer?

4. How could Pastor Sally help Janet manage her suffering as a Christian?

5. How could Pastor Sally help Janet reach out for help before attempting again?

Introduction

Generation Z (born between the late 1990s and early 2010s) is significantly more likely than other generations (including millennials and Gen Xers) to report their mental health as fair or poor.[1] Their mental health struggles match their struggles with suicide. The Centers for Disease Control and Prevention tell us that about one in six high schoolers seriously considers suicide annually, and about one in fourteen young adults ages eighteen to twenty-five has serious thoughts about suicide annually.[2] In 2018 in the United States, suicide was the *second* leading cause of death among people ages ten to thirty-four.[3] Suicide is a serious problem among young people. It makes sense to dedicate a chapter to preaching and teaching youth and young adults.

In this chapter, you will read about general preaching and teaching approaches for young adults and youth. This chapter is shorter than the others, but in appendix H we have included specific teaching activities for adolescents and young adults using the seven fences that help prevent suicide: preaching and teaching on connectedness, the worth and dignity of every human, hope, moral objections to suicide and reasons to live, self-control and the habit of choosing life, grief and suffering, and reaching out for help.

You might wish to avoid talking to young people about suicide. You might hope that if you could avoid the topic, they will, too. But the statistics above show young people face suicide. They are already talking about suicide amongst themselves and with other adult guides. Wouldn't it be better if young people explored suicide from the point of view of the Bible? One parachurch worker said that the more we can talk about these things from a Biblical worldview, the more young people will keep attending our faith-based gatherings, and the more they will invite their friends to attend because suicide is a relevant conversation.[4]

If the church ignores this conspicuous topic, young people might think God or the church is indifferent or ignorant about it. Rev. James T. Clemons wrote this about preaching about suicide: "When preachers don't address significant issues in some way, regardless of how controversial or difficult they may be, one of two messages comes thundering through the silence: Either preachers don't care or they don't know what to say."[5] Nothing could be further from the truth. Pastors care, and there is a lot to say about suicide because God has a lot to say about life. Appendix H will equip you with seven Bible studies for young adults and seven Sunday School or youth group suicide-related activities for adolescents. These are biblically based activities.

Approaches to Suicide Prevention for Young People

Rather than restate various principles we've already discussed in this book—which apply to young people, too—it is better to leave youth workers with several general approaches to suicide prevention.

Be relevant

Young people face a lot of challenges, such as the breakup of families, breakups with romantic partners, anxiety about the future, questions about vaping and sex, *and* a high suicide rate. Pastors tell us that to engage young people, it is important to engage the questions of life that are relevant to them, to connect to their real struggles. Suicide is one of their real struggles. Clinton Faupel at RemedyLIVE reports that of the 30,363 young people they surveyed in 2018–2019, 61 percent knew someone who struggles with suicidal thinking.[6] But these young people may not be sure how to help each other. And they are not sure who is a safe adult to talk to about their questions.[7]

Be a safe person

The most important gift you can offer young people is to be that safe person. They need a trusted adult to come to with any question they have. Pastors tell us that young people need to know trusted adults *before a crisis* so that they know they can reach out, knowing without a shadow of doubt that they will not be judged. They can be sure they won't be judged because of the kind of community pastors foster. Young people need a community where they are known and unconditionally loved. This non-judgmental love communicates the young person's innate value and fosters connectedness. One parachurch worker said, "We try to connect in a meaningful way with teenagers so they have a person they can trust, an adult who cares about them and earns the right to be heard, who they can confide in and turn to when they are struggling or hurting and feel low." This same parachurch worker added that young people also need faith-based guidance. "Teenagers need a faith-centered place where they can process and communicate how they feel without judgment, and instead with guidance and love."[8]

It is in this type of community that a young person can learn about wise living, about moral objections to suicide and narratives of hope in the midst of suffering. In this context, young people learn the seven fences of connectedness, the worth and dignity of every human, hope, moral objections to suicide and reasons to live, self-control and the habit of choosing life, grief and suffering, and that they can reach out for help. These fences merge into the fence of an authentic genuine community. And where better than in a church or parachurch organization? One senior pastor told us that every adolescent in her church has a mentor who prays for them daily and is available to meet if the adolescent reaches out.[9] Churches foster this type of community for young people in many ways.

Be equipped

Pastors have told us they feel under-equipped and are trying to learn on the job.[10] Pastors also tell us that it is important to equip everyone to recognize the signs of suicide and to help. The result of an authentic community where young people reach out in a crisis is that everyone must be ready to help. Pastors have told us that it's important to train everyone: pastors, small group leaders, volunteers, and mentors, as well as the young people themselves. This kind of training is called gatekeeper training; individuals are trained in knowledge and skills to identify those at risk and connect the suicidal person to resources, to open the gate to the help they need.[11] There are many gatekeeper trainings available.[12]

When acting as a gatekeeper, it is important to know that parents and legal guardians are responsible for the welfare of their minor child (a child under eighteen years old). If a minor is suicidal, their parent or legal guardian should be contacted. If the young person asked you to keep their confidence a secret, don't. Keeping a young person safe is a higher obligation than keeping their confidentiality.

In chapter 5, "Pastoral Care after a Suicide Crisis," we laid out several basic skills like developing a crisis plan, accessing the National Suicide Prevention Lifeline (1-800-273-TALK), and monitoring adolescents following a suicide because of their vulnerability to contagion and copycat suicide. At the end of this book, you'll find several additional resources. We lay out several specific steps in a response protocol in appendix D, and provide a sample letter to youth group parents about a suicide prevention Bible study series in appendix G. This letter is an important step in implementing suicide prevention activities for minors because their parents are responsible for the welfare of their children. In appendix H we have included those Bible studies and activities for young people, including creating a hope kit. A suicidal person can turn to a hope kit when their suicidal thoughts get strong. The hope kit contains a young person's reasons to live. Our personal hope is that every youth gathering in the United States would include making a hope kit for each young person.

More resources include a sample sermon on Psalm 13, a lament psalm (appendix A), a liturgy for World Suicide Prevention Day on September 10 (appendix B), advice for how parents can support their student following a suicide (appendix I), and a response protocol following a suicide (appendix D).

Be networked

Young people and their families need resources. As one parachurch worker said, "A lot of people say you just need more Jesus. ... Jesus is important, but there is a greater need. To make counseling services available for families, kids, and adults would be great. I have heard of churches that have counseling resources available for families and children and meeting their needs that way. ... [We] have one counselor on staff, and that is not enough anymore."[13] Utilizing resources at church are important, but what other ones are there?

One of the most important community resources is the Suicide Prevention Lifeline (1-800-273-TALK).[14] The lifeline provides free, 24/7 confidential support for people in distress and best practices for professionals. When a pastor calls the lifeline, the pastor will be connected to a national network of local crisis centers and your nearest crisis center may be able to suggest local resources. Another resource is the young person's school. Many US schools (elementary, middle, high school, undergraduate, and graduate schools) have trained counselors who are available to provide support to the young person. Many US communities also have mental health organizations to which to refer. To access these, some of your congregants must have health insurance. Health insurance that provides mental health or substance use disorder benefits should not impose less favorable benefit limitations on mental health benefits than on medical/surgical benefits.[15] One pastor told us that she has had her congregants bring in their insurance cards to church. They made sure that everyone understood their insurance plan and how to find a provider *before a crisis*.[16] But some communities are lacking in theses resources, and many health systems in the United States are fractured.[17] This makes referral particularly difficult for pastors. As quoted in chapter 1, one pastor told us that the lack of resources "is just about the scariest thing that I face."[18] To address that shortage, Orange County in California has developed an intentionally coordinated system of mental health and substance abuse services that includes churches.[19] The Hope and Healing Center & Institute in Houston, Texas, offers an integrated system of mental health services that includes churches. Developing these resources takes a great deal of vision, work, funding, and advocacy.

Suicide is an urgent priority

Pastors have also told us that it's not easy to find time to focus on suicide and get trained. Pastors face the fact that there are a "million" other issues that need to be addressed, many competing priorities that feel more urgent. As one pastor said, "[Suicide] gets pushed to the back burner until it comes up; then you say, ah man, I wish I could have been more prepared for that."[20] Many clergy will deal with suicide at some point[21] because clergy are as likely to be contacted by suicidal people as other professionals,[22] and suicide happens in faith communities.

Mental health is the twenty-first century mission field

Pastors have also told us that one way to focus on suicide prevention is by focusing on mental health. Pastors have said that people have left the church because their church experience feels disconnected from the real issues they face, including mental health. Several pastors have said that ministry to young people means dealing with mental health. One parachurch worker said, "Kids don't feel understood, and they don't feel like anyone gets what kind of climate is going on within that mind of theirs. ... We need to talk about mental health. ... Mental health is the mission field of this generation."[23]

There are many ways to include a focus on mental health. Many churches have mental health ministries or mental health professionals in their congregations who would like to contribute to such a focus. One example is Dr. Matthew Stanford's program called Gateway to Hope, which empowers congregations with a free faith-based mental health training at your church or parachurch location.[24] The program includes a section on suicide prevention.

You could also invite groups who specialize in this topic to come and start the conversation at your church. These include groups like RemedyLIVE or Soul Shop.[25] RemedyLIVE also has programs specifically for teens and parents.[26]

Summary

Suicide is a significant problem faced by young people. In order to reverse the growing tragedy of suicide in the next generation, churches and parachurch organizations need to help youth and young adults build lives worth living by providing one or more protective factors including a safe, connected community; a skilled, equipped community; and a well-networked community. The appendices provide specific examples of how to do so through biblically based life-affirming teaching.

CONCLUSION

In time, even hope demolished can become hope rebuilt, if it
is realistic and rooted, not just in the cross and empty tomb
but also in the garden and the sweat-like blood.

Zack Eswine, Spurgeon's Sorrows: Realistic Hope for Those
Who Suffer from Depression

THIS STUDY on preaching and suicide prevention ends where it
began. In the introduction, we noted that we would be addressing the
following questions: How can a pastor adequately prepare the congregation for a tragedy like suicide? What can pastors do to engender
the hope of the gospel in the regular rhythms of congregational life?
What does a pastor need to know as he or she prepares to preach to
the suicide bereaved?

As for helping a congregation prepare adequately for a tragedy
like suicide, in chapters one and two we laid out the facts and features of suicide and suicide prevention. In chapter three, we discussed
how those facts and features inform the shape and vision of one's
preaching: instilling the hope of the gospel into the regular rhythm
of a pastor's preaching.

The case studies are also meant to help you prepare your congregation for the tragedy of suicide. The case studies are actual snapshots

from the lives of men and women whom both of us have served. The cases can be used in pastoral staff training or campus ministry situations, small groups or even the classroom. They tell the story to congregations that the matter of suicide is real and help to stimulate healthy discussion, further preparing them for a potential suicide calamity.

The second question, "What can pastors do to engender the hope of the gospel in the regular rhythms of congregational life?," was covered in chapter three and further explored in chapters four through seven. Pastoral care in the preparation for a funeral for the suicide bereaved is crucial—but this is only one aspect of cultivating hope in listeners. Hope is engendered with awareness, presence, and pastoral follow-up. Speaking about Christian hope at the funeral service is one thing, but demonstrating it in other aspects of pastoral ministry is another. Both are needed for strengthening the faith and life of a congregation.

We also established that pastors themselves need care in seasons rocked by suicide. The pastor is challenged emotionally, physically, and spiritually, especially since he or she is caring for the burdens of so many. Cared-for pastors are better equipped to preach and persuade people with hope if they are confident in the hope of the gospel themselves. Pastoral care for the pastor is crucial.

The third and final question, "What does a pastor need to know as he or she prepares to preach to the suicide bereaved?," is wrapped up in the entirety of this book. A pastor simply must understand the gravity of the situation and be at least somewhat familiar with the dynamics of suicide. This is why we determined to use real-life situations for the case studies, laid open the features of suicide statistics and what comprises the signs of suicide, and discussed strategies for preventing suicide. Preparedness for preaching a suicide funeral sermon is a time-consuming endeavor, but it is so important. A pastor must tenderly, solemnly, and yet with hope guide listeners through the denial, anger, numbness, grief, and a rush of other powerful emotions of those present. They are gathered to grieve, and many hope and need to hear a clear word from God.

We have an immensely holy task in front of us as we bring God's word to God's people, and to those who do not yet know him. Now we are aware of the prominent place suicide has within our culture. For many of us, a suicide death has already punctured the ministry God has given us. For others, you shudder to think that sometime in the days ahead you will be called upon to preach to a grieving group of the suicide bereaved. You are reading this book because you want to be better prepared to serve the people under your care as they grapple with the awfulness of suicide. This book is an attempt to address this need by awareness, by thoughtful integration of hope in one's preaching, by teaching young adults about issues surrounding suicide, by encouraging pastoral follow-up, and by understanding the people to whom you minister.

We have learned a lot in researching and writing this book. We trust that you, too, have benefitted from our discoveries and the insights shared. Our prayer is that God will use this book to encourage you in the ministry to which he has called you—as you encounter men and women and boys and girls who have lost hope. For in Christ, our only hope, is hope eternal.

ACKNOWLEDGMENTS

From Scott

"Of the making of books there is no end," notes wise Solomon. I'm not sure if Solomon had assistance in the writing of his books, but I certainly did in the crafting of this book. Student assistants at Gordon-Conwell Theological Seminary called Byington Fellows were immensely helpful in gathering materials, conducting research, and searching for books and articles. Thanks to Tim Norton, Preston Conger, Angus Courtney, and Brent Clark who, as Byington Fellows, pushed forward this project with skill and patience. Thank you to the seminary trustees for the time to work on this project. Additionally, thanks to the staff (Ron, Ken, Nick, Dan, and Sarah) at Crave Café and Bakery in Beverly, MA, for a great place to work and enjoy gluten-free goodies. You're the best—and so are the baked goods.

Immense thanks to the pastors, funeral directors, and the suicide bereaved who participated in the various surveys that helped to undergird this book. Your input is invaluable!

Thanks goes to my colleague, Karen Mason, for approaching me to join with her in this most needed and interesting project. Her immense knowledge of suicide prevention is remarkable, and her grace in partnering in this book is encouraging and inspiring. Thank you, Karen, for the privilege of working with you, and for making pastors aware of what they can do to help protect against suicide and minister to the suicide bereaved.

I am constantly grateful to God for my wife, Rhonda, who unflaggingly supports this ministry of writing. She is an amazing follower of Christ and an incredible wife. Thank you, my dearest.

My portion of the dedication of this book is to Kenneth L. Swetland. Ken died before the publication of this book. Ken and I had known each other for almost forty years. He had been a professor, mentor, friend, colleague, and spiritual father to me. I am immensely grateful to God for his impress on my life, which is immense. He was one of the wisest men I've known. I am the person I am today in many ways because of Ken Swetland. I am thankful to God for Ken, for his love and care for me. Although undeserving, I am nevertheless profoundly thankful.

From Karen

I owe so much to Esther Kim, who has been my Byington Fellow during the writing of this book. Esther recruited several other youth pastors who joined her in testing the youth Bible studies in appendix H. Their excellent suggestions improved them significantly. Esther also has been a key research team member in the study of congregants and clergy. Esther formatted my chapters. A million thanks, Esther. Thanks also to Jared Doyle, who served as the Gordon-Conwell interlibrary loan assistant. His gracious help made the book possible. Thanks especially to Gordon-Conwell Theological Seminary trustees for their generous study leave policy.

I sat through a Doctor of Ministry preaching course with Scott as the professor and knew I wanted to partner with Scott to write this book. I was thrilled when Scott agreed. His massive knowledge and skill in homiletics were needed as we undertook this important but unchartered task. Discovering the overlap between homiletics and social science required Scott's foundational knowledge, his experience as a pastor, and his interest in the science of suicide prevention. Thank you, Scott!

By God's grace, my cup overflows with my family's support: my husband, Paul, my parents and siblings, and my two sons and their families. Their love sustains me.

My portion of the book is dedicated to Raymond Pendleton, colleague and mentor. Ray has been an invaluable model for me in seamlessly integrating psychology and theology. His life embodies that integration as a psychologist and a pastor. I have benefited from watching him think about integration and live it out. He has helped me to know where the theological boundary lines are while not getting caught up in holy crusades. Thanks, Ray, for your gift of integration.

From Both

Thank you to Bishop Claude Alexander of Park Church, Charlotte, North Carolina; Patrick Gray of Christ Church, Episcopal, Hamilton & Wenham, Massachusetts; William R. L. Haley of The Falls Church Anglican, Falls Church, Virginia; Paul A. Hoffman of the Evangelical Friends Church, Middletown, Rhode Island; and Tom Simmons of St. Peter's Episcopal Church, Purcellville, Virginia, for granting permission to publish your sermons as a resource for our readers. We are grateful for your help!

A very special thanks to Elliot Ritzema and Matthew Boffey at Lexham Press for their skillful editorial guidance. Elliot and Matthew, you have made our book even better. Elliot, you deserve particular recognition for your shepherding of our project through the dark hole of publication processes. Thank you.

APPENDIX A

TWO SERMONS THAT DEAL WITH SUICIDE

Psalm 13

(Karen Mason preached this sermon at the Mental Health Conference at the Chinese Bible Church of Greater Boston, Lexington, MA, April 10, 2016.)

- **Exegetical idea:** The psalmist calls out to God because 1) he has been suffering, and 2) he's certain that God is the one who hears his prayer and saves him, despite the current evidence.

- **Homiletical idea:** Despite the current evidence, all believers should call out to God when they are suffering because they are certain that God is the one who hears their prayer and will save them.

- **Purpose:** As a result of hearing this sermon, I want suffering people to not feel guilty if they are in a place of lament, and I want them to have the faith to call out to God in the midst of their suffering.

Introduction

If you're human, you've had troubles. Job 5:7 says, "Humans are born to trouble as surely as sparks fly upward."

A) But some troubles drag on and on and don't get resolved:

- You get expelled from school *again*

- Your classmates *continue* to bully you

- Micro-aggressions happen *again* in your school

- Your depression is *not* lifting

B) Those circumstances are bad enough, but as Christians the suffering we experience can be compounded by the sense of God being absent or slow to act. Suffering for Christians is not only the difficult circumstances (the child, the boss, the terrorism), but also the sense that God is not intervening. God promises us in Deuteronomy 31:6, "I will never leave you nor forsake you." But in times of suffering that drag on and on, we don't see the evidence. And without that evidence, we may feel lost, uncertain, worried, and fearful about what God is up to.

C) In the midst of those troubles, well-meaning people may have quoted to you: Phil 4:4—"Rejoice in the Lord, always; again, I say rejoice." But this may have felt like putting lemon juice on a paper cut or pouring vinegar on a wound:

> like vinegar poured on a wound,
> is one who sings songs to a heavy heart. (Prov 25:20)

Rejoicing is definitely a challenge for a suffering person whose trouble is dragging on.

As Christians, we affirm the truth of Philippians 4:4, but we *also* affirm that God offers us other words, like "*How long?*" God gives our suffering words in Psalm 13. God gives us lament psalms because it's hard to put suffering into words.

Lament psalms allow us to express our hurts to the one person who is powerful enough to change our circumstances and who can show himself present.

D) You may not be familiar with lament psalms, but almost half of the book of Psalms comprises lament psalms. Most of them have a specific structure:

- Protest—"God, the present circumstances are intolerable"

- Petition—A request and expectation that God will do something about the situation

- Praise—An expression of faith and certainty because God is a loving covenant God.

Body

How Psalm 13 fits the lament structure. Each section has two verses:

1. Protest (vv. 1-2)

2. Petition (vv. 3-4)

3. Praise (vv. 5-6)

1. PROTEST

¹ How long, LORD? Will you forget me forever?
　　How long will you hide your face from me?
² How long must I wrestle with my thoughts
　　and day after day have sorrow in my heart?
　　How long will my enemy triumph over me?

The protest in Psalm 13 is "How long?" David asks this question four times. *How long* will you forget me? *How long* will you hide your face from me? *How long* must I wrestle with my thoughts and have sorrow in my heart? *How long* will my enemy triumph over me?

A) In v. 2, David writes that he's wrestling with his thoughts and sorrows. The idea of "wrestle" is that of planning in order to get out of the difficulty, but the plans fail and just add sorrow to sorrow.

The psalm doesn't specify what suffering prompted the writing of Psalm 13. David had a lot of reasons to ask, "How long?"

- David is anointed king by Samuel (1 Sam 16) but about fifteen years go by before he is anointed king in Hebron (2 Sam 1), and another five years or so go by before he's finally anointed king over all Israel (2 Sam 5).

- David may have wondered if God had forgotten him, hidden his face from him, had left him to wrestle with his thoughts and sorrows, had let his enemy continually triumph over him. It took many years before he received what was rightfully his.

- And during that time, he suffered a number of devastating setbacks: having to leave his best friend, Jonathan; his wife, Michal; living on the run among the Philistines; the capture of his family by the Amalekites (1 Sam 30); and the treachery of his son, Absalom, who took the kingdom from him (2 Sam 15). Some commentators think David may have been writing about an illness.[1]

B) Have you ever been there? I have. Several years ago, I had a very bad boss who continually wronged me. She wouldn't follow through on meetings with me. She would have meetings with my direct report and not include me. She would criticize my work. My boss was bad enough, but I also wondered where God was. I prayed to God, "How long, Lord? How long?"

I knew that God is a God who reveals himself in nature (Ps 8:3–4; Rom 1:20), in Jesus (Heb 1:1–2; John 1:14) and through Scripture (2 Tim 3:16), but I couldn't see God intervening in my circumstances. I knew about Isaiah 49:14—God can't forget us, just as a nursing mother can't forget her child. But what happens when you can't see the evidence of God's presence and working?

You've had that experience, haven't you? You've been in (or might be in now) intolerable circumstances where there is no obvious solution to your suffering. You wrestle day after day with your thoughts and your sorrows. You fixate your thoughts on looking for a solution that is not forthcoming. You have the sense that the wrong person or thing is winning: your enemy, your child's drug addiction, your boss, institutionalized racism, depression, or terrorism.

C) In these moments David doesn't compose a psalm of praise. He composes a psalm of lament. He protests the fact that the evidence of God's working in David's life is long in coming. David protests his long wait.

When we get to this point, the appropriate response is to tell God. Lament psalms give us the words we need. They allow us to express our hurts to the one person who is powerful enough to change our circumstances: God. And we start with a protest: "How long, God, am I going to have to put up with these intolerable circumstances? How long, God, are you going to *not* intervene?"

In these types of situations, some people give up on God. Some think, he's forgotten me. He's too distant. He doesn't care. He's not powerful enough. But when God seemed distant, David addressed God. Instead of turning from God, he turned to him. Instead of complaining to people about God, David complained to God about circumstances. God is the right person to protest to and to petition.

2. PETITION

The next section of this lament psalm is David's requests and his expectation that God will do something about the situation.

> [3] Look on me and answer, LORD my God.
>   Give light to my eyes, or I will sleep in death,
> [4] and my enemy will say, "I have overcome him,"
>   and my foes will rejoice when I fall.

A) The petition here is for God to see David (to not hide his face from David), to answer, and to give light to his eyes.

In v. 3, when David asks to be given some light to his eyes, this might mean he wants God to revive him (1 Sam 14:29; Job 33:30) and give him relief (Ezek 9:8). The same word is used in 1 Sam 14:29. Saul and Jonathan (with Israel) are fighting the Philistines and not eating. When Jonathan eats some honey, he says, "See how my eyes brightened when I tasted a little of this honey." Here David calls out to God to give light to his eyes, that is, to revive him, because he's close to giving up, to being overcome.

Petition is the language and behavior of relationship. You make petitions of people with whom you have a relationship. You don't say to a complete stranger, "Give me $10!" David here is appealing to his relationship with God. Right at the beginning of the petition in v. 3, David emphasizes his relationship with God. David calls God "Yahweh, *my* God." Yahweh was the name that God revealed to Moses: I am who I am (Exod 3:14), a name which evokes the covenant relationship. David is appealing here to Yahweh, *his* God, with whom he is in a covenant relationship as an Israelite (Exod 19:5) and as a person.

Commentators have also noted that if God doesn't answer David, David's enemy will declare victory and rejoice. David says that his defeat would become God's defeat because they are joined together in a relationship.

David here is depending on God to be the right person to petition to because God has entered into a relationship with Israel and with him. And God has done so because he is a God of love. David knows that God revealed his character of love to Moses in Exodus 34:6–7: "The Lord, the Lord, a God merciful and gracious, slow to anger, and abounding in *steadfast love* and faithfulness, ⁷ keeping *steadfast love* for the thousandth generation, forgiving iniquity and transgression and sin, yet by no means clearing the guilty, but visiting the iniquity of the parents upon the children and the children's children, to the third and the fourth generation."

B) We, like David, are in a covenant relationship with God, and every time we celebrate the Lord's Supper we affirm that (Matt 26:26–29; Mark 14:22–25; Luke 22:14–20; 1 Cor 11:25). We are in this relationship because God is love (1 John 4:8); the greatest example is the cross. It is in God's character to care what happens to us and to show his love to us. It is on the basis of our relationship with him that we petition him in the midst of suffering.

If we were in a contractual relationship with God, that would mean that if one of the parties would violate the contract, the contract would be voided. God would walk away or we would walk away—especially in the midst of great suffering. But a covenant is different because a violation doesn't void the covenant. There will be consequences to a violation (Deut. 28), but both parties agree to maintain the relationship despite violations.

We often talk about the difference between contracts and covenants in the context of marriage. That's why the marriage vow is "in good times and in bad, in sickness *and* in health," in other words, in all circumstances. Jesus talks about some rare and unusual circumstances where the breaking of the covenant occurs (Matt 19:8–9). But these are just that: rare and unusual. While there are consequences to violations, the covenant stands.

So David here is saying to God, "You're in a relationship with me, and I anticipate that you will be present and intervene."

C) Now what David is *not* saying is:

- *You have to answer in the way I want you to.* We have the example of Paul in 2 Corinthians 12:8–9 who pleaded three times with the God to take away his thorn in the flesh. But God did not.

- *You have to answer me now.* Psalm 37:7: "Be still before the LORD and wait patiently for him."

- *You have to eliminate all my pain and only give me what's good.* Job 2:10: "Shall we accept good and not trouble?"

David is asking for God to intervene. It makes sense to petition God because he is in a relationship with us and has the character of a person who wants to intervene in our lives.

D) The famous preacher Charles Spurgeon was walking through the English countryside with a friend. He noticed a barn with a weather vane. At the top of the vane were the words, "God is love." Spurgeon remarked that this was an inappropriate place for such a message, because weather vanes are changeable, but God's love is constant. But Spurgeon's friend disagreed. "You misunderstood the meaning," he said. "That weather vane is stating the truth that no matter which way the wind blows, God is love."

E) I can tell you that in times of suffering it is hard to lean into the covenant and God's character of love. It is hard to ask God to intervene in a problem he hasn't intervened in yet—as far as we can tell. The real test of faith is asking God in the absence of the evidence of his presence and intervention.

Even in the face of no evidence, when everything feels hopeless, believers call out to God because God is in a covenant relationship with us and because he is a God of love.

Our last section emphasizes that we call out to God because he is in the business of the redemption of hopeless situations.

3. PRAISE

> [5] But I trust in your unfailing love;
>   my heart rejoices in your salvation.
> [6] I will sing the LORD's praise,
>   for he has been good to me.

A) This section starts with "but," which is "the fulcrum on which David's faith turns."[2] David has not yet been saved. But he boldly praises God. David says that he "trusts in God's unfailing love and his heart rejoices in God's salvation" (v. 5). When he says "unfailing love," David uses the word *hesed*, God's covenant love, God's unfailing love, because it's love expressed in the context of a covenant. He hasn't yet seen God intervene in this situation, but David is obstinately depending on God. Even though David hasn't seen the answer yet, he trusts in God's covenant and character of love.

In the future tense, David says that he will sing Yahweh's praise, because God has been good to him, or has dealt bountifully with him (v. 6).[3]

B) We don't engage in the praise element of lament in a flippant, careless way. We praise God in the midst of pain because of his extraordinary past redemptions. For example, we just celebrated Easter, the fact that God took the shame of the cross by dying on it and turned shame and what looked like defeat into the victory over our sin. His death looked like a hopeless, dead-end situation to the disciples, but it was followed by an unexpected triumph over death, the resurrection. Do we need any more proof that God can take hopeless circumstances and turn them into triumph? The praise element of lament psalms essentially affirm that God is in the business of redeeming hopeless situations, those in the past and ours in the present.

Have you ever seen a burl on a tree? It's a rounded outgrowth on the tree trunk, caused by some stress that the tree has undergone. An injury or a virus could cause it. My brother-in-law takes tree burls and stumps left to decay and crafts crosses out of them, to symbolize the redemption of the injury to the tree and to our lives. It's this expectation that drives David's praise. God will bring good out of this intolerable circumstance.

Conclusion/Application

Despite the current evidence, all believers should call out to God when they are suffering because they are certain that God is the one who hears their prayer and will save them—even if it takes 20 years, as it did for David.

When you find yourself in an intolerable circumstance, protest and complain to God, make your request known to him, and hang on by faith to the belief that he will intervene.

The most powerful narrative that illustrates Psalm 13 is the story of a seventeen-year-old boy named Joseph in Genesis 37. As he's in a cistern, is he calling out to God, "How long, O LORD, how long"? As he's sold into slavery by his jealous brothers and force-marched to Egypt, is he calling out to God, "How long, O LORD, how long"? After Joseph is thrown into prison unjustly because of Potiphar's wife's lies, is he calling out to God, "How long, O LORD, how long"? After interpreting the cupbearer's dream, Joseph was two more years in prison. During those two years, is he calling out to God, "How long, O LORD, how long"? In these moments of suffering and shame, Joseph didn't know the end of the story. He didn't know that God would take those years of suffering and shame in Joseph's life and turn them into the deliverance of the people of Israel, so that Jacob's family wouldn't die in the famine. God redeemed the suffering, such that Joseph tells his brothers in Genesis 50:20, "You intended to harm me, but God intended it for good to accomplish what is now being done, the saving of many lives."

We don't know the end of our story and our suffering. All we know is that God loves us, has redeemed us, and has redeemed the suffering of others. It is on the basis of that—that in our suffering, we can ask, "How long, O Lord, how long?"—that we ask for salvation from our intolerable circumstances, and that we look for salvation, because we are certain that our loving God is the one who hears our prayer and will save us.

Psalm 55

Claude Alexander

In August of 2014, the entertainment industry and indeed the United States was rocked by the news of the unexpected and tragic death of Robin Williams by suicide. For those of us who grew up in the seventies, this was a particularly sharp blow. His career paralleled our coming of age. We remember him first appearing on *Happy Days* as that time-traveling comedic force Mork from Ork. We tuned into the sitcom *Mork and Mindy*. Somehow, the awkwardness of our adolescence was more understandable as we saw his awkwardness mirror our own. As we laughed at him, somehow we were able to laugh at ourselves. As we saw him find his legitimate place, we were encouraged to know that we would find our own place. We witnessed Robin mature and transition from comedic maverick to dramatic actor. With equal aplomb, we saw him excel. While he entertained us, he subtly taught us to stretch, to take chances, to never take ourselves too seriously, and to always find a time for laughter. In the '80s, he demonstrated social responsibility through Comic Relief. He, along with Billy Crystal and Whoopi Goldberg, lent their comedic and social influence to the cause of homelessness. They not only raised money, but they also raised the consciousness and public awareness of the scandal behind the alarming rate of homelessness in our country. I'll never forget one of Whoopi Goldberg's lines in the first Comic Relief, "The homeless are looking more like us because more of us are becoming homeless."

Robin Williams was a uniquely gifted person who leveraged that gift to bring joy, laughter, relief, and hope to so many. Perhaps one of my favorite roles that he played, which didn't receive as much acclaim, was the role of Patch Adams, a medical student who used humor to help his patients. That was more than a role for Williams. It was a part of his life. He was widely known for visiting pediatric cancer patients, making them feel special, and filling their lives with joy.

It is so ironic that one who spent his life filling the lives of others with such joy and happiness could be in such emotional pain that he would take his own life. You are made to wonder what it must have taken for Robin to offer himself as a channel for joy and laughter while bearing such personal and private pain. I am readily aware that, like Williams, there are many individuals who give of themselves in very public and prolific ways who wrestle with intense personal and private pain. Depression is a personal reality that people find hard to admit having. This is due in part to the wrongful stigmatization of mental illness. While there is a spiritual dimension to depression, known as heaviness, there is also a biochemical dimension to depression. It is one of the consequences of the fall. Because of that, many people are biochemically prone to battle with this throughout their lives. There is a medical dimension to it that must be taken seriously and addressed. Unfortunately, for some, the wrestling with it has caused and continues to cause them to consider the option that Robin Williams ultimately took.

I wish that I had the chance to talk to Robin Williams before he made that choice. While I didn't have the chance to talk with him, I do have the chance to talk with somebody today. There is somebody who knows where Robin Williams was because it is where you currently are. Like with Williams, no one knows that this is where you are. There are some who say that this isn't for you, but I guarantee you that it is for someone that you know but are unaware of the personal and private pain that has them at a place of considering taking a permanent solution to a temporary problem. I am on a specific assignment to tell you what I would have told Robin Williams had I been given the opportunity.

Had I been able to talk with him, I would have told him that I know what it is to equate the internal pain of life with life itself, and to desire the pain to end so badly that you see ending life as the appropriate and sensible solution. Mental and emotional pain can be so intense and seem so pervasive that it appears to possess its own rationality. The immediacy of the pain is such that you only see the pain, and nothing beyond it. You imagine no future without it. The deceit of it is that it is permanent. As a teenager, wrestling with matters of esteem due to my biological father's lack of support and the spiritual warfare of discerning God's call on my life, I suffered a depression that had me at the point of considering ending my life several times. No one knew that I had such considerations. My mother, a psychiatrist, knew of my depression, but not to the extent that it was.

It wasn't that I didn't want to live. It's just that the mental and emotional battle was such that the battle had become synonymous with living. The need for an escape from the battle began to be seen as the need to escape life itself.

Lest we fool ourselves, the desire to escape is more common than we think. Suicide is the most drastic attempt to escape. There are less drastic forms of escape in which individuals engage on a daily basis. The abuse of drugs, alcohol, sex, pornography, and gambling are all self-defeating and self-destructive forms of escape. They are illegitimate responses to a legitimate need for relief from the pain and pressure of feeling overwhelmed by life.

This legitimate need for relief in the midst of feeling overwhelmed has nothing to do with a lack of spirituality. It has everything to do with you being human. I don't care who you are, how much Scripture you know, or how many bottles of oil you possess, life can hit you, circumstances can beset you in such a way that you feel overwhelmed. Problems and pressures can come in such a manner that you see yourself as a shrinking dot overshadowed by that which is beyond your control. The larger that they loom in your mind and spirit, the more helpless and hopeless you begin to feel. If left unchecked, you find yourself open to anything that advertises a modicum of relief. Sometimes, the only option of relief is escape.

This is where the psalmist finds himself in Psalm 55. This is a lament psalm of David. The occasion of this is the betrayal of one of his closest advisors, Ahithophel, who joins Absalom in his rebellion against David. You can read the background of this in 2 Samuel 15–16.

David describes his mental and emotional state throughout the psalm. In verse 2, he says, "I am overwhelmed by my troubles."[4] In verse 4, he says, "My heart pounds in my chest. The terror of death assaults me." In verse 5, he says, "Fear and trembling overwhelm me and I can't stop shaking." The word picture for overwhelmed in verse 2 is that of being tossed about. It describes a restlessness akin to roaming about aimlessly. The word picture for troubles is to be stirred about. He is severely agitated. His blood pressure is elevated as his heart pounds in his chest. He is emotionally assaulted by terror and fear. He is gripped by fear and feels totally eclipsed by this situation. The word picture for overwhelmed in verse 5 is that of being concealed. That which he faces is so dominant that he can no longer recognize himself independent of it. It obscures him. It swallows him. It is to such a degree that he cannot stop shaking.

Its presence and predominance is such that escape is a considerable option. He wants to be as far from it as possible. That's why he says in verse 6, "Oh, that I had wings like a dove; then I would fly away and rest! I would fly far away to the quiet of the wilderness." He pauses and resumes with verse 8, saying, "How quickly I would escape—far from this wild storm of hatred." Spiritually shaken, mentally torn, and emotionally battered, David—in need of relief—desires escape. Those who know David's story know that David ends up facing what he wants to flee. He resists the pull toward self-destruction. He discovers that his answer is not in fleeing but in facing. I had to look at how he did it. There is somebody here who needs to know that permanent flight from the painful aspects of life is not the solution. There is a better way. It's not fleeing. It's facing. It's not in escaping. It's in courageously confronting. There is a way to face the painful. There is a way to overcome being overwhelmed.

Take your pain to God

David makes a conscious decision. He pours out to God. He vents to God. He does not keep it within himself. He pours it out to God. In verse 1, David says, "Listen to my prayer, O God. Do not ignore my cry for help. Please listen and answer me."

In the midst of emotional wounding and distress, we choose how we respond. There are those who choose to keep stuff within themselves. They hold onto it. They allow it to fester within until it becomes a source of bitterness. Others respond vindictively. Others resign and check out from life and living altogether.

David instructs us to take our hurt to God. We are to take it to God with honesty and specificity. Listen to David's honesty: "I am overwhelmed by my troubles. My heart pounds in my chest. The terror of death assaults me. Fear and trembling overwhelm me. ... Everything is falling apart."

When you find yourself emotionally wounded to the point of wanting to give up on life, you need to know that you can take that pain to God. When you don't feel comfortable taking it to anybody else, you can take it to God. You take it to him in the rawest of language. This is a lament psalm. It's a psalm of complaint. It's a psalm with an edge to it. There is nothing dressed up or pretty about it. It is raw.

A real relationship with God is such that you don't have to dress it up or make it look or sound pretty when what you are feeling is not pretty. In Psalm 142:2, David puts it this way, "I pour out my complaints before God and tell him all my troubles."

You need not carry those thoughts and feelings within yourself by yourself. Pour out those thoughts and feelings to God. Pour them out in honesty and specificity. "God, I'm torn. God, I'm confused. God, I'm weary of life itself. God, I'm tired of feeling the way that I feel and I need some degree of relief. God, I'm at the end of my rope and I feel that I'm losing my grip. God, I need something from you that lets me know that you're still around. Not another second, not another minute, not an hour, nor another day, but at this moment with my arms outstretched. I need you to make a way. As you have done many times before through a window or an open door. I stretch my hands to thee. Come rescue me. I need you right away." You've got to pour out your heart and tell him, "If I ever needed you before to show up and restore all of the faith that I let slip while I was searching the world for more, now is the time. You're the truest friend I have, indeed. You're my best friend I know in need. I stretch my hands to thee; come rescue me. I need you right away. I need you now, Lord; I need you now. I need you now, right now. I need you now."

In the midst of feeling overwhelmed to the point of giving up on life, there is another option. Call out to the Lord with honesty and specificity. David expresses his resolve again in verse 16, "But I will call on God." In verse 17, he says, "Morning, noon, and night I cry out in my distress." He consistently and persistently pours himself out to God. He is not ashamed of pouring himself out to God more than one time. The matter is too pressing for him. He says, "Morning, noon, and night I cry out in my distress, and the Lord hears my voice." He pours himself out to God confident that God hears him. He is assured that God listens to him. He is certain that God takes notice of him. He remembered Hagar's testimony in the wilderness: "God hears." He remembered God telling Moses, "I have heard their cry by reason of their taskmasters." He remembered Hannah's testimony in 1 Samuel 1:27, "I asked the Lord to give me this boy, and he granted my request."

You can pour yourself out to God, knowing that God hears you and that God will hear you. David does more than pour his heart out to God. He does something else which he advises us to do.

Count on God to respond

Look again at verse 16, "But I will call on God, and the Lord will rescue me." Now look at verse 18, "He ransoms me and keeps me safe from the battle waged against me, though many still oppose me." There is a subtle shift in his expression. He moves from saying what the Lord will do to what the Lord is doing. David's faith is being realized. The Lord is responding. As the Lord listens, the Lord is responding.

When you cry out to God in the midst of being overwhelmed, you can count on God to respond. God promises to respond. Hear God promise in Psalm 50:15, "Call upon me in the day of trouble; I will deliver you." Psalm 91:15, "He shall call upon me, and I will answer him; I will be with him in trouble; I will deliver him, and honor him. With long life will I satisfy him and show him my salvation."

You can count on God to respond. In fact, the response of the Lord occurs as David prays. While David prays, the help is coming. While David calls, the answer is being given.

In the midst of David pouring out to God, God pours into David. This is an important realization especially when you're feeling over-whelmed. There is the tendency to be so focused on what is against you, on what is hurting you, and on what is pressing you that you don't realize what God is doing in the midst. In the midst of the hurt, in the midst of the pressure, in the midst of the pain, in the midst of the disappointment, God is still doing some things. God is keeping you alive. You're alive to feel. You're alive to cry. You're alive to get angry. You're alive to complain. I know that it may seem like a small thing but what it says is that regardless of how painful life has been, it has not taken you out. Regardless of how deep the hurt may be or how awful the disappointment may be, it hasn't overridden God's keeping you alive. No matter how ugly it may look or how threatening it may sound, God has still sustained you. God still pours breath into you. God still pumps blood through your veins. God still gives strength and activity to you. God still pours sanity into your mind. God still pours defiance into your spirit.

Somebody can testify that as you've poured out to God, God has poured into you. As you've called out to him, he has responded to you. As you sought him, he was answering you. In fact, your praying was indicative of his already acting. He was the one who gave you the presence of mind to pray. He was the one who gave you the faith to pray. He was the one who gave you the strength to pray. He was the one who prompted you to pray. In prompting you to pray, God sustained you while praying. God encouraged you in praying. God protected you. God kept you safe.

God promises as much in Isaiah 65:24: "And it shall come to pass, that before they call, I will answer; and while they are yet speaking, I will hear." You can count on God to respond because He knows what you need before you ask. Therefore, before you call, he's already answering. Before you speak, he's already hearing. He knows your thoughts from afar. More than knowing your thoughts, he knows your needs. You can count on God to respond not just based upon the content of your cry, but upon the intent of His sovereign purpose. When God responds to our prayers, it's with respect to his intent and not their content. This is important because God's intent always has more in mind than my prayer's content. The content of my prayers comes out of the context of my feelings. The content of my prayers comes out of the context of my limited understanding. God's intent is within the context of His will for my life. His will for my life is far more extensive than my current situation. It is more expansive than my present experience. Therefore, when God responds, it's always more than I anticipated. Count on the Lord to respond according to his intent. His intent is further than you can see. It's greater than you can imagine. I'm glad about it, because at 16 with suicide on my mind, I didn't see what God intended for me to be at age 50. I'm so glad that my content at 16 didn't frustrate his intent for me at 50. I want somebody to know that I don't care how bad it looks for you right now, it can't compare to the intent of God for your future. Whatever it looks like right now, there is one word to describe it: temporary. It's not going to be this way always. Down home, people had a saying, "Trouble don't last always."

Therefore, I want to encourage you not just to take your pain to God and to count on God to respond, but also to release the burden.

Release the burden

David moves into a point of self-exhortation, saying, "Give your burdens to the Lord, and he will take care of you." Sometimes in the secret of your own heart and mind, you must exhort yourself. This is not the first time that David has done so. Earlier in his life, when the city of Ziklag was burned into rubble and his men wanted to stone him, David encouraged himself in the Lord his God. Here he is again providing self-exhortation, "Give your burdens to the Lord, and he will take care of you." David tells himself that he has a choice. He can try to carry the weight by himself. He can try to bear it by himself. He can try to resolve it by himself. Or he can choose to shift the weight. He can choose to transfer the burden. He remembers what he sang in Psalm 37:5, "Commit your way to the Lord." The word for "commit" means to "roll it over." When the weight of life gets heavy, you need to choose to roll it over to the Lord. Give it to him. I want to encourage somebody to give your burdens to the Lord. Give what's weighing you down to the Lord; give what's been keeping you up at night to the Lord. Give what's been invading your quiet moments to the Lord. Give what's been stealing your joy to the Lord. Give what's been disturbing your peace to the Lord. Release the burden. Release the load. Release the weight. Release the strain. Release the stress. Release the heaviness. Stop carrying what the Lord is already handling. Stop bearing what the Lord is already fighting. Stop stressing over what the Lord is already solving.

David ends the psalm with the resolution, "I'm trusting you to save me." Rather than me taking the wings of a dove and flying away, I'm trusting you, Lord, to save me. I'm trusting you to take care of me. I'm releasing the burden and trusting you.

Isn't that what Jesus did when he was overwhelmed? Looking at the cup of suffering, Jesus was exceedingly sorrowful, even to the point of death. When he sought to escape the pain, he released the burden unto his Father and trusted the Father with the burden. God answered the prayer based upon God's intent rather than Jesus' content. God gave Jesus the strength for what God intended. God gave him the power for his intent. God gave him the stamina for his intent. As a result, Jesus became the offering for sin that God intended. Jesus became the savior that God intended. Jesus became the redeemer that God intended. God gave Jesus the victory that God intended.

I'm glad that Jesus overcame being overwhelmed. I want to encourage you: don't you give up. Take the pain to the Lord. Pour it out upon him. Count on him to respond. Release the burden.

Release the burden and he will take care of you. He will watch over you. He will protect you. He will provide for you. He will hold you together. He will not let you lose it altogether. Even should you let go, he will still hold you. He will hold you close.

I just want to pause and thank the Lord for keeping me close when I would have let go. I want to thank him for keeping his hand on my life when I couldn't see what he saw for me. I want to thank the Lord for keeping the pills and the guns out of my reach. I want to thank the Lord for tempering the thoughts of my mind. I want to thank the Lord for holding me until he broke through to me. I want to thank the Lord for giving me a high school English teacher as rope until he broke through to me. I want to thank the Lord for giving me my uncle Willis until he broke through to me. I want to thank the Lord for breaking through to me on June 24, 1980, in St. Louis, Missouri, at the National Baptist Congress of Christian Education, letting me know that I could cast my cares upon him because he cared for me. He loved me. He had a plan for my life that was more than I could ever imagine. He had a calling for me to fulfill. I want to thank the Lord for showing me, for directing me to my destiny. I know what I'm here for. I can testify that if you release the burden, he's able to take care of you. He will take care of you. He will restore you. He will renew you. He'll be a firm foundation, your salvation, your solid rock.

APPENDIX B

SAMPLE LITURGY FOR WORLD SUICIDE PREVENTION DAY (SEPTEMBER 10)

The celebrant says the words in normal text. The people say the words in italics. All stand during the processional song, acclamation, prayers, and singing.

[Insert processional song here.]

Acclamation

If the LORD had not been on our side—
    let Israel say—
if the LORD had not been on our side
    when people attacked us,
they would have swallowed us alive
    when their anger flared against us;
the flood would have engulfed us,
    the torrent would have swept over us,
the raging waters
    would have swept us away.

Praise be to the LORD,
    who has not let us be torn by their teeth.
We have escaped like a bird
    from the fowler's snare;
the snare has been broken,
    and we have escaped.
Our help is in the name of the LORD,
    the Maker of heaven and earth. (Ps 124)

Blessed be God, Father, Son, and Holy Spirit, who sustain us through the assaults of this life.
And blessed are the poor in spirit, for theirs is the kingdom of heaven (Matt 5:3).

Prayers

The Lord be with you.
And also with you.
Let us pray.

Almighty God, you alone give life and take it (Deut 32:39; Exod 20:13), but life is not easy. With the psalmist, we proclaim that without you we would be swallowed alive, torn up and engulfed by the floods, and swept away by the torrents of this life. Preserve us, Father. We put our hope in you, Father, Son, and Holy Spirit. *Amen.*

[Insert song here.]

Our loving and merciful Father, we pray for those who were overcome by the floods and torrents of this life and who died by suicide. We bitterly lament their loss among us. We seek comfort from each other in this gathered community and from you, our compassionate comforter, along with the Lord Jesus Christ and the Holy Spirit. *Amen.*

[The people sit.]

Scripture Readings and Sermon

A reading from the book of Genesis:

> When Joseph's brothers saw that their father was dead, they said, "What if Joseph holds a grudge against us and pays us back for all the wrongs we did to him?" So they sent word to Joseph, saying, "Your father left these instructions before he died: 'This is what you are to say to Joseph: I ask you to forgive your brothers the sins and the wrongs they committed in treating you so badly.' Now please forgive the sins of the servants of the God of your father." When their message came to him, Joseph wept. His brothers then came and threw themselves down before him. "We are your slaves," they said. But Joseph said to them, "Don't be afraid. Am I in the place of God? You intended to harm me, but God intended it for good to accomplish what is now being done, the saving of many lives. So then, don't be afraid. I will provide for you and your children." And he reassured them and spoke kindly to them. (Gen 50:15–21)

A reading from the book of Psalms:
[Read responsively or sing antiphonally.]

> I will exalt you, LORD,
>> for you lifted me out of the depths
>> and did not let my enemies gloat over me.
> *LORD my God, I called to you for help,*
>> *and you healed me.*

You, Lord, brought me up from the realm of the dead;
  you spared me from going down to the pit.
Sing the praises of the Lord, you his faithful people;
  praise his holy name.
For his anger lasts only a moment,
  but his favor lasts a lifetime;
weeping may stay for the night,
  but rejoicing comes in the morning.
When I felt secure, I said,
  "I will never be shaken."
Lord, when you favored me,
  you made my royal mountain stand firm;
but when you hid your face,
  I was dismayed.
To you, Lord, I called;
  to the Lord I cried for mercy:
"What is gained if I am silenced,
  if I go down to the pit?
Will the dust praise you?
  Will it proclaim your faithfulness?
Hear, Lord, and be merciful to me;
  Lord, be my help."
You turned my wailing into dancing;
  you removed my sackcloth and clothed me with joy,
that my heart may sing your praises and not be silent.
  Lord my God, I will praise you forever. (Ps 30)

A reading from the apostle Paul's epistle to the Romans:

If God is for us, who can be against us? He who did not spare
his own Son, but gave him up for us all—how will he not also,
along with him, graciously give us all things? Who will bring

any charge against those whom God has chosen? It is God who justifies. Who then is the one who condemns? No one. Christ Jesus who died—more than that, who was raised to life—is at the right hand of God and is also interceding for us. Who shall separate us from the love of Christ? Shall trouble or hardship or persecution or famine or nakedness or danger or sword? As it is written:

"For your sake we face death all day long;
we are considered as sheep to be slaughtered."

No, in all these things we are more than conquerors through him who loved us. For I am convinced that neither death nor life, neither angels nor demons, neither the present nor the future, nor any powers, neither height nor depth, nor anything else in all creation, will be able to separate us from the love of God that is in Christ Jesus our Lord. (Rom 8:31–39)

[The people stand.]

The Gospel of our Lord Jesus Christ according to Mark.
Glory to you, Lord Christ.

Then they came to Jericho. As Jesus and his disciples, together with a large crowd, were leaving the city, a blind man, Bartimaeus (which means "son of Timaeus"), was sitting by the roadside begging. When he heard that it was Jesus of Nazareth, he began to shout, "Jesus, Son of David, have mercy on me!" Many rebuked him and told him to be quiet, but he shouted all the more, "Son of David, have mercy on me!" Jesus stopped and said, "Call him." So they called to the blind man, "Cheer up! On your feet! He's calling you." Throwing his cloak aside, he jumped to his feet and came to Jesus. "What do you want me to do for you?" Jesus asked him. The blind man said, "Rabbi, I want to see." "Go," said Jesus, "your faith has healed you." Immediately he received his sight and followed Jesus along the road. (Mark 10:46–52)

The Gospel of the Lord.
Praise to you, Lord Christ.

[The people sit.]

[Insert sermon here.]

[Insert the Apostle's Creed or the Nicene Creed here if desired. The people stand.]

The Prayers of the People

[The people kneel.]

As Jesus, God's only Son, taught us, let us pray together.

> *Our Father in heaven,*
> *hallowed be your name,*
> *your kingdom come,*
> *your will be done,*
>   *on earth as it is in heaven.*
> *Give us today our daily bread.*
> *And forgive us our debts,*
>   *as we also have forgiven our debtors.*
> *And lead us not into temptation,*
>   *but deliver us from the evil one. (Matt 6:9–13)*

We pray to you, Father,

> For all those in despair
> *That they would choose life.*

> For those facing devastating loss
> *That they would remember your presence and intercession for them.*

> For all those who feel they are a burden
> *That they would love themselves as you love them.*

> For all those without hope
> *That they would find in you, Father, a reason to live.*

> For those who feel alone
> *That they would find in our gathered community a reason to live.*

> For those facing evil in this world
> *That they would remember your redemption of the evil done to Joseph.*

> For all those suffering the misery of depression and other psychological pain
> *That they would reach out for help like blind Bartimaeus.*

> For all those in despondent desolation
> *That we would reach out to them.*

Let us confess our sins against God and our neighbor.[1]
[Brief period of silence]

> *Most merciful God,*
> *We confess that we have sinned against you*
> *In thought, word, and deed,*
> *By what we have done,*
> *And by what we have left undone.*

We have not loved you with our whole heart;
We have not loved our neighbors as ourselves.
We are truly sorry and we humbly repent.
For the sake of your Son Jesus Christ,
Have mercy on us and forgive us;
That we may delight in your will,
And walk in your ways,
To the glory of your Name. Amen.

Almighty God have mercy on you, forgive you all your sins through our Lord Jesus Christ, strengthen you in all goodness, and by the power of the Holy Spirit keep you in eternal life. *Amen.*

The peace of the Lord be always with you.
And also with you.

[Standing, the people pass the peace. Consider reading Matthew 5:23–24 beforehand.]

[If desired, include the taking of communion.]

Communion

[The people kneel.]
God so loved the world that he gave his one and only Son, that whoever believes in him shall not perish but have eternal life. For God did not send his Son into the world to condemn the world, but to save the world through him. Whoever believes in him is not condemned, but whoever does not believe stands condemned already because they have not believed in the name of God's one and only Son ...

[who] though in very nature God,
made himself nothing ...

And being found in appearance as a man,
>   he humbled himself
>   by becoming obedient to death—
>   even death on a cross! (John 3:16–18; Phil 2:6–8)

Through Jesus' death on the cross, God in his mercy, grace, and kindness redeemed us to himself. Once we were not a people, but now we are the people of God; once we had not received mercy, but now we have received mercy (1 Pet 2:10). We remember God's new covenant with us, his people, in the breaking of the bread and the drinking of the cup.

The Lord Jesus, on the night he was betrayed, took bread, and when he had given thanks, he broke it and said, "This is my body, which is for you; do this in remembrance of me." In the same way, after supper he took the cup, saying, "This cup is the new covenant in my blood; do this, whenever you drink it, in remembrance of me." For whenever you eat this bread and drink this cup, you proclaim the Lord's death until he comes (1 Cor 11:23–26).

We do not presume to come to this your table, merciful Lord, trusting in our own righteousness, but in your manifold and great mercies. We are not worthy so much as to gather up the crumbs under your table. But you are the same Lord whose nature is always to have mercy. Grant us therefore, gracious Lord, to evermore dwell in your Son Jesus Christ, and he in us. Amen.[2]

[The people take communion.]

[Insert a song here.]

> But now, this is what the LORD says—
>   he who created you, Jacob,
>   he who formed you, Israel:

"Do not fear, for I have redeemed you;
>   I have summoned you by name; you are mine.
When you pass through the waters,
>   I will be with you;
and when you pass through the rivers,
>   they will not sweep over you.
When you walk through the fire,
>   you will not be burned;
>   the flames will not set you ablaze.
For I am the LORD your God,
>   the Holy One of Israel, your Savior;
I give Egypt for your ransom,
>   Cush and Seba in your stead.
Since you are precious and honored in my sight,
>   and because I love you,
I will give people in exchange for you,
>   nations in exchange for your life.
Do not be afraid, for I am with you. (Isaiah 43:1–5)

[Insert song here. The people stand.]

[Recessional. The people stand.]

SAMPLE HANDOUT FOR SURVIVORS FOLLOWING A SUICIDE

Suicide is an unexpected, shocking loss. Grief following suicide is more intense and disorganizing than grief after other losses.

Most people don't have a lot of experience with suicide, so they may not know how to support you. Tell people what you need and don't need. Don't spend time with people who judge you. Avoid time with people who add to your burden (Job 16:2), offer empty platitudes (Job 42:7–9), or speak hurtfully (Prov 15:1–4).

God sees your pain: "You have noted my lamentation, put my tears in your bottle" (Ps 56:8). As you ask God many questions, pray using the lament psalms (e.g., Pss 13; 55).

Your local suicide prevention coalition may be able to get you in touch with other suicide loss survivors who can walk with you through this tragic loss. To find your local coalition, go to www.sprc .org/states.

Read a book written for survivors so that you know you are not alone and you are not "losing your mind." Start with J. Jordan and B. Baugher, *After Suicide Loss: Coping with Your Grief*.[1] It will help you with practical suggestions. Here are some of their ideas (with page numbers where applicable so you can read further):

- The police may investigate the suicide, not because suicide is against the law, but to make sure that the death isn't really a homicide made to look like a suicide. Neither you nor your loved one has committed a crime. If the police take some of your loved one's belongings, be sure to ask for an inventory so that you can get them back (p. 11).

- Someone may need to identify the body, but that doesn't have to be you. Even if the body has been identified, you can ask to view the body and have time alone with your loved one. Make sure to have a friend or relative with you at the time. If an autopsy is done, you have the right to ask for a copy of the autopsy report (pp. 12–14).

- Telling others about the suicide is hard, but most survivors are glad they decided to be honest about the facts of the death (p. 15).

- It's best to be honest but not detailed with children. You don't want to have children hear about the death from someone else or another source (p. 40).

- Get children connected to a children's bereavement or grief support group. Check your local hospital, hospice, or the Dougy National Center for Grieving Children and Families (dougy.org). At some point, you may also want to join a suicide survivor support group. To find one in your area, go to afsp.org or suicidology.org, or call your local United Way 211 number.

- You are under no obligation to speak to the media. As a family, you may want to designate a spokesperson (p. 17).

- By being honest in the obituary about the suicide, you give people the opportunity to support you.

- You and your loved ones will most likely grieve differently. Allow each other to grieve in your own way, while still finding common ways to acknowledge your own experience (p. 36). Remember that there is not one right way.

Christian Books for Survivors

Biebel, D.B., and S. L. Foster. *Finding Your Way after the Suicide of Someone You Love.* Grand Rapids: Zondervan, 2005.

Bolton, I., with C. Mitchell. *My Son ... My Son ... : A Guide to Healing After Death, Loss or Suicide.* Roswell, GA: Bolton Press Atlanta, 2005.

Hubbard, M. G. *More Than an Aspirin: A Christian Perspective on Pain and Suffering.* Grand Rapids: Discovery House Publishers, 2009.

Hsu, A. Y. *Grieving a Suicide: A Loved One's Search for Comfort, Answers and Hope.* 2nd ed. Downers Grove, IL: InterVarsity Press, 2017.

Punnett, I. *How to Pray When You're Pissed at God: Or Anyone Else for That Matter.* New York: Harmony Books, 2013.

Books for Children

Cammarata, D. *Someone I Love Died by Suicide: A Story for Child Survivors and Those Who Care for Them.* Jupiter, FL: Limitless Press LLC, 2009.

Requarth, M. *After a Parent's Suicide: Helping Children Heal.* Sebastopol, CA: Healing Hearts Press, 2006.

Rubel, B. *But I Didn't Say Goodbye: For Parents and Professionals Helping Child Suicide Survivors.* Kendall Park, NJ: Griefwork Center Inc, 2000.

Survivor Support Groups

- American Foundation for Suicide Prevention (afsp.org)

- American Association of Suicidology (suicidology.org)

- Dougy National Center for Grieving Children and Families (dougy.org)

- National Alliance for Grieving Children (childrengrieve.org)

- Samaritans (samaritansusa.org)

- The Compassionate Friends (compassionatefriends.org)

SAMPLE RESPONSE PROTOCOL FOLLOWING A SUICIDE[1]

1. **Inform pastors if needed.**

2. **Provide pastoral care and obtain facts.** The pastor provides support to the family and also verifies facts, obtains accurate information, and asks what information the family is comfortable sharing.

3. **Inform lay leaders in a meeting or by phone.** In order to ensure a unified response, the pastor informs lay leaders so they can inform members of their groups (e.g., Sunday School, choir, small group). The following may be discussed:

   - Facts of the suicide

   - The lay leaders' emotions

   - The lay leaders' theological questions

   - How to care for the family

   - How to inform members in their groups

- How to identify and monitor vulnerable individuals in their groups (close friends of the deceased, attempt survivors, survivors, etc.)

- How lay leaders can care for themselves and their group members

- List of resources (mental health professionals, support groups, National Suicide Prevention Hotline, books, websites)

- Prayer

4. **Make sure that the family of the deceased is receiving concrete helps** like meals and babysitting.

5. **Issue a brief church-wide announcement regarding the death** with support, resources, and small group meeting times. Disclose only relevant facts—do not provide details of method or location of suicide.

6. **Lay leaders meet with members in groups.** The following may be discussed:

- Relevant facts of the suicide (omitting method and location)

- The members' emotions

- The members' theological questions

- How to care for the family

- How to encourage and support one another (make sure members know how to reach out and to whom)

- How to identify and monitor vulnerable individuals in their groups (close friends of the deceased, attempt survivors, survivors, etc.)

- How members can care for themselves

- List of resources (mental health professionals, support groups, National Suicide Prevention Hotline, books, websites)

- Prayer

7. **Prepare and provide prayer teams** who can minister to those in need on consecutive Sundays after the death.

8. **Address the suicide from the pulpit.** The pastor teaches the congregation how to mourn together as a community, prevent suicide, and reach out to the family of the deceased.

9. **Hold an open forum** if necessary for members to process grief, guilt, or anger after the church service.

10. **Provide additional support services**, including referral to mental health professionals, resources, and support groups.

11. **Debrief lay leaders** one week after the death and review the status of congregation members and leaders. Provide space for lay leaders to grieve and share.

12. **Identify at-risk individuals** within the congregation, evaluate how they are doing, and actively reach out to support them. Be alert for signs of contagion or clustering.

13. **Provide information about funeral arrangements** to relevant people. Arrange to attend the funeral as a community and with others.

14. **Evaluate upcoming church activities** and decide whether there is a need to cancel.

15. **Continue to offer pastoral care** to the family of the deceased.

16. **Make a note to provide pastoral care to the family and the church as the anniversary of the death approaches.**

APPENDIX E

FOUR FUNERAL SERMONS FOLLOWING A SUICIDE

Sermon One

Patrick Gray

In the Name of the Father, and of the Son, and of the Holy Spirit. Amen.

I think we're all going to need a little forgiveness, a little mercy; we're going to have to cut each other some slack over the course of these coming days and weeks. I love Mark,[1] and you do, too. And I'm upset at what happened. And I'm going to miss him very much. And I'm upset at why it is I'm going to miss him very much. The reason we are here is not right, and I'm angry about it. And there is nothing romantic or poetic about what has happened. But we love Mark, and that's why we're here, and we are going to miss him very much.

Things have started to come back to me, memories of times together; I'm sure it's happening to you, too. Just being in this place, here at the Church of the Advent [Boston, MA], which is where I first met him, down in the garden, after the service, him coming up and doing his Mark thing. "I'm Mark. Sup?" And during the course of the conversation, him doing his little laugh, bouncing as he did it. It's coming back. And I laugh, and then I cry.

I want to talk about God. I want to talk about the God Mark loves. I want to talk about the God that loves Mark. Because God does love Mark. He always has. He always will. Nothing separates us from the love of God. But lots of things try to. Lots of things want to get between you and God. And this is a problem. This is not right. Lots of things try to put a "no" where a "yes" should be. But this God doesn't take "no" for an answer. No matter who we are, no matter what we think, no matter how we feel, no matter what we do, this God says, "I know who you are, and I have not forgotten you. I'm going to make all your problems my problem. All that has gone wrong, horribly, horribly, wrong, I will make right. I'm going to do something about it. But it won't go away with a wave of my hand. But it will take my hand. In fact, because of what has happened, it will take both my hands."

What has happened to you, what has happened to Mark, what has happened to this world will take both hands. The Christian God is the God that reaches out and that reaches into our lives with both hands. With one hand he takes away the weight, all those things that hold you down, all those things that trip you up, all those things that make you fall, he takes away, he clears it all away with one hand; and with the other hand he reaches in and grabs ahold of you, and never lets you go. With one hand he takes ahold of death, and darkness— he grabs it by the scruff of the neck, he grabs that old dog—and he shakes it, shakes it till it shakes out, shakes out the way it was meant to be, the way God intended it to be. To paraphrase his prophet Bruce Cockburn, he shakes death and darkness until they bleed life and light. And with the other hand, the other hand that has grabbed you—this hand will never let you go—he lifts you up. God will lift you up. No matter how far down you go, God will lift you up. God will raise you up, and, to quote God's other prophet Johnny Cash, "Ain't no grave can hold my body down." God needs both hands to take care of what's happened to us. God reaches in, and God reaches out; he stretches out his arms of love on the hard wood of the cross so that he might draw the whole world to himself. This is the Christian God. This is the God that Mark loves. This is the God that loves Mark.

And I've seen a lot of imitation of this God this week. I've seen a lot of people using both hands to hold these dear people. Sweet Sally, George and Jane, Samuel and Tracy—you have reached out to them with your hands and your heart, but as you can imagine, they will need you to continue to do this. They're going to need both your hands for some time. But they're not the only ones. You don't only reach out to those that are hurting. You reach out if *you* are hurting. If you're in a bad place, you need to reach out. And if you don't know where to start, anyone with a white collar on in this room is a fine place to start. Clergy, I admit, are a funny bunch. There's a reason we wear collars—God has to keep us on a short leash. But whoever it is, don't suffer alone.

Now we come to the touchy-feely part of the sermon. Mark would have hated this, but I want to make sure you get this. I want you to repeat after me. Ready? "When I am in trouble, I will reach out with both hands. When I am in a bad place, I will reach out with both hands. When I am in a tight spot, I will reach out with both hands." Reach out with both hands to someone who will be happy to hold them, and to hold you.

I have one more thing I want to say, and it's for a specific group, you'll know who you are. ... You are the ones who maybe grew up Christian, or you are the ones who converted to Christianity with great enthusiasm, you are the ones who most likely brushed up against evangelical Christianity at some time, and you thought that was a healthy plant you brushed up against, and now you're pretty convinced it was poison ivy. ... You are folks who have your eyes wide open, and you didn't like what you saw. ... But something is still going on with you. You want to believe. Or maybe you want to want to believe. You still think there might be a place for you. But you don't go. You don't go. And I get it. Believe me, I get it. ... I'm here to tell you this morning, it's time. It's time. If ever you needed it, you need it now. … Wherever it is, it's time for you to find a church. It starts now. And you need to find a church where they worship and give thanks to the God that reaches out with both hands. You need to go and find that place. And when you show up that Sunday morning, you might be so out of your element, there might not be a skinny jean in sight, but you will know if this is a place where they worship the God who reaches out with both hands. Because you need that God, now more than ever, and you need to be with people who worship that God, now more than ever. But you'll have to see for yourself, because as I said, you are people with your eyes wide open. But in places like I'm talking about, my brothers and sisters, you will see in that place, you will see that the Christian God is a God who reaches out to us with both hands, who never lets us go. And you will see people of all kinds doing their best to imitate this God. That's a church you want to go to. And all of you, all of you, now more than ever, imitate this God even if you don't believe in him. With both hands, reach out.

Sermon Two

William R. L. Haley

On this most difficult day, we are surrounded by a great company of fellowship, a very strong and loving embrace. We are with each other, holding onto each other, as family, and friends, husbands and wives, mothers and fathers, brothers and sisters, holding each other up for support and comfort. We are surrounded by the heavenly hosts, angels, and the communion of saints, and loved ones gone before us. We are surrounded by God—Father, Son, and Holy Spirit—and held in God's very strong and loving embrace.

And we are surrounded by these mountains. They, too, are part of our service today, honoring the life of our beloved Edward. They are strong, and offer perhaps the best response on a day like today, a reverent silence. It is like they are bearing witness, keeping vigil, standing guard. And they are reminding us of something very import-ant. These mountains have been here a long time, and will be. A hun-dred years ago, before any of us were born, they were here, looking like this. And a hundred years from now, when we will not be here, they will be, looking like this. These mountains remind us that life on earth is short.

For Edward, his life on earth was far too short. Life became too hard for him, and we have many questions. The best answers right now to all the questions … is silence, because words fail. And we look to the mountains. As the psalmist wrote and we prayed together, "I lift up my eyes to the hills. From where does my help come from? My help comes from the LORD, who made heaven and earth" (Ps 121:1–2 ESV).

But even though Edward's life on earth was short, you loved him! I was, as were so many of us, blessed by Reena's reflections about Edward written last week, what was great about him, and a gift about him. You wrote, "Edward is a lot of words starting with P. Passionate, precise, particular, perceptive. And he is still precious to us." There is no doubt that the gifts of Edward's life will keep on giving, like seeds that have been planted, and will grow, and bear fruit.

While you had him, you loved him, and love him still!

There is some comfort to think that now, where he is, Edward is loving you better than he was able to on earth. That's what happens when we meet Jesus face to face. We become like him. We're made perfect. Not only is our pain taken away and our troubled souls given rest, but we're able to love perfectly for the first time. I'm sure that if Edward knew what he knows now, he'd make different choices. I'm sure that if we knew what Edward knows now, we'd make different choices too.

And now Edward is at peace, and rest. His pain is over, and he knows love. And he knows that he is loved.

On this side, we know loss. We must take our pain to God, even when words fail, and take our heartache to each other, when sharing tears is more helpful than talking. And we look forward in hope to the resurrection. We heard the words of God through the prophet Isaiah, that "he will swallow up death forever, and wipe away tears from all faces." There is comfort in this hope, that death does not have the last word, but that God does.

And God's loudest word on death was the Word, his Son, Jesus Christ, the Good Shepherd, who laid down his life for his sheep, for us, and for Edward, so that death wouldn't get the last word. Rather, Jesus conquers death through his own death, by rising from the dead, so that we, too, can rise, and those we love. In this there is hope, and on a day like today, our only hope. But it is a solid hope.

So today, we mourn, we weep; we are sad and heavy-hearted. The mountains bear witness and keep a reverent silence. We hold onto each other and hold each other up. We look to God for help, and put our hope in Jesus, who will one day raise all of his own from the dead, and Edward, too.

Sermon Three

Paul A. Hoffman
Romans 8:28–39

We are gathered here this morning to celebrate and give thanks to God for the life of Stephanie Gilcrest.

Although it is true that recently she was in great pain, waging an internal battle and struggling deeply with bulimia, I don't want the way she left this world to overshadow the way she lived in this world. I just want to briefly mention a few things I noticed about Stephanie in the short time I knew her.

Stephanie displayed a servant's heart. She served our country in the Navy and was a deacon here at First Presbyterian. She helped in many ministries: the soup kitchen ministry and the children's and youth ministries. She also had a strong interest in missions.

Stephanie possessed an energetic and vibrant personality. She enjoyed riding her bike, running, playing with her dogs. She loved being in nature. A couple of months back she wrote an email to a friend and said, "Hi! Brrr ... where is the sunshine? I went for a walk today on the Cliff Walk and I was very thankful for all of God's beauty!" She must have forgotten that she lived in Rhode Island!

Stephanie was compassionate. She was studying nursing at the local university.

But I think the most important thing about Stephanie was her passion for Jesus Christ. That Jesus loved her, and she loved him. That love shined through in so many ways in her life. A passage which reflects that love is Romans 8:28–39. Let me read the text for you:

> And we know that in all things God works for the good of those who love him, who have been called according to his purpose. For those God foreknew he also predestined to be

conformed to the image of his Son, that he might be the first-born among many brothers and sisters. And those he predestined, he also called; those he called, he also justified; those he justified, he also glorified.

What, then, shall we say in response to these things? If God is for us, who can be against us? He who did not spare his own Son, but gave him up for us all—how will he not also, along with him, graciously give us all things? Who will bring any charge against those whom God has chosen? It is God who justifies. Who then is the one who condemns? No one. Christ Jesus who died—more than that, who was raised to life—is at the right hand of God and is also interceding for us. Who shall separate us from the love of Christ? Shall trouble or hardship or persecution or famine or nakedness or danger or sword? As it is written:

"For your sake we face death all day long;
we are considered as sheep to be slaughtered."

No, in all these things we are more than conquerors through him who loved us. For I am convinced that neither death nor life, neither angels nor demons, neither the present nor the future, nor any powers, neither height nor depth, nor anything else in all creation, will be able to separate us from the love of God that is in Christ Jesus our Lord.

If you don't remember anything else I say this morning, I want you to remember this: God's love holds fast. How do you and I know that to be true in a time such as this? Well the apostle Paul gives us a few reasons. Number one, before Stephanie was even born, God called her to be his own. He set her apart to love him and serve him. And Stephanie did that with all her heart and soul.

But Stephanie could do that because, number two, she had experienced the grace and mercy of God. That God sent his son Jesus to die on a cross for her. The apostle Paul puts it this way, "God did not spare his own son but gave him up for us all." Isn't that a powerful truth? That God gave you his all out of his love for you? That blows my mind! There is no other way to explain a life like Stephanie's, is there? So, God not only called Stephanie but gave his son for her. God's love holds fast.

But there is a third reason. Paul asserts in verse 34 that Jesus was raised to life. After Jesus died on the cross, he rose from the dead. And Paul tells us in 1 Corinthians 15 that because Jesus was raised from the dead, everyone who believes in Jesus will also be raised from the dead. Stephanie believed in Jesus, and because of that, we believe that she will be raised from the dead. That she is in the presence of Jesus Christ right now. There is no suffering, no pain, only joy. God's love holds fast.

Lastly, the apostle Paul says in verses 35–39 that *nothing* can separate a follower of Jesus Christ from the powerful love of Jesus Christ. Christ binds us to himself with unbreakable cords of love. Ultimately, our salvation, our eternal life, is not based on us, but on him. It is not based on what we have done, but on what God has done on the cross and through the resurrection. God is a conqueror, and because of the unbreakable love he offers you and me, we are conquerors, too. We conquer all things, especially death. It cannot stand in our way because all-powerful God is on our side.

God's love holds fast. Stephanie was called. She was saved through the cross. And she believed in Jesus, who was raised from the dead. And his unbreakable love made her a conqueror.

Stephanie would have wanted nothing more than everyone who is here to experience the salvation, love, and hope that is in Jesus Christ. The key word here is in verse 37: "Through Christ." You must choose to embrace God's love demonstrated on the cross, just like Stephanie did. It is only through Jesus' blood that your sins can be forgiven. It is only through Jesus Christ that you can be reconciled to God and receive eternal life. The eternal life we believe Stephanie is experiencing right now in heaven. God's love holds fast.

Sermon Four

Tom Simmons
Romans 5:1–11

This week we suffered a horrible, shocking, tragic loss. Our friend and brother Jim Schooley died on Thursday, by his own hand. We will gather on Saturday afternoon for Jim's funeral. It's scary when sudden death comes shattering into our lives. It reminds us that every day is a matter of life and death—literally.

But let's step back from that terrible precipice to think of your life last week and next week, the day-in-day-out situations of disappointment, suffering, and loss, times when we're angry about how things turned out, feeling sorry for ourselves, complaining, nursing our grudge, "what we deserve," holding onto the picture in our mind of how life "should be," casting blame on ourselves, others, or even God when life falls short of our ideal.

We all do it—some more than others.

When we read about the Israelites in Exodus 17, I can really sympathize with them questioning God in their sufferings. They'd been uprooted from everything familiar. It was lousy being slaves in Egypt, but at least it was familiar! Now they're out in the desert, hot, thirsty, wandering around, and they're feeling a little … grumpy. With all their discomfort, disappointment, and irritation, they are doubting God's goodness, questioning his motives. "Did God bring us out here to kill us!?" Israelites are inclined to think it's true.

In Genesis 3, we see that when the deceiver asked Eve, "Did God *really* say?" he was sowing doubt about God's good intentions. "He's keeping some vital information from you … he's just trying to keep you down." Since that time, doubting God is the default mode of the human heart, our first reflex. People will blame God for just about everything! Chaos and death and the evil that men do strike again ... and guess who gets the blame! Satan struck first by ruining our trust in God's goodness.

But God struck back. Paul tells us in Romans 5:7–8 that God proved his love in this: that though one will scarcely die for a good person, Christ died for us while we were still sinners.

It's a love proved in pain—his pain.

God feels his love for you that strongly!

Do you need more proof?!

We could just end the sermon there with that ringing declaration of God's good intentions.

But let's take it another step and think through the implications of this stunning fact.

First, Paul makes very clear the impact of Jesus' death. He suffered as our substitute. He took what we deserve so that we could get what he deserves. He took rejection so we could get access. When you feel guilty, or afraid, or humiliated, or exposed, or alone, or powerless, or rejected, or betrayed, or accused, know this: Jesus was suffering all those things in full to save you through them. He shows you his scars to prove his *love* for you. "These scars mean peace with God. Access."

It is love proved in pain.

Second, this shows us a new path through suffering and loss, danger and disappointment. His love conquers anger and despair and guilt. No matter how bad your plight may seem, God is in it, transforming it for good. The gospel gives us a new way to deal with loss, from the death of a child or spouse to daily stresses in traffic, and everything in between. His love is being "poured out into our hearts through the Holy Spirit."[2] As we let that love trickle deeper and deeper into the core of who we are, down into the dark recesses and crevices of our heart, it dissolves our insecurity and fear of being lost or rejected or abandoned by God or by people we love. We don't have to live anxiously protecting ourselves or promoting ourselves.

Paul shows us how, instead of driving us away from God in anger or despair, suffering in hope changes us for the better. He says in Romans 5, "we boast in the hope of the glory of God. Not only so, but we also glory in our sufferings, because we know that suffering produces perseverance; perseverance, character; and character, hope. And hope does not put us to shame, because God's love has been poured out into our hearts through the Holy Spirit, who has been given to us."

When we allow the Holy Spirit to be active in our lives, infusing us with the Father's love, suffering leads us to deeper experience of God's love being poured into us. See how God doesn't save us from suffering? He saves us through it.

It's a love proved in pain. Our pain.

But there's another thing I want to highlight here. It's the pervasive use of the word "we" and "us," those plural pronouns that make it abundantly clear who Paul is addressing. He's not talking to a bunch of individuals in their personal spiritual journeys. He's not writing to "the individual believers in Rome." He's writing to the church in Rome, the body of Christ, linked together, arm-in-arm like your body's organs. He's describing our life together as *one*, not our lives as many individuals who attend church most Sundays.

Here is where all that he's describing plays out in the drama of our lives. Here is where we share that access. Here is where we pass the peace Paul talks about. Here is where we learn to walk that journey of faith, which Jim began with us about five years ago. Here is where we support each other with prayers and meals and hugs and counsel and tears and truth and putting up with one another. Here is where we share our lives and receive the support we need for the difficult journey, turning suffering into endurance, into character, into hope. Here is where we are safe to share our hearts and let grace happen.

But how can grace happen if we keep our suffering bottled up inside, secret from our brothers and sisters? Maybe Jim's death can spur us to find new ways for St. Peter's to be a place where no one stands alone. *Or dies alone.* The only way to experience these things with God is by sharing them with one another.

Here is where love is proved in pain. Our pain, borne together.

SAMPLE FUNERAL LITURGY FOLLOWING A SUICIDE

The people say the words in italics. The celebrant says the words in upright text. [All stand during the processional, acclamation, prayers, and singing.]

Acclamation

"I am the resurrection and the life. The one who believes in me will live, even though they die…" (John 11:25)

> *"Where, O death, is your victory?*
>> *Where, O death, is your sting?"*
> *The sting of death is sin, and the power of sin is the law. But thanks*
>> *be to God! He gives us the victory through our Lord Jesus*
>> *Christ. (1 Cor 15:55–57)*

I know that my redeemer lives,
  and that in the end he will stand on the earth.
And after my skin has been destroyed,
  yet in my flesh I will see God;
I myself will see him
  with my own eyes—I, and not another. (Job 19:25–27)

Blessed be God, Father, Son and Holy Spirit, who alone has the right to give life and take life (Deut 32:39; Exod 20:13).

And blessed be those who mourn because they will be comforted (Matt 5:4).

Prayers

The Lord be with you.
And also with you.
Let us pray.

Our loving Father, whose mercies are infinite, hear our prayers for [name]. Jesus, Son of the living God, have mercy on [name] who was deceived into believing death was the only way out and that death would unburden others from [her/his] pain. May [name] find eternal life and gladness with you, God the Father, Jesus Christ the Son and the Holy Spirit, who live and reign together forever and ever. *Amen.*[1]

[Insert song here.]

Praise be to the God and Father of our Lord Jesus Christ, the Father of compassion and the God of all comfort, who comforts us in all our troubles, so that we can comfort those in any trouble with the comfort we ourselves receive from God (2 Cor 1:3–4). We deeply lament the bitter loss of [name] and we seek comfort from you, God, and from each other. Our world has been diminished because [name] is no longer among us. Surround us with your love, that we may not be overwhelmed by our loss, but have confidence in your goodness, and strength to meet the days to come,[2] through our Lord Jesus Christ, who lives and reigns with you and the Holy Spirit. *Amen.*

Scripture Readings and Sermon

[The people sit.]

A reading from the lamentations of the prophet Jeremiah:

Because of the LORD's great love we are not consumed,
    for his compassions never fail.
They are new every morning;
    great is your faithfulness.
I say to myself, "The LORD is my portion;
    therefore I will wait for him."
The LORD is good to those whose hope is in him,
    to the one who seeks him;
it is good to wait quietly
    for the salvation of the LORD. ...
For no one is cast off
    by the Lord forever.
Though he brings grief, he will show compassion,
    so great is his unfailing love.
For he does not willingly bring affliction
    or grief to anyone. (Lam 3:22–26, 31–33)

A reading from Psalm 90:
[Read responsively or sing antiphonally.]

Lord, you have been our dwelling place
    throughout all generations.
Before the mountains were born
    or you brought forth the whole world,
from everlasting to everlasting you are God.
You turn people back to dust,
    saying, "Return to dust, you mortals."
A thousand years in your sight
    are like a day that has just gone by,
    or like a watch in the night.
Yet you sweep people away in the sleep of death—
    they are like the new grass of the morning:

In the morning it springs up new,
    but by evening it is dry and withered.
We are consumed by your anger
    and terrified by your indignation.
You have set our iniquities before you,
    our secret sins in the light of your presence.
All our days pass away under your wrath;
    we finish our years with a moan.
Our days may come to seventy years,
    or eighty, if our strength endures;
yet the best of them are but trouble and sorrow,
    for they quickly pass, and we fly away.
If only we knew the power of your anger!
    Your wrath is as great as the fear that is your due.
Teach us to number our days,
    that we may gain a heart of wisdom. (Ps 90:1–12)

A reading from the apostle Paul's epistle to the Romans:

I consider that our present sufferings are not worth comparing with the glory that will be revealed in us. For the creation waits in eager expectation for the children of God to be revealed. For the creation was subjected to frustration, not by its own choice, but by the will of the one who subjected it, in hope that the creation itself will be liberated from its bondage to decay and brought into the freedom and glory of the children of God. We know that the whole creation has been groaning as in the pains of childbirth right up to the present time. Not only so, but we ourselves, who have the firstfruits of the Spirit, groan inwardly as we wait eagerly for our adoption to sonship, the redemption of our bodies. For in this hope we were saved. But hope that is seen is no hope at all. Who hopes for what they already have? But if we hope for what we do not yet have, we wait for it patiently. ... Who will bring any charge against those whom God has chosen? It is God who justifies. Who then is the one who condemns? No one. Christ Jesus who died—more than that, who was raised to life—is at the right hand of God and is also interceding for us. Who shall separate us from the love of Christ? Shall trouble or hardship or persecution or famine or nakedness or danger or sword? ... No, in all these things we are more than conquerors through him who loved us. For I am convinced that neither death nor life, neither angels nor demons, neither the present nor the future, nor any powers, neither height nor depth, nor anything else in all creation, will be able to separate us from the love of God that is in Christ Jesus our Lord. (Rom 8: 18–25, 33–35, 37–39).

[The people stand.]

The Gospel of our Lord Jesus Christ according to John.
Glory to you, Lord Christ.

"Lord," Martha said to Jesus, "if you had been here, my brother would not have died. But I know that even now God will give you whatever you ask."

Jesus said to her, "Your brother will rise again."

Martha answered, "I know he will rise again in the resurrection at the last day."

Jesus said to her, "I am the resurrection and the life. The one who believes in me will live, even though they die; and whoever lives by believing in me will never die. Do you believe this?"

"Yes, Lord," she replied, "I believe that you are the Messiah, the Son of God, who is to come into the world" (John 11:21–27).

The Gospel of the Lord.
Praise to you, Lord Christ.

[Insert sermon here. The people sit.]

[Insert the Apostle's Creed or the Nicene Creed here if desired. The people stand.]

The Prayers of the People

[The people kneel.]

As Jesus, God's only Son, taught us, let us pray together:

> *Our Father in heaven,*
> *hallowed be your name,*
> *your kingdom come,*
> *your will be done,*
> > *on earth as it is in heaven.*
> *Give us today our daily bread.*
> *And forgive us our debts,*
> > *as we also have forgiven our debtors.*
> *And lead us not into temptation,*
> > *but deliver us from the evil one.* (Matt 6:9–13)

Bless the Lord who is faithful and just and will forgive us our sins (1 John 1:9).
His mercy endures forever (Ps 136).

We have not always remembered your loving presence with us.
His mercy endures forever.

We have not always remembered your ongoing intercession for us (Rom 8:24; Heb 7:25).
His mercy endures forever.

We have not always remembered that you are a very present help in our trouble (Ps 46:1).
His mercy endures forever.

We have not always trusted you to redeem evil.
His mercy endures forever.

We have not always courageously faced our lives full of trouble (Job 14:1).
His mercy endures forever.

We have lost hope repeatedly.
His mercy endures forever.

We have not always affirmed the unshakable value of the life you gave us.
His mercy endures forever.

We have not always treated each other with worth and dignity.
His mercy endures forever.

We have not always borne each other's burdens (Gal 6:2).
His mercy endures forever.

We have not always worked out our relationships with love and truth.
His mercy endures forever

We have not always worked to alleviate the suffering of others.
His mercy endures forever.

Let us confess our sins against God and our neighbor.

[Brief period of silence]

> *Most merciful God,*
> *We confess that we have sinned against you*
> *In thought, word, and deed,*
> *By what we have done,*
> *And by what we have left undone.*
> *We have not loved you with our whole heart;*
> *We have not loved our neighbors as ourselves.*
> *We are truly sorry and we humbly repent.*
> *For the sake of your Son Jesus Christ,*
> *Have mercy on us and forgive us;*
> *That we may delight in your will,*
> *And walk in your ways,*
> *To the glory of your Name. Amen.*[3]

Almighty God have mercy on you, forgive you all your sins through our Lord Jesus Christ, strengthen you in all goodness, and by the power of the Holy Spirit keep you in eternal life.
Amen.

The peace of the Lord be always with you.
And also with you.[4]

[Standing, the people pass the peace (Matt 5:23–24).]

[Insert song here. The people stand.]

[Insert two to three eulogies here. The people sit.]

[If desired, include the taking of communion.]

Communion

[The people kneel.]

God so loved the world that he gave his one and only Son, that who-ever believes in him shall not perish but have eternal life. For God did not send his Son into the world to condemn the world, but to save the world through him. Whoever believes in him is not con-demned, but whoever does not believe stands condemned already because they have not believed in the name of God's one and only Son ... (John 3:16–18)

> [who] though in very nature God ...
>> made himself nothing ...
> And being found in appearance as a man,
>> he humbled himself
>> by becoming obedient to death—
>> even death on a cross! (Phil 2:6–8)

Through Jesus' death on the cross, God in his mercy, grace, and kind-ness redeemed us to himself. Once we were not a people, but now we are the people of God; once we had not received mercy, but now we have received mercy (1 Pet 2:10). We remember God's new cove-nant with us, his people, in the breaking of the bread and the drink-ing of the cup.

The Lord Jesus, on the night he was betrayed, took bread, and when he had given thanks, he broke it and said, "This is my body, which is for you; do this in remembrance of me." In the same way, after supper he took the cup, saying, "This cup is the new covenant in my blood; do this, whenever you drink it, in remembrance of me." For whenever you eat this bread and drink this cup, you proclaim the Lord's death until he comes (1 Cor 11:23–26).

*We do not presume to come to this your table, merciful Lord, trusting in
our own righteousness, but in your manifold and great mercies. We are
not worthy so much as to gather up the crumbs under your table. But
you are the same Lord whose nature is always to have mercy. Grant us
therefore, gracious Lord, to evermore dwell in your Son Jesus Christ, and
he in us. Amen.*[5]

[The people take communion.]

The Lord be with you.
And also with you.
Let us pray.

We thank you, Father, for nourishing us in our grief with a foretaste
of the marriage supper of the Lamb (Rev 19:9). Comfort us who are
burdened with sorrow, with the assurance of your everlasting love
for us, with your peace that passes all understanding, and with your
hope for today and eternity. Grant that we comfort others with your
comfort. We eagerly wait for you to make all things new (Rev 21:5),
for the day when you will destroy the enemy, death (1 Cor 15:25–26),
and for when you bring us to your heavenly kingdom, where there
will be no more mourning or crying or pain (Rev 21:4). Come, Lord
Jesus! (Rev 22:20). Through Jesus Christ our Lord who reigns with
God the Father and the Holy Spirit.
Amen.

Into your hands, merciful Savior, we commend [name]. Acknowledge,
we humbly beseech you, a sinner of your own redeeming. Receive
[name/him/her] in the arms of your mercy.[6]
Amen.

Let us go forth in the name of Christ.
Thanks be to God.

[Recessional. The people stand.]

[Insert a song here.]

For none of us lives for ourselves alone, and none of us dies for ourselves alone. If we live, we live for the Lord; and if we die, we die for the Lord. So, whether we live or die, we belong to the Lord. For this very reason, Christ died and returned to life so that he might be the Lord of both the dead and the living (Rom 14:7–9).

But Christ has indeed been raised from the dead, the firstfruits of those who have fallen asleep. … So will it be with the resurrection of the dead. The body that is sown is perishable, it is raised imperishable; it is sown in dishonor, it is raised in glory; it is sown in weakness, it is raised in power; it is sown a natural body, it is raised a spiritual body. … Therefore, my dear brothers and sisters, stand firm. Let nothing move you (1 Cor 15:20, 42–44, 58).

But for you who revere my name, the sun of righteousness will rise with healing in its rays. And you will go out and frolic like well-fed calves (Mal 4:2).

Note: Another resource is Melinda Moore and Daniel A. Roberts, eds., The Suicide Funeral (or Memorial Service): Honoring Their Memory, Comforting Their Survivors *(Eugene, OR: Resource Publications, 2017).*

SAMPLE LETTER TO YOUTH GROUP PARENTS ABOUT THE SUICIDE PREVENTION BIBLE STUDIES SERIES

This and the following two appendices are directed to adolescents and their parents. Below is a sample letter to youth group parents about the suicide prevention Bible studies series (appendix H). This letter is an important step in implementing suicide prevention activities for minors because their parents are responsible for their welfare.

Dear youth group parents,

In the United States, suicide is the *second* leading cause of death among ten- to thirty-four-year-olds.[1]

It makes sense to dedicate the next seven weeks to suicide prevention. We'll be studying the Bible and teaching your student about seven ways that help prevent suicide:

1. Connectedness with others

2. The worth and dignity of every human

3. Hope

4. Why suicide is wrong

5. Self-control

6. Suffering

7. Reaching out for help.

Please call or email with any questions or concerns.

BIBLE STUDIES FOR YOUTH AND YOUNG ADULTS

While Esther Kim (MDiv, MACO) was the youth coordinator at City*life* Presbyterian Church, Boston, she recruited several other youth pastors who joined her in testing these youth Bible studies. Their excellent suggestions improved them significantly. Before implementing these Bible studies and activities, let the parents know that over the next several weeks the focus will be on suicide prevention. A sample letter to parents is found in appendix G.

Lessons for Young People

Lesson one: Connectedness

- Supplies: Bibles, image distortion program on the internet, notecards, envelopes, and stamps, as well as the names of each student in the group on folded papers in a bowl or the church's directory with addresses of congregants.

- Exegetical idea: Paul wrote letters to address distorted views.

- Study idea: Encouraging notes help people alter their distorted view of being disconnected.

Using a distortion program on the internet, demonstrate distortion.[1] Depressed and suicidal people distort reality. They think they are alone. The apostle Paul wrote many letters to address distorted views.

Read Ephesians 6:21–22.

1. What are ways that our views of ourselves can become distorted?

2. Paul wrote letters to address distorted views. What are some letters that the apostle Paul wrote?

3. What distorted view is Paul addressing in Ephesians 6:21–22?

4. In what situations have you needed encouragement?

5. What are some other situations where people need encouragement?

6. Why do people need this kind of encouragement?

Read 1 Thessalonians 5:9–11.

1. How does 1 Thessalonians 5:9–11 tell us to encourage others?

2. What kind of encouragement do depressed or suicidal Christians need?

3. Why do notes help us feel that we are not alone?

Everyone needs to know they are not alone. One way to help someone know that they are not alone is by sending them an encouraging note.

Ask each student to draw the name of a student in the group or choose one person from church who needs to hear that they are not alone.

Write the student or person a note. Give the note to the student or use the church directory to address the envelopes.

Ask, "What did you learn that you want to take with you this week?"

Close in prayer for students and other people who may be feeling lonely.

Lesson two: Worth and dignity

- Supplies: Bibles, 2–4 video cameras (e.g., 2–4 phone cameras), the capability to play back and project the video, a ream of copy paper, and markers.

- Exegetical idea: God has created us (Group 1), he has loved us (Group 2), nothing can separate us from his love (Group 3), and he has made us his people (Group 4).

- Study idea: God gives us reasons to live.

Divide into 2–4 groups. Read the passages. Find as many reasons to live as you can in each passage. Write each reason to live on a piece of copy paper. Video each member of the group holding up each reason to live found in the passages. Add other reasons to live, like finishing school, getting married, making a scientific discovery, helping others, learning to ski, planting flowers and watching them grow, etc.

- Group 1: Psalm 8; Psalm 139:14

- Group 2: Jeremiah 31:3; Zephaniah 3:17; John 3:16

- Group 3: Romans 8:31–39

- Group 4: 1 Peter 2:9–10; Revelation 1:5b–6

Play back the videos for the whole group. While watching, students write down their top 10 reasons for living. Keep these lists for the next Bible study activity (developing a hope kit).

Ask, "What did you learn that you want to take with you this week?"

Close in prayer, thanking God for the reasons to live that he gives us.

Lesson three: Hope

- Supplies: Bibles, a shoe box for each student, the reasons to live from the previous youth group activity (see above), old magazines, and scissors.

- Exegetical idea: Paul prevented the jailer's suicide by giving him a reason to live.

- Study idea: Prevent suicide by giving people reasons to live.

Begin by reading Acts 16:23–34.

1. How were Paul and Silas treated when they were thrown into prison?

2. What were Paul and Silas doing, and what were the other prisoners doing?

3. Why did the jailer want to kill himself?

4. When people like the jailer feel hopeless or like a failure, what helps them?

5. What did Paul do to stop the jailer from killing himself?

6. Why was "We are all here!" a reason to live for the jailer?

7. Last week we made a long list of reasons to live. How are the jailer's reasons the same or different from yours?

8. How can you give other people reasons to live when they have suicidal thoughts?

9. How can you remind yourself of your reasons to live when you feel hopeless?

Emphasize the need to remind others of their reasons to live and to remind ourselves of our own reasons to live.

Read James 1:17.

1. What good and perfect gifts does God give us?

2. What are some of the good and perfect gifts that God has given you?

Explain that one way to remind ourselves of our reasons to live is a hope kit. The adult helper can show their own hope kit by way of example. Tell students to use their list of reasons to live from the previous youth group activity, and find reminders of these in the magazines. Students will cut out reminders of their reasons to live and put them in their hope box. They will bring their hope box home and use it to remind them of their reasons to live when they are feeling hopeless.

Ask, "What did you learn that you want to take with you this week?"

Close in prayer, asking God to remind us of the hope we have because of our faith in him.

Lesson four: Moral objections to suicide

- Supplies: Bibles, blue painter's tape for shackles, yard stick for sword, eight student volunteers (one jailer, Paul, Silas, five prisoners).

- Exegetical idea: Paul prevented the jailer's suicide because God alone gives life and takes it, even the life of a jailer.

- Study idea: God prohibits suicide because he alone gives and takes life.

Begin by reading Acts 16:23–34. Recruit eight students to act out the passage: one jailer, Paul, Silas, and five prisoners. Following the performance, facilitate a discussion about Paul's intervention with the jailer.

1. Today we're talking about a "bad guy." Why was the jailer a "bad guy"?

2. Why did the jailor want to kill himself?

3. When the jailor drew his sword, what did Paul do?

4. Last week, we talked about Paul giving the jailer a reason to live ("We're all here!"). This week, we want to ask why Paul stopped a "bad guy" from killing himself. Why is the suicide of a "bad guy" wrong?

5. Read Deuteronomy 32:39. What does it mean that God is the one who puts to death and brings to life?

6. If you have a friend who talks about suicide, what would you do?

7. If your friend asks you to keep their suicidal thinking a secret, why shouldn't you? Why didn't Luke keep it a secret when he wrote the book of Acts?

8. Who are trusted adults that you could turn to if your friend talks about suicide?

9. What did you learn that you want to take with you this week?

Conclude by thanking God for the worth he has given everyone and by praying for students who might be struggling with thoughts of suicide.

Lesson five: Self-control

- Supplies: Bibles, favorite food (e.g., cookies, pretzels), 1–2 student volunteers.

- Exegetical idea: Self-control develops through the work of the Holy Spirit.

- Study idea: As Christians mature, they develop self-control through the work of the Holy Spirit and practice.

Begin by reading Galatians 5:22–23.

1. What illustration is this verse using to describe the work of the Spirit?

2. Why is Scripture using the tree/fruit illustration?

3. When does fruit appear on a tree?

4. What is the evidence that the Holy Spirit is working in a Christian's life?

5. Do the fruit of the Spirit show up right away in a Christian's life?

6. What is self-control?

7. Why does the Holy Spirit help Christians develop self-control? What is so important about self-control?

Recruit a student volunteer. Ask the student to sit in front of *one piece* of his/her favorite food. Tell the student that he/she can eat this piece now, OR, if he/she waits ten minutes without eating the food while you are out of the room, you will give him/her *two pieces* of his/her favorite food when you return. Leave the room for ten minutes (to give the students a chance to see *if* and *how* the volunteer delays gratification.) Repeat with another student volunteer if desired to see *if* and *how* the volunteer delays gratification.

1. How did you/they show self-control?

2. Were there challenges to delaying the eating of the favorite food? What were they?

3. What did you/they do to delay eating your/his/her favorite food? What kinds of thoughts were going through your mind?

4. Read Proverbs 14:8, 15. What is the opposite of self-control?

5. One way Christians show self-control is to think carefully before acting. What decisions do you, your friends or family, or anyone you know need to think carefully about?

6. How could a Christian think carefully first and control the impulse to _____ (insert answers from previous question)?

7. Sometimes suicide attempts are impulsive. How could a Christian think carefully first and control this impulse?

8. If you want more self-control, how does it develop?

9. As we're practicing self-control, who is helping us?

10. What part does the Holy Spirit play, and what part does your self-control play?

11. What did you learn that you want to take with you this week?

Close in prayer, asking for help as we all develop self-control through practice and the work of the Holy Spirit.

Lesson six: Suffering

- Supplies: Bibles, paper, and pens.

- Exegetical idea: The psalmist laments to God because 1) he has been suffering and 2) he is certain that God is the one who hears his prayer and saves him, despite the current evidence.

- Study idea: Christians call out to God when they are suffering because they are certain that God is the one who hears their prayer and will save them.

When something bad happens, like a classmate bullies you or your parents divorce or your boyfriend/girlfriend breaks up with you, some people attempt suicide. But a better choice is to write an ancient prayer called a lament psalm. A lament psalm is an expression of sadness, a prayer to God, and many examples are found in the book of Psalms in the Bible. It is a kind of poem.

1. What kinds of poems have you learned about in school?

2. What is the structure of a haiku poem?

    -   Three lines

    -   The first line is five syllables

    -   The second line is seven syllables

    -   The third line is five syllables, like the first

A lament psalm also has a structure, but a different one from a haiku[2]:

-   Part one: protest—a complaint ("God, the present situation is horrible").

-   Part two: petition—a request ("God, do something about the situation").

-   Part three: praise—an expression of faith ("I will praise you, God, because you will do something about this horrible situation").

Let's read Psalm 13 with this structure in mind.[3]

1. Which verses are the protest, a complaint to God about the situation?

2. Which verses are the petition, a request that God do something about the situation?

3. Which verses are the praise, an expression of faith and certainty that God will do something?

4. Here is a current-day lament written by a student who is being bullied. Where is the protest, petition, and praise?

Listen up, God, as I voice my complaint;
protect me from the tyranny of the popular,
from the morality of the cool.
Hide me from the conspiracy of the insecure,
from the kids who cover over their failings by exploiting others.
I do not feel attractive, I may not be athletic,
but you are my God.
You know how I am disgraced and shamed;
all my enemies are before you.

Charge [the cool], God, with crime upon crime;
do not let them share in your salvation.
May they be blotted out of the book of life
and not be listed among the righteous.
I am in pain and distress;
may your salvation, O God, protect me.

I will praise God's name in song
and glorify God with thanksgiving.
This will please the Lord more than those
whose pledge of allegiance is only lip service at the flagpole.
The meek will see and be glad;
those who seek God, may your hearts live!
The Lord hears the pleas of the nerdy
and does not despise those held captive by bad skin, teeth,
    and hair.

Let heaven and earth praise God,
for God will save the uncool in their math clubs
and rebuild their broken spirits;
their children will be many,
and someday they will finally know love and acceptance.
Amen.[4]

Or you can use this lament written by a lonely, desperate student. Where is the protest, petition, and praise?

> Hey you, O Lord? Remember me?
> The person who has always been committed to you?
> How long will you hide your face from me?
> How long must I struggle with my darkest doubts
> without the comfort of your voice?
> I feel you have abandoned me!
> Has this been a one-way relationship all along?
> When will it be my turn to succeed and thrive?
> Is this fun for you?
>
> Look me in the eye and answer me, O Lord my God.
> Either give me light or I will just die in the dark.
> If I go down, those people who take pleasure
> in the ruin of my life will say, "I win."
> They will laugh and rejoice.
> Is that what you want?
> Remember, I've always been on your side, God!
>
> I trust in your love; my heart rejoices in your salvation.
> I will sing to the Lord, for God has been good to me.
> Even if right now all I can think of is how [bad] things are.
> Amen.[5]

Have students pick a horrible situation and write a lament psalm with protest, petition, and praise. (It could be a horrible situation in the student's life or in the world.) Students can add their lament psalms to their hope boxes as a reminder of God's presence and what to do when they feel sad.

Ask, "What did you learn that you want to take with you this week?"

Close in prayer for people who are suffering.

Lesson seven: Reaching out for help

- Supplies: Bibles, chairs, two blindfolds, one set of ear plugs, three student volunteers (two who will walk blindfolded and one who will guide one of the blindfolded students through the maze).

- Exegetical idea: Blind Bartimaeus reached out for help.

- Study idea: Just as blind Bartimaeus reached out for help, so depressed people can reach out for help.

Ask for two student volunteers to walk blindfolded through a maze of chairs. After the two student volunteers leave the room, create a maze by setting up chairs randomly between the door of the room to the other side of the room. Ask the class to time each student and to observe what is different with each blindfolded student's performance. When the first blindfolded student returns, have the third student volunteer to tell the blindfolded student volunteer where the chairs are. When the second blindfolded student volunteer enters, the class should not help. Check the time after each blindfolded student arrives at the other side of the room.

When the two students arrive at the other side of the room, debrief.

1. Both students were blindfolded. What was different?

2. Why was getting help so crucial in this game?

3. We're going to read the story of a blind man named Bartimaeus who reached out for help.

Read Mark 10:46–52.

1. What did Bartimaeus do when he heard that Jesus was walking by?

2. What did he shout?

3. Imagine what Bartimaeus was feeling or thinking when he was shouting.

4. What did Jesus do?

5. Why do you think Jesus asked Bartimaeus what he wanted?

6. When Jesus asked what Bartimaeus wanted, what did Bartimaeus say?

7. What did Jesus do?

8. Bartimaeus needed help. What would you do if you needed help?

9. What would make you reach out? To whom would you reach out?

10. If you had suicidal thoughts, what would you do?

11. Who could you reach out to for help?

12. What are obstacles that keep you from reaching out?

13. Role play (a) reaching out for help, (b) helping a friend who reaches out, or (c) helping a friend tell his or her parent about suicidal thoughts. Consider role playing all three.

14. What did you learn that you want to take with you this week?

As we come to the end of our suicide prevention Bible studies, let's review what we've studied and then pick one specific thing you want to remember:

1. Stay connected

2. Your reasons for living

3. Hope (we developed a hope box)

4. Why suicide is wrong

5. Self-control instead of impulsiveness

6. Suffering by writing a lament psalm

7. Reaching out for help

Lessons for Young Adults

Lesson one: Connectedness

- Exegetical idea: Genuine, sincere love must be put in action in community.

- Study idea: Christians suffer in community.

One 2012 study found that 27 percent of families who attend church had mental illness.[6] These families reported twice as much stress as other families on average. What is staggering is that the families wanted help with the mental illness but felt ignored by the congregation.

Read Romans 12:9–21.

1. How does Paul define "genuine/sincere love" in this passage?

2. Why is "weep/mourn with those who weep/mourn" an important mark of a Christian? (v. 15) How does this phrase fit with the context?

3. What circumstances might have happened to those who are weeping?

4. Why does weeping need to happen with others? Why not weep alone?

5. How might a depressed person need to weep with others—especially when depressed people tend to isolate?

6. If you have ever been depressed, what did you need or want in a friend at the time?

7. If you have ever been a friend to a depressed person, what did you—as a friend—need or want at the time?

8. If you have ever been the family member of a depressed person, what did you—as a family member—need or want in a friend at the time?

9. If you are depressed now, how can friends make a difference for you?

10. What resources exist in your community for depressed people?

11. What specifically can a friend or family member do to connect a depressed person to resources?

12. How specifically will you put Romans 12:9–21 into practice over this next week?

13. What did you learn that you want to take with you this week?

Close in prayer by praying for those who are depressed, have a depressed family member, or have a friend who is depressed.

Lesson two: Worth and dignity of every human

- Exegetical idea: God creates all people in his image and all have God-given purpose.

- Study idea: People's dignity is not related to productivity.

What does being created "in the image of God" mean? Authors Paul Brand and Philip Yancey write that in different eras, people have focused on human characteristics that image God: the capacity to make moral judgments (Victorians), the capacity for artistic creativity (Renaissance), the capacity for reason (Enlightenment), the spiritual faculty (Pietism), or the capacity for relationship (Barth/psychology).[7]

But author John Kilner argues, "Viewing attributes (likenesses to God) as the basis of human worth opens the door to reductionism—focusing only on those characteristics of people that one thinks are most important."[8] He goes on to say that being created in the image of God means that we are created to be conformed to the image of Christ. He writes, "While [people] do not warrant the title of God's image' yet, they have dignity grounded in their destiny to become God's image—and so warrant that title once they are fully conformed to Christ. Until then, people are just 'in' or 'according to' God's image—always accountable to the standard of God's image, and developing toward that image as God enables and people endeavor."[9]

Read Genesis 1:26–28.

1. Based on Genesis 1:26–28, why should all people be treated with dignity?

2. Which types of people are at risk of not being treated with dignity?

3. What purpose has God given all people?

4. What other purpose besides the general purpose to care for creation does God give to Christians?

5. People often confuse being productive with having worth. Why is dignity not related to fulfilling one's purpose?

6. When a society confuses dignity with productivity, unproductive people aren't valued. What type of people might be unproductive?

7. Why are some depressed and suicidal people unproductive?

8. William James said that religion made life worth living in the face of contemplated suicide because of the belief that we are needed to redeem "something really wild in the universe."[10] Why does being needed help to prevent suicide?

9. When a society doesn't value unproductive people, these people begin to lose a sense of their dignity. What could Christians do to help depressed and suicidal Christians keep a sense of their dignity?

10. What can Christians do about the undervaluing of unproductive people?

11. What specifically could you do this next week to maintain the dignity of all humans?

12. What did you learn that you want to take with you this week?

Close in prayer for depressed and suicidal people who don't value themselves because of their lost productivity.

Lesson three: Hope

- Exegetical idea: Paul prevented the jailer's suicide by giving him a reason to live.

- Study idea: Protect against suicide by reminding people of their reasons to live.

Albert Hsu (pronounced Shee) wrote a book called *Grieving a Suicide: A Loved One's Search for Comfort, Answers, and Hope*. In reflecting on Acts 16, Hsu writes:

> Paul's model of suicide prevention is one we can follow today. He intervened in the jailor's crisis. He stopped him from harming himself. He gave him a reason to live. We can do the same. If we see others who are despairing of life, we, like Paul, can call out to them, "Don't harm yourself! We are all here!" We need to show them that we are in fact here for them. We are here, your loved ones, friends, and family members, and we don't want you to harm yourself.[11]

Read Acts 16:23–34.

1. Why did the jailer want to kill himself?

2. What did Paul do to stop the jailer from killing himself?

3. Why was "We are all here!" a reason to live for the jailer?

4. When people like the jailer feel hopeless or like a failure, what helps them?

5. How does the jailer's newfound faith give him a reason to live?

6. How can you give other people reasons to live when they have suicidal thoughts?

7. What are your reasons to live?

8. Using the Virtual Hope Box app on your phone or using a paper, list your reasons to live. (Some people collect their reasons to live in an actual box.) Here are some reasons to live that might be in a virtual hope box or written list or an actual hope box:

   - Any reasons to live, including God's love and presence, finishing school, getting married, making a scientific discovery, helping others, learning to ski, planting flowers and watching them grow, etc.

   - Bible verses that give you reasons to live, such as Isaiah 43:1–3, 5; Jeremiah 29:11; Lamentations 3:20–26; Habakkuk 3:17–19; and John 16:33

   - Reminders of times you've served God faithfully (e.g., mission trip)

   - Pictures that remind you of a time you felt God's presence

   - Pictures that remind you of a time you grew in your faith

   - Pictures of loved ones

   - Pictures of a best friend

   - Pictures of a group you belong to

- Pictures that remind you of people who helped you through a difficult time

- A photograph of someone who gives you hope

- Letters/notes from loved ones

- Reminders of having had an impact on others (e.g., volunteering)

- Pictures that remind you of a time when you felt proud of yourself

- Compliments you've received

- Pictures of something that gives you hope

- Pictures of special days

- A quote that gives hope, such as, "Hope lies in dreams, in imagination, and in the courage of those who dare to make dreams into reality" (Jonas Salk, developer of the polio vaccine), or "Never, ever ever ever ever give up" (Winston Churchill, prime minister of the United Kingdom during World War II).

- Any keepsake

9. Discuss some of your reasons to live with the rest of the group.

10. When will you need your list the most? Discuss when you will access the virtual hope box or list (or actual box) to remind yourself of your reasons to live.

11. What did you learn that you want to take with you this week?

Close in prayer and ask God to remind you of your reasons to live in difficult times.

Lesson four: Moral objections to suicide

- Exegetical idea: God prohibits murder and he alone gives and takes life.

- Study idea: God prohibits suicide but we also focus on reasons for living.

1. The Bible mentions six suicides but doesn't comment on them as sin or not.

    a. Abimelek (Judg 9:54—"'Draw your sword and kill me.' ")

    b. Samson (Judg 16:30—"'Let me die with the Philistines!' ")

    c. Saul (1 Sam 31:4—"Saul took his own sword and fell on it.")

    d. Ahithophel (2 Sam 17:23—"He put his house in order and then hanged himself.")

    e. Zimri (1 Kgs 16:18—"When Zimri saw that the city was taken, he went into the citadel of the royal palace and set the palace on fire around him.")

    f. Judas (Matt 27:5—"Then he went away and hanged himself"; Acts 1:18).

2. We have to look elsewhere for why God prohibits suicide.

    a. Bonhoeffer argued that the silence of the Bible on suicide is not a basis for condoning suicide.[12]

b. The sixth commandment declares, "Do not murder" (Exod 20:13; Deut 5:17). Augustine argues, "Since the sixth commandment does not have the qualification 'your neighbor,' as do the ninth and tenth commandments, ... the commandment applies both to other people *and* to oneself."[13]

c. In Deuteronomy 32:39, God says, "I put to death and I bring to life." God *alone* decides when life begins and ends; life should not be cut short. 1 Corinthians 6:19 confirms this: "... you are not your own." John Calvin said, "Let us wait for the highest commander, who sent us into this world, to call us out of it."[14]

d. Bonhoeffer writes, "It is because there is a living God that suicide is wrongful as a sin of lack of faith. ... Lack of faith takes no account of the living God. That is the sin."[15] Bonhoeffer makes the point that suicide is a lack of belief in God. He suggests that a person in the midst of a suicide crisis may resolve that God is incapable of intervening in intolerable circumstances. In Matthew 14:30–31, Jesus calls us to faith in him in the midst of stormy circumstances: "Then Peter got down out of the boat, walked on the water and came toward Jesus. But when he saw the wind, he was afraid and, beginning to sink, cried out, 'Lord, save me!' Immediately Jesus reached out his hand and caught him. 'You of little faith,' he said, 'why did you doubt?' " Bonhoeffer says that suicide is prohibited because Jesus calls us to faith in God's living presence and power in the midst of life's storms.

3. God forgives sin.

a. The only unpardonable sin is blasphemy against the Holy Spirit (Matt 12:31) and the sin unto death (1 John 5:16).

b. The following verses emphasize that God focuses on his covenant with us, not on a transactional repentance of every sin. Nothing can separate us from God's love (Rom 8:38–39). God is merciful (Exod 34:6–7) and deals with our sin not as we deserve (Ps 103:10). God can be trusted to be a fair judge (Isa 61:8) because he is a "friend of sinners" (Luke 7:34). Bonhoeffer writes, "Insufficient, too, is the argument which is widely used in the Christian Church to the effect that suicide rules out the possibility of repentance and, therefore, also of forgiveness. Many Christians have died sudden deaths without having repented of all their sins. This is setting too much store by the last moment of life."[16]

4. So why is suicide wrong?

5. These verses tell us what not to do. What should we do instead?

6. What can we do in difficult moments when we're thinking about suicide?

7. What did you learn that you want to take with you this week?

Close in prayer for people who are struggling with thoughts of suicide.

Lesson five: Self-control

- Exegetical idea: Torn between life and death, Paul chooses life.

- Study idea: Paul's self-control can help suicidal people choose life.

Read Philippians 1:19–26.

1. Paul is in prison (Phil 1:13). He knows he could be executed (v. 20). Paul is willing to live but prefers to die (v. 21; 2 Cor 5:8). Why are both life and death good for Paul?

2. What hardships has Paul experienced (Phil 3:5–8; 2 Cor 11:23–28)?

3. What are Paul's reasons to live (vv. 22, 24–26)?

4. What is Paul's reason to die (v. 23)?

5. What takes Paul's focus away from dying (vv. 24–26)?

6. What is ultimately of most importance to Paul (Phil 1:18; 1 Cor 9:23)?

7. Where do you see Paul showing great self-control in making this decision?

8. Suicidal people are torn between life and death. A part of them wants to live, and a part of them wants to die. How could Paul's example of self-control help them to choose life?

9. Social science research has found that self-control is related to better health, less substance use, better academic performance, less violence, less risky sex, and

less attempted suicide—and therefore longer life. Why is self-control so important in life?

10. Social science research has also shown that self-control improves over time just as a muscle is strengthened through use. How could you strengthen your self-control?

11. How could a suicidal person get better and better at self-control?

12. What did you learn that you want to take with you this week?

Close in prayer for self-control in all our major decisions.

Lesson six: Grief and suffering (Ps 13)

- Exegetical idea: The psalmist laments to God because 1) he has been suffering and 2) he is certain that God is the one who hears his prayer and saves him, despite the current evidence.

- Study idea: Christians call out to God when they are suffering because they are certain that God is the one who hears their prayer and will save them.

When difficult situations happen, like a romantic breakup or your academic or employment future becomes dim, some people attempt suicide. But a better choice is to write an ancient prayer called a lament psalm. A lament psalm is a prayer to God that is an expression of suffering, and examples are found in the book of Psalms in the Bible.

A lament psalm has a particular structure.[17]

- Part one: protest—a complaint ("God, the present situation is horrible").

- Part two: petition—a request ("God, do something about the situation").

- Part three: praise—an expression of faith ("I will praise you, God, because you will do something about this horrible situation").

Let's read Psalm 13 with this structure in mind. (A sermon on Psalm 13 is included in Appendix A and can be used as an explanation of lament psalms.)

1. Which verses are the protest, a complaint to God about the situation?

2. Which verses are the petition, a request that God do something about the situation?

3. Which verses are the praise, an expression of faith and certainty that God will do something?

Here is a current-day lament written by a lonely, desperate person. Where is the protest, petition, and praise?

Hey you, O Lord? Remember me?
The person who has always been committed to you?
How long will you hide your face from me?
How long must I struggle with my darkest doubts
without the comfort of your voice?
I feel you have abandoned me!
Has this been a one-way relationship all along?
When will it be my turn to succeed and thrive?
Is this fun for you?

Look me in the eye and answer me, O Lord my God.
Either give me light or I will just die in the dark.
If I go down, those people who take pleasure

in the ruin of my life will say, "I win."
They will laugh and rejoice.
Is that what you want?
Remember, I've always been on your side, God!

I trust in your love; my heart rejoices in your salvation.
I will sing to the Lord, for God has been good to me.
Even if right now all I can think of is how [bad] things are.
Amen.[18]

Or you can use this lament written by a depressed person during the holidays. Where is the protest, petition, and praise?

As a dog pants for a bowl of water,
so my soul thirst for you, O God.
My soul thirst for any sign of God,
for a living, not historical, God.
But I'm still like a dog because you do not feed,
and I only get by on what I am eating from my lawn.
Is there someplace where God will meet me halfway?
My tears have been my food day and night,
while people say to me, "Where is your God?
If you believe, why won't your God heal you?
If you are not healed then maybe God does not believe in you!"

These things I remember as I pour out my soul:
I used to go to church;
I sang in the choir in the house of God,
with shouts of joy and thanksgiving among the festive throng.
And then depression gripped me,
and now my house of worship
might as well be a house of pancakes.

The joy of the holidays became my enemy,
and holiday decorations mocked my soul.
I am haunted by the difference between what I once had
and the way I live now.
Where shall you go, O my soul, until the New Year?
Why are you so disturbed within me?
I yell at myself, "Put your hope in God!
Remember when God did great things for you!"

I once heard God calling me from the roar of waterfalls;
waves and breakers swept over me once.
Now I can no longer hear God through the fog of my depression.
I say to God, "Why have you forgotten me?
Will you ever break me free of this?"

But you are God and I am not.
I fear I am nothing.[19]

Pick a difficult situation and write a lament psalm with protest, petition, and praise. (It could be a difficult situation in your life or in the world.) Add your lament psalm to your hope box as a reminder of God's presence and of what to do in the midst of suffering.

What did you learn that you want to take with you this week?

Lesson seven: Reaching out for help

- Exegetical idea: Suffering is not in itself good though God can redeem it. Christians are waiting patiently for a world without suffering.

- Study idea: Psychological suffering is a result of the fall, and Christians can help alleviate it by helping depressed Christians find help.

Christians have a long tradition of alleviating suffering. Paul took up an offering for the church in Jerusalem (1 Cor 16:1–4). Early Christians cared for the sick during epidemics and used their free-will offerings to feed the poor, bury the dead, provide for orphans, and bring relief to prisoners and the aged. Medieval monasteries sheltered travelers and cared for the sick and the poor. William Wilberforce worked relentlessly to abolish societal evils, including slavery. Elizabeth Fry, a Quaker, brought the gospel and reformation to women's prisons and insane asylums in Europe because she believed that these women and their children should hear the gospel and be treated humanely. Missionaries in the nineteenth and twentieth centuries brought the gospel *and* medical care, education, and orphanages, and then trained local nurses, doctors, and teachers, because they believed that all people had, as Belle Jane Allen and Caroline Atwater Mason put it, "a sacred right to life temporal and life eternal."

Read Romans 8:19–30.

1. Compare Romans 8:20 to Genesis 3:17–19. How was "the creation subjected to frustration"?

2. Compare Romans 8:21 to Revelation 21:4. What liberation is creation waiting for?

3. Creation and humans are groaning (Rom 8:22–23). How does having depression fit with the idea of the brokenness of the world and humans?

4. What is creation eagerly waiting for (Rom 8:19)? What are we hoping for and patiently waiting for (vv. 24–25)?

5. In the midst of our suffering who is praying for us (Rom 8:27)? What does that mean to you?

6. Reading verses 28 to 30 in the context of the previous verses, suffering is redeemed by God, but is it inherently good?

7. When Jesus announced the kingdom of God, he also healed the sick (Matt 5:35). How does Jesus' healing of the sick fit with Romans 8:19–30?

8. Where does alleviating psychological suffering fit in the long tradition of Christian alleviation of suffering?

9. Why should Christians get help for psychological suffering like depression?

10. What stigmas exist that get in the way of Christians getting help for psychological suffering like depression?

11. Where could Christians get help for depression?

12. How could you help suffering Christians get the help they need?

13. What did you learn that you want to take with you this week?

Close in prayer for those who are suffering with depression.

As we come to the end of our suicide-prevention Bible studies, let's review what we've studied and then pick one specific thing you want to remember:

1. Suffering in community

2. All people have dignity (including unproductive people)

3. Hope and reasons to live (using a hope box)

4. Why suicide is wrong

5. Self-control instead of impulsiveness

6. Suffering by writing a lament psalm

7. Reaching out for help

APPENDIX I

HELP FOR PARENTS IN SUPPORTING THEIR STUDENTS FOLLOWING A SUICIDE

The following advice for parents is excerpted from Jack Jordan and Bob Baugher, *After Suicide Loss: Coping with Your Grief*, 2nd ed. (Newcastle, WA: Caring People Press, 2016), 53–59.

Suicide is an unexpected, shocking loss. Grief following suicide is more intense and disorganizing than grief after other losses.

Directly ask your student how he or she is coping with the suicide. Adolescents are between childhood and young adulthood. Developmentally, they are developing their sense of identity as separate from their parents and are very concerned about fitting in with their peers. Because their brain is not yet fully developed, they may struggle with regulating emotions and thinking realistically about the suicide. Unless they exhibit warning signs that they are suicidal, respect their way of coping with the death.

Watch for these warning signs that your student may be suicidal:

- Talking about wanting to die or kill him- or herself

- Looking for a way to kill him- or herself

- Talking about not having reasons to live

- Talking about being a burden to others

- Talking about feeling hopelessly trapped

- Increasing reckless behaviors (using alcohol or drugs, risky sexual behaviors, driving too fast)

- Withdrawing from others

- Mood swings with irritability, agitation, and depression

If you see some of these warning signs, ask your student if he or she is thinking about suicide directly. Asking won't plant the idea in their mind. If your student says "yes," get them help such as calling the National Suicide Prevention Lifeline (1-800-273-TALK) or going to your local emergency department for an evaluation.

Be as honest as possible about the suicide with your student. Adolescents are very sensitive to "phoniness."

Help your student work through any false guilt about the suicide being their fault. Ask your student, "Sometimes when someone dies we think that it is because of something we said or did. Do you ever feel that way?" Help your student understand that the person died because of enormous pain, not because of anything your student did or didn't do, no matter what it was.

Help your student understand that the person who died by suicide did not reach out for help but your student can. Help your student understand that they have other options when psychological pain becomes that intense.

Expect your student to have concerns about how the suicide will affect their relationship with peers. If your student is concerned about how a suicide will change how they look with their friends, this is not a sign of selfishness.

Help your student transition back to school. For some students, they may welcome a "return to normal" in their life, while others may find going back to school work and peers overwhelming. Offer them reassurance and support, and help them identify trusted adults at their school with whom they can talk if needed.

Resources

In addition to giving parents the preceding advice, you may want to distribute a handout that lists resources in your area. It should include at least the following information.

Crisis lines

- The National Suicide Prevention Lifeline (1-800-273-TALK, suicidepreventionlifeline.org)

- List others for your area (e.g., the Samaritans)

Mental health professionals

- List trusted professionals in your area

Support groups for survivors of suicide loss

- One resource for finding support groups in your area is the American Foundation for Suicide Prevention's "Find a Support Group" page: afsp.org/find-a-support-group/

- Another is the American Association of Suicidology

- You can also call your local United Way 211 number or check your local hospital or mental health center

- List support groups in your area (call your local United Way 211 number or check your local hospital or mental health center)

NOTES

INTRODUCTION

Epigraph: Lee Eclov, *Pastoral Graces: Reflections on the Care of Souls* (Chicago: Moody Publishers, 2012), 71.

1. This finding is based on a subset of evangelical clergy from a larger dataset published in Karen Mason, Esther Kim, and W. Blake Martin, "Clergy Use of Suicide Prevention Competencies," *OMEGA—Journal of Death and Dying* (2018), https://doi.org/10.1177/0030222818777373. In order from least used: 1) When a suicidal person talks to me, I know the right questions to ask. 2) When a suicidal person talks to me, I'm confident about next steps. 3) When a suicide death happens, I know how to care for the friend(s) and family member(s) / the survivor(s). 4) I can talk to my congregation (preach or teach) about suicide (average rating: 3.6—Sometimes/Somewhat like me).
2. Jackson W. Carroll, *God's Potters: Pastoral Leadership and the Shaping of Congregations* (Grand Rapids: Eerdmans, 2006), 100, 254.
3. S. Pridmore and G. Walter, "Suicide Prediction and Prevention," *Australasian Psychiatry* 21, no. 4 (2013): 410–11.

CHAPTER 1

1. All names and identifying details have been changed to protect the identity of individuals in case studies.
2. Rae Jean Proeschold-Bell, Andrew Miles, Matthew Toth, Christopher Adams, Bruce W. Smith, and David Toole, "Using Effort-Reward Imbalance Theory to Understand High Rates of Depression and Anxiety among Clergy," *The Journal of Primary Prevention* 34, no. 6 (2013): 439–53.
3. David Kinnaman and Gabe Lyons, *Good Faith: Being a Christian When Society Thinks You're Irrelevant and Extreme* (Grand Rapids: Baker, 2016), 246–47. In a study of Lutheran pastors, forty were moderately to severely depressed;

Jackson W. Carroll, *God's Potters: Pastoral Leadership and the Shaping of Congregations* (Grand Rapids: Eerdmans, 2016), 13.

4. Karen Mason, *Preventing Suicide: A Handbook for Pastors, Chaplains and Pastoral Counselors* (Downers Grove, IL: InterVarsity Press, 2014), 42.

5. American Psychiatric Association, *Diagnostic and Statistical Manual of Mental Disorders*, 5th ed. (Washington, DC: American Psychiatric Association, 2013), 161.

6. Mason, *Preventing Suicide*, 42–44.

7. Karen Mason, Monica Geist, and Mollie Clark, "A Developmental Model of Clergy Engagement with Suicide: A Qualitative Study," *OMEGA—Journal of Death and Dying* 79, no. 4 (2019), 347–63.

8. Centers for Disease Control and Prevention (CDC), National Center for Injury Prevention and Control. Web-based Injury Statistics Query and Reporting System (WISQARS) [online] (2005): cdc.gov/injury/wisqars.

9. 2018 is the latest US data available at the time of the writing of this book.

10. 1990–1992 National Comorbidity Survey and the 2001–2003 National Comorbidity Survey-Replication. For every 14 suicides per 100,000 people each year, approximately 500 people per 100,000 attempt suicide, and 3,000 people per 100,000 think about suicide. Ronald Kessler et al., "Trends in Suicide Ideation, Plans, Gestures, and Attempts in the United States, 1990–1992 to 2001–2003," *The Journal of the American Medical Association* 293, no. 20 (2005): 2487–95. The same general trend was found in the World Mental Health Survey Initiative by WHO. Among 84,850 people in 17 countries, 9.2 percent reported suicidal ideation, 3.1 percent had a suicide plan, 2.7 percent attempted suicide. Matthew Nock, American Psychological Association Convention, Orlando, FL (August 2012).

11. David Jobes, "Collaborative Assessment and Management of Suicidality: an Evidence-Based Approach for Clinicians" (paper presented at the 124th American Psychological Association Annual Convention, Denver, CO, August 2016).

12. Karen Mason, Monica Geist, Richard Kuo, Marshall Day, and James D. Wines, Jr. "Predictors of Clergy's Ability to Fulfill a Suicide Prevention Gatekeeper Role," *Journal of Pastoral Care and Counseling* 70, no. 1 (2016): 34–39.

13. Matthew K. Nock et al., "Mental Disorders, Comorbidity, and Suicidal Behavior," in Matthew K. Nock, Guilherme Borges, and Yutaka Ono, eds., *Suicide: Global Perspectives from the WHO World Mental Health Surveys* (New York: Cambridge University Press, 2012), 148–63.

14. 82 percent of people with suicidal thoughts had a mental health disorder; 94.5 percent of those who made a suicide plan and 88.2 percent of those who had attempted suicide in the previous twelve months had a mental health disorder. Ronald Kessler et al., "Trends in Suicide Ideation," 2487–95. In the World Health Organization study of 55,299 people in 21 countries, a smaller number of suicide attempters had a mental health disorder (23.5 percent).

Matthew K. Nock et al., "Mental Disorders, Comorbidity, and Suicidal Behavior," 148–63.

15. David M. Fergusson, Annette L. Beautrais, and John L. Horwood, "Vulnerability and Resiliency to Suicidal Behaviours in Young People," *Psychological Medicine* 33, no. 1 (2003): 61–73.

16. "Suicide Rising Across the US," Vitalsigns, CDC (June 2018), accessed February 8, 2020, cdc.gov/vitalsigns/pdf/vs-0618-suicide-H.pdf.

17. Among the eleven studies of patients with mood disorders, the association between suicidal ideation and later suicide was not significant. Clare Louise Chapman et al., "Meta-Analysis of the Association between Suicidal Ideation and Later Suicide among Patients with Either a Schizophrenia Spectrum Psychosis or a Mood Disorder," *Acta Psychiatrica Scandinavica* 131, no. 3 (2015): 162–73. "Arguably the most difficult aspect of the prediction of suicidal behavior is the finding replicated worldwide and over time that only a small subset of those who think about suicide go on to attempt, and even fewer will die by suicide." Kimberly A. Van Orden et al., "The Interpersonal Theory of Suicide," *Psychological Review* 117, no. 2 (2010): 575–600.

18. Suicide among the mentally ill population is six to twelve times higher than in the general population. David Covington, "Toward Zero Suicide in Health Care: Values, Systems, and Practices Reducing Suicide" (paper presented at the 124th American Psychological Association Annual Convention, Denver, CO, August 2016).

19. Reasons given include a desire to escape (N = 29), reduced functioning and autonomy (N = 24), psychological problems, including depression (N = 24), somatic problems and physical pain (N = 16), perceived burdensomeness (N = 13), social problems that reflected either thwarted belongingness or family conflict (N = 13), and lack of meaning in life (N = 8); forty-one participants provided more than one reason. Kimberly A. Van Orden et al., "Reasons for Attempted Suicide in Later Life," *The American Journal of Geriatric Psychiatry* 23, no. 5 (2015): 536–44.

20. Pere Castellví et al., "Exposure to Violence, a Risk for Suicide in Youths and Young Adults. A Meta-Analysis of Longitudinal Studies," *Acta Psychiatrica Scandinavica* 135, no. 3 (2016).

21. Gabrielle Campbell et al., "Prevalence and Correlates of Suicidal Thoughts and Suicide Attempts in People Prescribed Pharmaceutical Opioids for Chronic Pain," *The Clinical Journal of Pain* 32, no. 4 (2016): 292–301.

22. Joyce P. Chu, Koyun Chi, Ken Chen, and Amy Leino, "Ethnic Variations in Suicidal Ideation and Behaviors: A Prominent Subtype Marked by Nonpsychiatric Factors among Asian Americans," *Journal of Clinical Psychology* 70, no. 12 (2014): 1211–26. M. Mercedes Perez-Rodriguez et al., "Relationship between Acculturation, Discrimination, and Suicidal Ideation and Attempts among US Hispanics in the National Epidemiologic Survey of Alcohol and Related Conditions," *Journal of Clinical Psychiatry* 75, no. 4 (2014): 399–407.

23. Rhiannon Evans, Jonathan Scourfield, and Graham Moore, "Gender, Relationship Breakdown, and Suicide Risk: A Review of Research in Western Countries," *Journal of Family Issues* 37, no. 16 (2016): 2239–64.

24. Karen Mason, Esther Kim, W. Blake Martin, and Rashad J. Gober, "The Moral Deliberations of 15 Clergy on Suicide and Assisted Death: A Qualitative Study," *Pastoral Psychology* 66, no. 3 (2016): 335–51.

25. Shneidman writes, "I have never known anyone who was 100 percent for wanting to commit suicide without any fantasies of possible rescue. Individuals would be happy not to do it, if they didn't 'have to.' It is this omnipresent ambivalence that gives us the moral imperative for clinical intervention." Edwin S. Shneidman, *The Suicidal Mind* (New York: Oxford University Press, 1996), 133.

26. Guilherme Borges et al., "Prevalence, Onset, and Transitions among Suicidal Behaviors," in Matthew K. Nock, Guilherme Borges, and Yutaka Ono, eds. *Suicide: Global Perspectives from the WHO World Mental Health Surveys* (New York: Cambridge University Press, 2012), 65–74.

27. Alexander J. Millner, Michael D. Lee, and Matthew K. Nock, "Describing and Measuring the Pathway to Suicide Attempts: A Preliminary Study," *Suicide and Life-Threatening Behavior* 47, no. 3 (2017): 353–69.

28. Amanda M. Raines, Joseph Currier, E. S. McManus, J. L. Walton, M. Uddo, and C. L. Franklin, "Spiritual Struggles and Suicide in Veterans Seeking PTSD Treatment," *Psychological Trauma: Theory, Research, Practice, and Policy* 9, no. 6 (2017): 746–49.

29. Yasmin C. Cole-Lewis, Polly Y. Gipson, Kiel J. Opperman, Alejandra Arango, and Cheryl A. King, "Protective Role of Religious Involvement against Depression and Suicidal Ideation among Youth with Interpersonal Problems," *Journal of Religion and Health* 55, no. 4 (2016): 1172–88; Kanita Dervic et al., "Religious Affiliation and Suicide Attempt," *The American Journal of Psychiatry* 161, no. 12 (2004): 2303–8; Robin E. Gearing and Dana Lizardi, "Religion and Suicide," *Journal of Religion and Heath* 48, no. 3 (2008): 332–41; Leilani Greening and Laura Stoppelbein, "Religiosity, Attributional Style, and Social Support as Psychosocial Buffers for African American and White Adolescents' Perceived Risk for Suicide," *Suicide & Life Threatening Behavior* 32, no. 4 (2002): 404–417; Dana Lizardi et al., "Perceived Reasons for Living at Index Hospitalization and Future Suicide Attempt," *The Journal of Nervous and Mental Disease* 195, no. 5 (2007): 451–55; Daniel Rasic, Jennifer A. Robinson, James Bolton, O. Joseph Bienvenu, and Jitender Sareen, "Longitudinal Relationships of Religious Worship Attendance and Spirituality with Major Depression, Anxiety Disorders, and Suicidal Ideation and Attempts: Findings from the Baltimore Epidemiologic Catchment Area Study," *Journal of Psychiatric Research* 45, no. 6 (2011): 848–54.

30. In a study of 1,245 university students, strength of religious faith was the strongest predictor for reasons for living among serious suicidal ideators when looking towards the future. Slade J. Rieger, Tracey Peter, and Lance

W. Roberts, "'Give me a reason to live!' Examining reasons for living across levels of suicidality," *Journal of Religion and Health* 54, no. 6 (2015): 2005–2019.

31. Karen Mason, Monica Geist, and Mollie Clark, "A Developmental Model of Clergy Engagement with Suicide: A Qualitative Study," *OMEGA—Journal of Death and Dying* 79, no. 4 (2019), 347-363.

32. Scott D. Miller, "The Evolution of Psychotherapy: An Oxymoron" (paper presented at the Evolution of Psychotherapy conference, Anaheim, CA, 2013); Daryl Chow, "The Study of Supershrinks: Development & Deliberate Practices of Highly Effective Psychotherapists" (PhD diss., Curtin University, 2014), available at espace.curtin.edu. au/bitstream/handle/20.500.11937/45/200923_Chow%202014. pdf?sequence=2&isAllowed=y.

33. Craig J. Bryan, Luther E. Dhillon-Davis, and Kieran K. Dhillon-Davis, "Emotional Impact of a Video-Based Suicide Prevention Program on Suicidal Viewers and Suicide Survivors," *Suicide and Life-Threatening Behavior* 39, no. 6 (2010): 623-32. See also Craig Bryan et al.,"Technology-Facilitated Assessment of Cognitive and Behavioral Indicators of Suicide Risk" (paper presented at the 124th American Psychological Association Annual Convention, Denver, CO, August 2016); Rahel Eynan et al., "The Effects of Suicide Ideation Assessments on Urges to Self-Harm and Suicide," *Crisis: The Journal of Crisis Intervention and Suicide Prevention* 35, no. 2 (2014): 123–31; Madelyn S. Gould et al., "Evaluating Iatrogenic Risk of Youth Suicide Screening Programs: A Randomized Controlled Trial," *JAMA: The Journal of the American Medical Association* 293, no. 13 (2005): 1635–43; Mary Kate Law et al., "Does Assessing Suicidality Frequently and Repeatedly Cause Harm? A Randomized Control Study," *Psychological Assessment* 27, no. 4 (2015): 1171–81; David M. Rudd et al., "The Emotional Impact and Ease of Recall of Warning Signs for Suicide," *Suicide & Life-Threatening Behavior* 36, no. 3 (2006): 288–95.

34. Some research suggests that up to two thirds of people who are evaluated for suicidal ideation say, "No, I'm not suicidal," but then kill themselves; Katie A. Busch, Jan Fawcett, and Douglas G. Jacobs, "Clinical Correlates of Inpatient Suicide," *Journal of Clinical Psychiatry* 64, no. 1 (2003): 14–19; David W. Coombs et al., "Presuicide Attempt Communications between Parasuicides and Consulted Caregivers," *Suicide and Life-Threatening Behavior* 22, no. 3 (1992): 289–302; Richard C. W. Hall, Dennis E. Platt, and Ryan C. Hall, "Suicide Risk Assessment: A Review of Risk Factors for Suicide in 100 Patients Who Made Severe Suicide Attempts: Evaluation of Suicide Risk in a Time of Managed Care," *Psychosomatics: Journal of Consultation and Liaison Psychiatry* 40, no. 1 (1999): 18–27; Maria Kovacs, Aaron T. Beck, and Arlene Weissman, "The Communication of Suicidal Intent: A Reexamination," *Archives of General Psychiatry* 33, no. 2 (1976): 198–201.

35. Karen Mason, Monica Geist, and Mollie Clark, "A Developmental Model of Clergy Engagement with Suicide: A Qualitative Study," *OMEGA—Journal of Death and Dying* 79, no. 4 (2019), 347-363.

36. Learn more at www.livingworks.net, www.qprinstitute.com, or www.theconnectprogram.org.

37. When calling herself a "quivering mass of availability," this respondent was quoting Stanley Hauerwas as quoted in William Willimon, *Pastor: The Theology and Practice of Ordained Ministry* (Nashville: Abingdon Press, 2002), 60.

38. Mark R. McMinn, Daniel C. Aikins, and Allen R. Lish, "Basic and Advanced Competence in Collaborating with Clergy," *Professional Psychology: Research and Practice* 34, no. 2 (2003): 197–202.

39. Karen Mason et al.., "Clergy Referral of Suicidal Individuals: A Qualitative Study," *Journal of Pastoral Care & Counseling* 65, no. 3 (2011): 6.

40. Total participants: n=55,302. Low perceived need was the most important reason for not seeking help (58 percent), followed by attitudinal barriers such as the wish to handle the problem alone (40 percent) and structural barriers such as financial concerns (15 percent). Only 7 percent of respondents endorsed stigma as a reason for not seeking treatment. Ronny Bruffaerts et al., "Treatment of Suicidal People around the World," *British Journal of Psychiatry* 199, no. 1 (2011): 64–70; Ronny Bruffaerts et al., "Treatment of Suicidal Persons around the World," in Matthew K. Nock, Guilherme Borges, and Yutaka Ono, eds., *Suicide: Global Perspectives from the WHO World Mental Health Surveys* (New York: Cambridge University Press, 2012), 199–212.

41. Karen Mason, Monica Geist, and Mollie Clark, "A Developmental Model of Clergy Engagement with Suicide: A Qualitative Study," *OMEGA—Journal of Death and Dying* 79, no. 4 (2019), 347–63.

42. Cheryl A. Chessick et al., "Current Suicide Ideation and Prior Suicide Attempts of Bipolar Patients as Influences on Caregiver Burden," *Suicide and Life-Threatening Behavior* 37, no. 4 (2007): 482–91.

43. Andrew J. Weaver et al., "Mental Health Issues among Clergy and Other Religious Professionals: A Review of Research," *Journal of Pastoral Care & Counseling* 56, no. 4 (2002): 393–403.

44. Thomas E. Joiner, Jr., *Why People Die by Suicide* (Cambridge, MA: Harvard University Press, 2005); Annette L. Beautrais, "Further Suicidal Behavior Among Medically Serious Suicide Attempters," *Suicide and Life-Threatening Behavior* 34, no. 1 (2004): 1–11.

45. Jayne Cooper et al., "Suicide after Deliberate Self-Harm: A 4-Year Cohort Study," *The American Journal of Psychiatry* 162, no. 2 (2005): 297–303; Clare E. Harris, and Brian Barraclough, "Suicide as an Outcome for Mental Disorders: A Meta-Analysis," *British Journal of Psychiatry* 170, no. 3 (1997): 205–28; Madelyn S. Gould et al., "Youth Suicide Risk and Preventive Interventions: A Review of the Past 10 Years," *Journal of The American*

Academy of Child & Adolescent Psychiatry 42, no. 4 (2003): 386–405; Keith Hawton, *Prevention and Treatment of Suicidal Behavior* (New York: Oxford University Press, 2005), 6.

46. Eve K. Mościcki, "Epidemiology of Suicide," in Douglas G. Jacobs, ed., *The Harvard Medical School Guide to Suicide Assessment and Intervention* (San Francisco: Jossey-Bass, 1999), 40–51.

47. Keith Hawton and Louise Harriss, "How Often Does Deliberate Self-Harm Occur Relative to Each Suicide? A Study of Variations by Gender and Age," *Suicide and Life-Threatening Behavior* 38, no. 6 (2008): 650–60.

48. The research team in England and Wales mentioned earlier that studied 2,177 suicides found that 519 (24 percent) suicides occurred within three months of hospital discharge, the highest number occurring in the first week after discharge. Most people who died by suicide were thought to have been at no or low immediate risk at the final contact. Louis Appleby et al., "Suicide Within 12 Months of Contact with Mental Health Services: National Clinical Survey," *British Medical Journal (Clinical Research Ed.)* 318, no. 7193 (1999): 1235–39. See also Jayne Cooper et al., "Suicide After Deliberate Self-Harm: A 4-Year Cohort Study," *The American Journal of Psychiatry* 162, no. 2 (2005): 297–303.

49. A research team followed 3,690 people who had been hospitalized for a suicide attempt and found that the risk of reattempt remained high for ten years but the risk is greatest in the first two years following discharge. Sheree J. Gibb, Annette L. Beautrais, and David M. Fergusson, "Mortality and Further Suicidal Behaviour after an Index Suicide Attempt: A 10-Year Study," *Australian and New Zealand Journal of Psychiatry* 39, no. 1–2 (2005): 95–100.

50. The Supreme Court of California (Case 47 Cal. 3d 286) heard this case. Here is an excerpt: "On the afternoon of March 12, Pastors MacArthur and Rea visited Nally at the hospital. Nally, who was still drowsy from the drug overdose, separately told both pastors that he was sorry he did not succeed in committing suicide. Apparently, MacArthur and Rea assumed the entire hospital staff was aware of Nally's unstable mental condition, and they did not discuss Nally's death-wish comment with anyone else." See www.law.justia.com/cases
/california/cal3d/47/278.html.

51. David Jobes, "Collaborative Assessment and Management of Suicidality: An Evidence-Based Approach for Clinicians" (paper presented at the 124th American Psychological Association Annual Convention, Denver, CO, August 2016).

52. According to a meta-analysis with more than 177,000 participants, people's personal and friendship networks have shrunk over the last 35 years. Cornelia Wirzus, Martha Hänel, Jenny Wagner, and Franz Neyer, "Social Network Changes and Life Events across the Life Span: A Meta-Analysis," *Psychological Bulletin* 139, no. 1, (2013): 53–80.

53. US Surgeon General Vivek Murthy, "Matter of Fact with Soledad O'Brien," interview by Fernando Espuelas, Matter of Fact, June 18, 2016.

54. US Surgeon General Vivek Murthy, "Live a Connected Life," commencement speech at the University of Arizona (May 17, 2016), www.time.com/4337454/vivek-murthy-commencement-speech-arizona.

55. Kimberly A. Van Orden et al., "Reasons for Attempted Suicide in Later Life," *The American Journal of Geriatric Psychiatry* 23, no. 5 (2015): 536–44.

56. A meta-analysis of 148 studies comprising more than 308,000 people found that participants with stronger social relationships were 50 percent more likely to survive over the studies' given periods than those with weaker connections. Julianne Holt-Lunstad, Timothy B. Smith, and Bradley J. Layton, "Social Relationships and Mortality Risk: A Meta-Analytic Review," *PLoS Med* 7, no. 7 (2010): www.journals.plos.org/plosmedicine/article?id=10.1371/journal.pmed.1000316.

57. Jerome A. Motto, "Suicide Prevention for High-Risk Persons Who Refuse Treatment," *Suicide: A Quarterly Journal of Life-Threatening Behavior* 6, no. 4 (1976): 223–30.

58. Motto, "Suicide Prevention," 223–30.

59. Motto, "Suicide Prevention," 223–30; Jerome A. Motto and Alan G. Bostrom, "A Randomized Controlled Trial of Postcrisis Suicide Prevention," *Psychiatric Services* 52, no. 6 (2001): 828–33.

60. Thomas E. Joiner, Jr., *Why People Die by Suicide* (Cambridge, MA: Harvard University Press, 2005), 47.

61. Karen Mason, Monica Geist, and Mollie Clark, "A Developmental Model of Clergy Engagement with Suicide: A Qualitative Study," *OMEGA—Journal of Death and Dying* 79, no. 4 (2019), 347–63.

62. Mason, Geist, and Clark, "Developmental Model."

63. Marilyn Armour, "Violent Death: Understanding the Context of Traumatic and Stigmatized Grief," *Journal of Human Behavior in the Social Environment* 14, no. 4 (2006): 53–90.

64. Ilanit Tal Young et al., "Suicide Bereavement and Complicated Grief," *Dialogues in Clinical Neuroscience* 14, no. 2, (2012): 177–86.

65. Ann M. Mitchell et al., "Complicated Grief in Survivors of Suicide," *Crisis: The Journal of Crisis Intervention And Suicide Prevention* 25, no. 1 (2004): 12–18.

66. Social constraints are associated with more depressive symptoms, perceived stress, somatic symptoms, and worse health. Vanessa Juth et al., "Social Constraints Are Associated with Negative Psychological and Physical Adjustment in Bereavement," *Applied Psychology: Health and Well-Being* 7 (2015): 129–48.

67. Mason, Geist, and Clark, "Developmental Model."

68. Kay R. Jamison, *Night Falls Fast: Understanding Suicide* (New York: Vintage Books, 1999), 279–80.

69. American Foundation for Suicide Prevention, Annenberg Public Policy Center, Columbia University Department of Psychiatry, National Alliance

on Mental Illness (NAMI), NAMI New Hampshire, Substance Abuse and Mental Health Services Administration, "Recommendations for Reporting on Suicide," reportingonsuicide.org.

70. Suicide Prevention Resource Center, *After a Suicide: Recommendations for Religious Services and Other Public Memorial Observances* (Newton, MA: Education Development Center, Inc., 2004).

71. Mason, Geist, and Clark, "Developmental Model."

72. Eve K. Mościcki, "Epidemiology of Suicide," in Douglas G. Jacobs, ed., *The Harvard Medical School Guide to Suicide Assessment and Intervention* (San Francisco, CA: Jossey-Bass, 1999), 40–51.

73. L. J. Nicoletti, "Morbid Topographies: Placing Suicide in Victorian London," in Lawrence A. Phillips, ed., *A Mighty Mass of Brick and Smoke: Victorian and Edwardian Representations of London* (Brill, 2007), 13–14.

74. Peter S. Bearman and James Moody, "Suicide and Friendships among American Adolescents," *American Journal of Public Health* 94, no. 1 (2004): 89–95; Gregory M. Zimmerman et al., "The Power of (Mis)perception: Rethinking Suicide Contagion in Youth Friendship Networks," *Social Science & Medicine* 157 (2016): 31–38.

75. Anna S. Mueller, Seth Abrutyn, and Cynthia Stockton, "Can Social Ties Be Harmful? Examining the Spread of Suicide in Early Adulthood," *Sociological Perspectives* 58, no. 2 (2015): 204–22.

76. Lauren Tingey et al., "Risk Pathways for Suicide among Native American Adolescents," *Qualitative Health Research* 24, no. 11 (2014): 1518–26.

77. Christine Ma-Kellams, Ji Hyun Baek, and Flora Or, "Suicide Contagion in Response to Widely Publicized Celebrity Deaths: The Roles of Depressed Affect, Death-Thought Accessibility, and Attitudes," *Psychology of Popular Media Culture* 7, no. 2 (2018): 164–70.

78. People who had known someone who died by suicide in the last year were 1.6 times more likely to have suicidal thoughts, 2.9 times more likely to have a plan for suicide, and 3.7 times more likely to have made a suicide attempt themselves. Alex E. Crosby and Jeffrey J. Sacks, "Exposure to Suicide: Incidence and Association with Suicidal Ideation and Behavior: United States, 1994," *Suicide and Life-Threatening Behavior* 32, no. 3 (2002): 321–28. Having had a friend who died by suicide increased the likelihood of suicidal ideation and attempts for both boys and girls. Bearman and Moody, "Suicide and Friendships among American Adolescents," 89–95.

79. A. Schmidtke and H. Häfner, "The Werther Effect after Television Films: New Evidence for an Old Hypothesis," *Psychological Medicine* 18, no. 3 (1988): 665–76.

80. Centers for Disease Control and Prevention, "CDC Recommendations for a Community Plan for the Prevention and Containment of Suicide Clusters," *MMWR* 37, no. S-6 (1988): 1–12.

81. Emile Durkheim, *Suicide: A Study in Sociology*, trans. John A. Spaulding and George Simpson (New York: The Free Press, 1951), 97.

82. H. Romilly Fedden, *Suicide: A Social and Historical Study* (London: Peter Davies Limited, 1938), 298.

83. US Department of Health and Human Services (HHS) Office of the Surgeon General and National Action Alliance for Suicide Prevention, "2012 National Strategy for Suicide Prevention: Goals and Objectives for Action" (Washington, DC: HHS, 2012).

84. Ferdi P. Kruger, "The Preacher's Vulnerable Attitudes in Naming Reality in a Neglected Society," *Verbum et Ecclesia*, 36, no. 1 (2015): 1–9. Professor Kruger is a researcher in the Unit for Reformational Theology and the Development of the South African Society at North-West University in South Africa.

85. Kruger, "Preacher's Vulnerable Attitudes," 8.

86. Kruger, "Preacher's Vulnerable Attitudes," 9.

87. Jackson W. Carroll, *God's Potters: Pastoral Leadership and the Shaping of Congregations* (Grand Rapids: Eerdmans, 2006), 25.

88. Unpublished interview from Karen Mason, Monica Geist, and Mollie Clark, "A Developmental Model of Clergy Engagement with Suicide: A Qualitative Study," *OMEGA—Journal of Death and Dying* 79, no. 4 (2019), 347–63.

89. Mason, Geist, and Clark, "Developmental Model."

CHAPTER 2

1. Jan Karon, *To Be Where You Are* (New York: G. P. Putnam's Sons, 2017), 191.

2. *It's a Wonderful Life*, directed by Frank Capra (1946; Los Angeles: Republic Pictures, 2001), DVD.

3. Louis Berkhof, *Systematic Theology*, 4th ed. (Grand Rapids: Eerdmans, 1941), 434.

4. Jackson W. Carroll, *God's Potters: Pastoral Leadership and the Shaping of Congregations* (Grand Rapids: Eerdmans, 2006), 26.

5. Michel de Montaigne, "A Custom of the Ile of Cea," *The Essays of Montaigne*, trans. Charles Cotton (Chicago: William Carew Hazlitt, 1977), thefullwiki. org/The_Essays_of_Montaigne/Book_II/Chapter_III.

6. Henry Romilly Fedden, *Suicide: A Social and Historical Study* (London, UK: Peter Davies Limited, 1938), 64.

7. Prudence J. Jones, *Cleopatra: A Sourcebook* (Norman, OK: University of Oklahoma Press, 2006), 180.

8. William Whiston, *The Genuine Works of Flavius Josephus: The Jewish Historian* (London: University of Cambridge, 1737), penelope.uchicago.edu/josephus/ war-7.html.

9. Michael Whitworth, *Authors in Context: Virginia Woolf* (Oxford, UK: Oxford University Press, 2005), 28.

10. Michael Scannell, *Koestler: The Literary and Political Odyssey of a Twentieth-Century Skeptic* (New York: Random House, 2009), xvi.

11. Scannell, *Koestler*, xvi.

12. Williams' widow, Susan Schneider Williams, said that Lewy body dementia was "the terrorist inside my husband's brain." CBS News, "Robin Williams' Widow on His Fight Against the 'Terrorist' Inside His Brain," CBS News, cbsnews.com/news/robin-williams-widow-susan-schneider-lewy-body-dementia-depression-brain-disease.

13. CBS Boston, "Aaron Hernandez Kills Himself in Prison," CBS News, https://boston.cbslocal.com/2017/04/19/aaron-hernandez-suicide-prison-hanging-souza-baranowski-correctional-center-shirley-new-england-patriots.

14. Jack Seward, *Hari-kiri: Japanese Ritual Suicide* (Rutland, VT: Charles E. Tuttle, Co., Inc., 1968).

15. Stephen Langdon, *Babylonian Wisdom* (London, UK: Luzac and Co., 1923), 80. It's important to note that though Ecclesiastes is similar literature, the conclusion is quite different.

16. John Sellars, *Stoicism* (Berkeley, CA: University of California Press, 2006), 109–110.

17. Jeffrey R. Watt, *Choosing Death: Suicide and Calvinism in Early Modern Geneva* (Kirksville, MO: Truman State University Press, 2001), 70.

18. Henry Romilly Fedden, *Suicide: A Social and Historical Study* (London, UK: Peter Davies Limited, 1938), 160.

19. Watt, *Choosing Death*, 110.

20. Montaigne, "A Custom of the Ile of Cea."

21. David Hume, *Essays on Suicide, and the Immortality of the Soul* (Ann Arbor, Michigan: University of Michigan Library, 2008), www.quod.lib.umich.edu/e/ecco/004780373.0001.000/1:3.1?rgn=div2;view=fulltext.

22. Arthur Schopenhauer, "On Suicide," *Essays of Schopenhauer*, www.gutenberg.org/files/11945/11945-h/11945-h.htm#link2H_4_0016.

23. William Carlos Williams, "The Descent of Winter," in *Imaginations* (New York: New Directions, 1970), 255.

24. A. Alvarez, *The Savage God: A Study of Suicide* (New York: Random House, 1972), 212.

25. Albert Camus, *The Myth of Sisyphus*, trans. J. O'Brien (London: Penguin Books, 1942), 3.

26. Schopenhauer, "On Suicide."

27. Henry Romilly Fedden, *Suicide: A Social and Historical Study* (London: Peter Davies Limited, 1938), 59.

28. Robert F. Worth, "How a Single Match Can Ignite a Revolution," *New York Times*, October 28, 2011, nytimes.com/2011/01/23/weekinreview/23worth.html?.

29. Thomas Joiner, *Why People Die by Suicide* (Cambridge, MA: Harvard University Press, 2005), 144.

30. Mark London Williams, *Cry of Pain: Understanding Suicide and Self-Harm* (London: Penguin Books, 1997), 115.

31. Franco De Masi, *The Enigma of the Suicide Bomber: A Psychoanalytic Essay,* trans. Philip Slotkin (London: Karnac Books Ltd, 2011), xxxvii.

32. John Keown, *Euthanasia, Ethics and Public Policy* (Cambridge: Cambridge University Press, 2002), 10.

33. Kelly Lawler, "Is '13 Reasons Why' More Controversial than Other Depictions of Suicide?," *USA Today,* May 5, 2017, www.usatoday.com/story/life/tv/2017/05/05/13-reasons-why-netflix-suicide-depiction-backlash-explained/101210380.

34. Sully Sullenberger, "The Devastating Impact of Suicide: My Personal Reflection," sullysullenberger.com/the-devastating-impact-of-suicide-my-personal-reflection.

35. Thomas Hobbes, *Leviathan* (1651), chapter XIV, "A Law Of Nature What," www.gutenberg.org/files/3207/3207-h/3207-h.htm.

36. Immanuel Kant, *Groundwork for the Metaphysics of Morals,* ed. and trans. Allen W. Wood (New Haven: Yale University Press, 2002), 47.

37. John Stuart Mill, *On Liberty* (The Walter Scott Publishing Co.), 195, www.gutenberg.org/files/34901/34901-h/34901-h.htm.

38. Femi Oyebode, "Choosing Death: The Moral Status of Suicide," *Psychiatric Bulletin* 20, (1996): 85–89.

39. Emiko Ohnuki-Tierney, *Kamikaze Diaries: Reflections of Japanese Student Soldiers* (Chicago, IL: Chicago University Press, 2006), xviii.

40. Ohnuki-Tierney, *Kamikaze Diaries,* 1.

41. Ohnuki-Tierney, *Kamikaze Diaries,* xiv, 22.

42. Williams, *Cry of Pain,* 111–12.

43. Herbert Hendin, *Seduced By Death: Doctors, Patients, and the Dutch Cure* (New York: W.W. Norton & Co, 1997), 160.

44. Kalman J. Kaplan and Matthew B. Schwartz, *A Psychology of Hope: A Biblical Response to Tragedy and Suicide* (Grand Rapids: Eerdmans, 2008), 196.

45. Kathryn A. Smith et al., "Predictors of Pursuit of Physician-Assisted Death," *Journal of Pain and Symptom Management* 49, no. 3 (2015): 555–61.

46. Linda Ganzini and Anthony Back, "From the USA: Understanding Requests for Physician-Assisted Death," *Palliative Medicine* 17, no. 2 (2003): 113–14.

47. Kaplan and Schwartz, *Psychology of Hope,* 196.

48. Linda Ganzini, Maria J. Silveira, and Wendy S. Johnston, "Predictors and Correlates of Interest in Assisted Suicide in the Final Month of Life among ALS patients in Oregon and Washington," *Journal of Pain and Symptom Management* 24, no. 3 (2002): 312–17.

49. Linda Ganzini et al., "Nurses' Experiences with Hospice Patients Who Refuse Food and Fluids to Hasten Death," *New England Journal of Medicine* 349, no. 4, (2003): 359–65.

50. Ganzini and Back, "From the USA," 113–14.

51. E. D. Pellegrino, "Doctors Must Not Kill," in *Euthanasia: The Good of the Patient, The Good of Society,* ed. R. I. Misbin (Frederick, MD: University Publishing Group, 1997), 27–41, quoted in Herbert Hendin, *Seduced By*

Death: Doctors, Patients, and the Dutch Cure (New York: W.W. Norton & Co, 1997), 182.

52. C. S. Lewis, *The Weight of Glory and Other Addresses* (New York: HarperOne, 2001), 46.

53. Bob Smietana, "1 in 3 Protestant Churchgoers Personally Affected by Suicide," *Christianity Today*, September 29, 2017, www.christianitytoday.com/news/2017/september/protestant-churches-pastors-views-on-suicide-aacc-liberty.html.

54. Smietana, "1 in 3."

55. Learn more at www.theactionalliance.org/faith-hope-life.

56. Learn more at www.sprc.org/states.

CHAPTER 3

1. Prevention ideas: year-round school, fence. Intervention ideas: lifeguard, CPR training.

2. Thomas E. Joiner, Jr, *Lonely at the Top: The High Cost of Men's Success* (New York: Palgrave MacMillan, 2011), 12.

3. Michele S. Berk et al., "A Cognitive Therapy Intervention for Suicide Attempters: An Overview of the Treatment and Case Examples," *Cognitive and Behavioral Practice* 11, no. 3 (2004): 265–77.

4. Virtual Hope Box was developed by the National Center for Telehealth and Technology: www.t2health.dcoe.mil/apps/virtual-hope-box.

5. William James, "Is Life Worth Living?," in *The Will to Believe and Other Essays in Popular Philosophy* (New York: Longmans, Green and Co., 1897), 61.

6. Marsha M. Linehan et al., "Reasons for Staying Alive When You Are Thinking of Killing Yourself: The Reasons for Living Inventory," *Journal of Consulting and Clinical Psychology* 51, no. 2 (1983): 276–86. See also Harold G. Koenig, Dana E. King, and Verna B. Carson, *Handbook of Religion and Health*, 2nd ed. (Oxford: Oxford University Press, 2012), 189.

7. Brett T. Litz et al., "Moral Injury and Moral Repair in War Veterans: A Preliminary Model and Intervention Strategy," *Clinical Psychology Review* 29, no. 8 (2009): 695–706.

8. Guilt denounces an action by the self and shame condemns the entire self. See Helen Block Lewis, *Shame and Guilt in Neurosis* (New York: International Universities Press, 1971).

9. Karen Mason, Monica Geist, and Mollie Clark, "A Developmental Model of Clergy Engagement with Suicide: A Qualitative Study," *OMEGA—Journal of Death and Dying* 79, no. 4 (2019), 347–63.

10. Karen Mason et al., "How Faith Communities Help Build Lives Worth Living" (poster session presented at the Annual Convention of the American Association of Suicidology, Portland, OR, April 25, 2020).

11. Matt Haig, *Reasons to Stay Alive* (Penguin Books, 2016). "If you hung in there, if you stuck it out, then things got better. They get better and then they get

worse and then they get better. Peaks and troughs, peaks and troughs" (p. 196). "Remember that the key thing about life on earth is change. Cars rust. Paper yellows, Technology dates. Caterpillars become butterflies. Nights morph into days. Depression lifts" (p. 242). See also, Jack Jordan and Bob Baugher, *After Suicide Loss: Coping with Your Grief* (Newcastle, WA: Caring People Press, 2002), 23, 26.

12. M. Gay Hubbard, *More than an Aspirin: a Christian Perspective on Pain and Suffering* (Grand Rapids: Discovery House, 2009), 278.

13. Karen Mason et al., "The Moral Deliberations of 15 Clergy on Suicide and Assisted Death: A Qualitative Study," *Pastoral Psychology* 66, no. 3 (2017): 335–51.

14. John F. Kilner, "The Bible, Ethics, and Health Care: Theological Foundations for a Christian Perspective on Health Care" (CACE, Wheaton College, 1992), www.wheaton.edu/media/migrated-images-amp-files/media/files/centers-and-institutes/cace/booklets/BibleEthicsHealthcare.pdf.

15. Kanita Dervic et al., "Religious Affiliation and Suicide Attempt," *The American Journal of Psychiatry* 161, no. 12 (2004): 2303–8. See also Ian Punnett, *How to Pray When You're Pissed at God: Or Anyone Else for That Matter* (New York: Harmony Books, 2013): "Although I have made many plans, I have never attempted suicide because I'm afraid that the suffering in this life will be worse in the next" (101).

16. James, "Is Life Worth Living?," 38.

17. Angela L. Duckworth and Martin E. P. Seligman, "Self-Discipline Outdoes IQ in Predicting Academic Performance of Adolescents," *Psychological Science* 16, no. 12 (2006): 939–44; Michael E. McCullough and Brian L. B. Willoughby, "Religion, Self-Regulation, and Self-Control: Associations, Explanations, and Implications," *Psychological Bulletin* 135, no. 1 (2009): 69–93; Walter Mischel, *The Marshmallow Test: Mastering Self-Control* (Boston: Little, Brown and Company, 2014). See also Mark J. Edlund et al., "Religiosity and Decreased Risk of Substance Use Disorders: Is the Effect Mediated by Social Support or Mental Health Status?" *Social Psychiatry and Psychiatric Epidemiology* 45, no. 9 (2010): 827–36. "Using a large, nationally representative community sample, we found a highly significant, negative relationship between religiosity and the presence of a substance use disorder in the past year. ... The mechanism(s) underlying this correlation remain poorly understood. ... We found little evidence for either our 'social support mediation' hypothesis or the 'mental health mediation' hypothesis [i.e., that 'the religious generally have better mental health']."

18. Daryl R. Van Tongeren, et al., "Self-Regulation Facilitates Meaning in Life," *Review of General Psychology* 22, no. 1. (2018), www.journals.sagepub.com/doi/full/10.1037/gpr0000121.

19. Mark Muraven and Roy F. Baumeister, "Self-Regulation and Depletion of Limited Resources: Does Self-Control Resemble a Muscle?" *Psychological Bulletin* 126, no. 2 (2000): 247–59; Cynthia Vieira Sanches Sampaio, Manuela

Garcia Lima, and Ana Marice Ladeia, "Meditation, Health and Scientific Investigations: Review of the Literature," *Journal of Religion and Health* 56, no. 2 (2017): 411–27.

20. Augustine, *Confessions*, 8.5, trans. Albert C. Outler, www.boap.org/LDS/Ancient-history-items/Early-Christian/Augustine/conbk08.txt.

21. David T. Neal, Wendy Wood, and Aimee Drolet, "How Do People Adhere to Goals When Willpower Is Low? The Profits (and Pitfalls) of Strong Habits," *Journal of Personality and Social Psychology* 104, no. 6 (2013): 959–75.

22. Karen Mason et al., "Unique Experiences in Religious Groups, in the U.S. and China—A Qualitative Study," *Journal of Mental Health, Religion and Culture* 21, no. 6 (2019): 609–24.

23. Peggy A. Thoits, "Mechanisms Linking Social Ties and Support to Physical and Mental Health," *Journal of Health and Social Behavior* 52 (2011): 145–61.

24. Ann Weems, *Psalms of Lament* (Westminster: John Knox Press, 1995).

25. Miroslav Volf, *Exclusion & Embrace: A Theological Exploration of Identity, Otherness, and Reconciliation* (Nashville: Abingdon, 1996), 124. Volf writes, "The main message of the imprecatory Psalms is this: rage belongs before God. … We place both our unjust enemy and our own vengeful self face to face with a God who loves and does justice."

26. Hubbard, *More Than an Aspirin*, 234. Hubbard writes, "It is a chosen community that reflects two basic facts. One: No one can do it alone. Two: Not everyone can help."

27. Ken Sande, *Peacemaker: A Biblical Guide to Resolving Personal Conflict* (Grand Rapids: Baker, 1997), 190.

28. We recommend Everett L. Worthington and Steven J. Sandage, *Forgiveness and Spirituality in Psychotherapy: A Relational Approach* (Washington, DC: American Psychological Association, 2015), as a good book about forgiveness.

29. Ravi Zacharias and Vince Vitale, *Why Suffering?: Finding Meaning and Comfort When Life Doesn't Make Sense* (New York: FaithWords, 2014), 51.

30. Mason et al., "Faith Communities."

31. Story shared by Robert Freedman, MD, when the Suicide Prevention Coalition of Colorado recognized his schizophrenia research as a vital contribution to suicide prevention.

32. Mark McMinn, *Sin and Grace in Christian Counseling* (Downers Grove, IL: IVP Academic, 2008), 154.

33. Rodney Stark, "Epidemics, Networks, and the Rise of Christianity," *Semeia* 56 (1991): 159–75.

34. Tertullian, *The Apology of Tertullian* 39, trans. and annotated by William Reeve (London: Griffith, Farran, Okeden & Welsh, 1709), 110, www.tertullian.org/articles/reeve_apology.htm.

35. Harold G. Koenig, Dana E. King, and Verna B. Carson, *Handbook of Religion and Health*, 2nd ed. (Oxford: Oxford University Press, 2012). "Medicine is taught in medical schools and as part of the education of the clergy" (p. 22). "The Knights Hospitallers … are monks who operate hospitals in Jerusalem

at the time of the crusades (1095–1291 AD)" (p. 23). "The Hotel Dieu in Paris expands in 1288 from twelve beds for the sick and the poor to over 1500 beds" (p. 24). "Aquinas writes about the importance of dreams and the workings of the unconscious (almost seven hundred years before Freud)" (p. 24). "The order of St. Francis (Franciscans) loses one hundred thousand priests to the plague, as they seek to minister to the sick" (p. 25).

36. Koenig, King, and Carson, *Handbook of Religion and Health*, 29.

37. Eric Metaxas, *Amazing Grace: William Wilberforce and the Heroic Campaign to End Slavery* (New York: Harper Collins, 2007), 71 and chapters 6–9.

38. Katharine Fry and Rachel Elizabeth Cresswell, eds., *Memoir of the Life of Elizabeth Fry: With Extracts from Her Journal and Letters*, vol. 1 (Philadelphia: H. Longstreth, 1847), 280–288, 401–403, 408–418, 428–432, 467–482, 493–496, 498–506. Samuel Marsden writes about the conditions of female convicts arriving in Australia: "The neglect of the female convicts in this country, is a disgrace to our national character, as well as a national sin" (p. 397). Elizabeth Fry writes, "No one knows what I go through in forming these institutions; it is always in fear, and mostly with many misgivings; wondering at myself for doing it. I believe the original motive is love to my Master, and love to my fellow-creatures; but fear is so predominant a feeling in my mind that it makes me suffer, perhaps unnecessarily, from doubts" (journal entry, p. 515).

39. Helen Mathers, "The Evangelical Spirituality of a Victorian Feminist: Josephine Baker, 1828–1906," *Journal of Ecclesiastical History* 52, no. 2 (2001): 282–312.

40. Belle Jane Allen and Caroline Atwater Mason, *A Crusade of Compassion for the Healing of the Nations: A Study of Medical Missions for Women and Children* (West Medford, MA: The Central Committee on the United Study of Foreign Missions, 1919), 16; see also Mary I. M. Causton, *For the Healing of the Nations: The Story of British Baptist Medical Missions, 1792–1951* (London: Kingsgate, 1951), 44–59.

41. Causton, *For the Healing of the Nations*, 169.

42. Jim T. Stout, *Bipolar Disorder: Rebuilding Your Life: A Bipolar's Story that Includes Practical Strategies, Techniques and Tips for Managing Moods* (Fort Bragg, CA: Cypress House, 2002).

CHAPTER 4

1. G. Lee Ramsey, Jr., *Care-full Preaching: From Sermon to Caring Community* (St. Louis: Chalice, 2000), 61.

2. Edgar N. Jackson, *A Psychology for Preaching* (Great Neck: Channel, 1961), 20.

3. Jackson, *A Psychology for Preaching*, 22.

4. See Scott M. Gibson, *Preaching with a Plan: Sermon Strategies for Growing Mature Believers* (Grand Rapids: Baker, 2012). This book offers pastors a

way to plan sermons that move listeners to spiritual maturity. Through the exercises, one is able to determine the spiritual maturity of one's congregation in order to plan preaching. These exercises are best done in cooperation with the leadership of the church.

5. Paul Tautges, *Comfort the Grieving: Ministering God's Grace in Times of Loss* (Grand Rapids: Zondervan, 2014), 21.

6. Arthur L. Teikmanis, *Preaching and Pastoral Care* (Englewood Cliffs, NJ: Prentice-
    Hall, 1964), 19.

7. Haddon W. Robinson, "Blending Bible Content and Life Application," in *Making a Difference in Preaching*, ed. Scott M. Gibson (Grand Rapids: Baker, 1999), 94.

8. Teikmanis, *Preaching and Pastoral Care*, 21.

9. Rick McKinniss, "Preparing the Congregation for Death," in Eugene Peterson, Calvin Miller, and others, *Wedding, Funerals and Special Events: The Personal Ministry of Public Occasions*, Leadership Library (Waco: Word, 1987), 73.

10. James T. Clemons, ed., *Sermons on Suicide* (Louisville: Westminster/John Knox, 1989), 8.

11. Clemons, *Sermons on Suicide*.

12. Zack Eswine, *Spurgeon's Sorrows: Realistic Hope for Those Who Suffer from Depression* (Fearn, Ross-shire: Christian Focus, 2014), 124.

13. Jackson, *A Psychology for Preaching*, 62.

14. Quoted in Jackson, *A Psychology*, 76.

15. Brian Croft, *Visit the Sick: Ministering God's Grace in Times of Illness* (Grand Rapids: Zondervan, 2014), 55.

16. Tauteges, *Comfort the Grieving*, 21.

17. Teikmanis, *Preaching and Pastoral Care*, 22.

18. Lee Eclov, *Pastoral Graces: Reflections on the Care of Souls* (Chicago: Moody, 2012), 42.

19. Jerry Bridges, *Discipline of Grace*, 46.

20. Eswine, *Spurgeon's Sorrows*, 125.

21. Roland Leavell, *Prophetic Preaching: Then and Now* (Grand Rapids: Baker, 1963), 69.

22. Leavell, *Prophetic Preaching*, 71–72.

23. Milton Vincent, *A Gospel Primer for Christians* (Bemidji, MN: Focus, 2008), 45, 47.

24. Vincent, *Gospel Primer*, 44.

25. Eclov, *Pastoral Graces*, 152.

26. Leavell, *Prophetic Preaching*, 74.

27. Brian Croft and Phil Newton, *Conduct Gospel-Centered Funerals: Applying the Gospel at the Unique Challenges of Death* (Grand Rapids: Zondervan, 2014), 13.

28. Vincent, *Gospel Primer*, 43.

29. Albert Y. Hsu, *Grieving a Suicide: A Loved One's Search for Comfort, Answers & Hope* (Downers Grove: InterVarsity, 2002), 70.

30. Jackson, *A Psychology for Preaching*, 84, 85.

31. Jackson, *A Psychology for Preaching*, 86.

32. Marty Thurber, "Suicide Affects Us All," *Ministry* 77.9 (September 2005): 10–11.

33. Jackson, *A Psychology for Preaching*, 171–72.

34. Eclov, *Pastoral Graces*, 162–63.

CHAPTER 5

1. See Glenn Stanton, "FactChecker: Misquoting Francis of Assisi," *The Gospel Coalition* (July 10, 2012), www.thegospelcoalition.org/article/factchecker-misquoting-francis-of-assisi.

2. Karen Mason, Monica Geist, and Mollie Clark, "A Developmental Model of Clergy Engagement with Suicide: A Qualitative Study," *OMEGA—Journal of Death and Dying* 79, no. 4 (2019): 347–63.

3. Mason, Geist, and Clark, "Developmental Model," 352.

4. Karen Mason et al., "The Moral Deliberations of 15 Clergy on Suicide and Assisted Death: A Qualitative Study," *Pastoral Psychology* 66, no. 3 (2017): 342.

5. Karen Mason et al., "Clergy Referral of Suicidal Individuals: A Qualitative Study," *Journal of Pastoral Care & Counseling* 65, no. 3 (2011). This is an unpublished quote from participant 5.

6. Mason et al., "Clergy Referral of Suicidal Individuals," 5.

7. Mason et al., "Clergy Referral of Suicidal Individuals," 5.

8. Karen Mason et al., "Predictors of Clergy's Ability to Fulfill a Suicide Prevention Gatekeeper Role," *Journal of Pastoral Care and Counseling* 70, no. 1 (2016): 34–39.

9. Mason, Kim, Martin, and Gober, "Moral Deliberations," 341.

10. Mason, Kim, Martin, and Gober, "Moral Deliberations," 341.

11. Mason, Kim, Martin, and Gober, "Moral Deliberations," 341.

12. Mason, Kim, Martin, and Gober, "Moral Deliberations," 340.

13. Mason et al., "Clergy Referral of Suicidal Individuals," 6.

14. Mason, Geist, and Clark, "Developmental Model," 353.

15. Mason et al., "The Moral Deliberations of 15 Clergy," 339.

16. R. Neal Davis et al., "Depressive Symptoms in Nonresident African American Fathers and Involvement with Their Sons," *Pediatrics* 124, no. 6 (2009): 1611–18; Peter Kane and Judy Garber, "The Relations Among Depression in Fathers, Children's Psychopathology, and Father-Child Conflict: A Meta-Analysis," *Clinical Psychology Review* 24, no. 3 (2004): 339–60; Peter Kane and Judy Garber, "Parental Depression and Child Externalizing and Internalizing Symptoms: Unique Effects of Fathers' Symptoms and Perceived Conflict as a Mediator," *Journal of Child And Family Studies* 18, no. 4 (2009): 465–72.

17. Learn more at www.stephenministries.org.

18. Thomas Joiner, *Lonely at the Top: The High Cost of Men's Success* (New York: Palgrave MacMillan, 2011).

19. Mason et al. "Clergy Referral of Suicidal Individuals," 4.

20. Mason et al. "Clergy Referral of Suicidal Individuals," 5.

21. Mason et al. "Clergy Referral of Suicidal Individuals," 6.

22. Mason, Geist, and Clark, "A Developmental Model, " 353.

23. Mason et al., "Clergy Referral of Suicidal Individuals," 6.

24. Glen Milstein et al., "Implementation of a Program to Improve the Continuity of Mental Health Care through Clergy Outreach and Professional Engagement (C.O.P.E.)," *Professional Psychology: Research and Practice* 39, no. 2 (2008): 218–28.

25. *Nally v. Grace Community Church*, 47 Cal. 3d 286, (Supreme Court of California, 1988). See regarding the wrongful death action brought against Grace Community Church of the Valley when pastors did not inform the hospital staff of their congregant's continued death wish. The California Supreme Court ruled in favor of the church in 1988.

26. Mason et al., "Moral Deliberations," 339.

27. Mason et al., "Moral Deliberations," 342.

28. Mason et al., "Moral Deliberations," 339.

29. Mason et al., "Moral Deliberations," 339.

30. Learn more at www.lifelineforattemptsurvivors.org/?_ga=2.112148100 .1852982159.1581950490-405761750.1577740005.

31. Learn more at www.afsp.org/find-support/voices-of-hope.

32. Learn more at www.suicidology.org/suicide-survivors/ suicide-attempt-survivors.

33. Learn more at www.beyondblue.org.au/the-facts/suicide-prevention/ recovery-and-support-strategies/support-after-a-suicide-attempt.

34. Unpublished interview with a family member following a suicide attempt.

35. See www.store.samhsa.gov/product/A-Guide-for-Taking-Care-of-Your-Family-Member-After-Treatment-in-the-Emergency-Department/sma18-4357eng, and www.resources.beyondblue.org.au/prism/file?token=BL/1161.

36. Elizabeth Stone and Erin Stone, *Valley of the Shadow* (Nashville: WestBow Press, 2014).

37. Jack Jordan and Bob Baugher, *After Suicide Loss: Coping with Your Grief* (Newcastle, WA: Caring People Press, 2016), 83.

38. Mason et al., "Clergy Referral of Suicidal Individuals," 5.

39. This and other quotes of anonymous pastors throughout this chapter come from unpublished interviews with five pastors about their experiences after a suicide in their faith community. The interviews were conducted by Karen Mason and Heather Thornburg.

40. Mason, Geist, and Clark, "Developmental Model," 354.

41. Learn more at www.afsp.org/find-support/ive-lost-someone/practical-information-for-immediately-after-a-loss.

42. Learn more at www.sprc.org/states.

43. Jordan and Baugher, *After Suicide Loss*, 61–62.

44. Mason, Geist, and Clark, "Developmental Model," 354.

45. Mason, Geist, and Clark, "Developmental Model," 354.

46. Jordan and Baugher, *After Suicide Loss*, 75.

47. Jordan and Baugher, *After Suicide Loss*, 8.

48. Jordan and Baugher, *After Suicide Loss*, 67. For a list of support groups, go to www.afsp.org/find-support/ive-lost-someone/find-a-support-group (afsp. org) or call your local United Way 211 number. Jordan and Baugher suggest attending the group two or three times before deciding to stop going.

49. Jordan and Baugher, *After Suicide Loss*, 72–73.

50. Jordan and Baugher, *After Suicide Loss*, 73.

51. Jordan and Baugher, *After Suicide Loss*, 11.

52. All quotes in this paragraph are from interviews of survivors for this book.

53. Biebel and Foster note, "Within two years of a suicide, at least 80 percent of survivors will either leave the church they were attending and join another or stop attending church altogether. The two most common reasons for this are (1) disappointment due to unmet expectations and (2) criticism or judgmental attitudes and treatment." David B. Biebel and Suzanne L. Foster, *Finding Your Way after the Suicide of Someone You Love* (Grand Rapids: Zondervan, 2005), 169.

54. Jordan and Baugher, *After Suicide Loss*, 76.

55. Jordan and Baugher, *After Suicide Loss*, 76.

56. Jordan and Baugher, *After Suicide Loss*, 86.

57. Jordan and Baugher, *After Suicide Loss*, 65–66.

58. Jordan and Baugher, *After Suicide Loss*, 86.

59. Jordan and Baugher, *After Suicide Loss*, 21.

60. Mason, Geist, and Clark, "Developmental Model, " 354.

61. Learn more at www.soulshopmovement.org.

CHAPTER 6

1. Melinda Moore, "Preface," in Melinda Moore and Daniel A. Roberts, eds., *The Suicide Funeral (or Memorial Service): Honoring Their Memory, Comforting Their Survivors* (Eugene, OR: Resource, 2017), xxv–xxvi.

2. Frederick Buechner, *Telling Secrets: A Memoir* (New York: HarperCollins, 1991), 7.

3. Buechner, *Telling Secrets*, 7–8.

4. For the development of the central idea for funeral sermons, see Scott M. Gibson, *Preaching for Special Services* (Grand Rapids: Baker, 2001).

5. Andrew Watterson Blackwood, *The Funeral: A Source Book for Ministers* (Philadelphia: Westminster, 1942), 189.

6. Karen Mason et al., "Clergy Referral of Suicidal Individuals: A Qualitative Study," *Journal of Pastoral Care & Counseling* 65, no. 3 (2011): 6.

7.   William R. Baird, Sr., and John E. Baird, *Funeral Meditations* (Nashville: Abingdon, 1966), 9.

8.   Brian Croft and Phil Newton, *Conduct Gospel-Centered Funerals: Applying the Gospel at the Unique Challenges of Death* (Grand Rapids: Zondervan, 2014), 67.

9.   See Blackwood, *The Funeral*, 190.

10. Emily Askew and O. Wesley Allen, *Beyond Heterosexism in the Pulpit* (Eugene, OR: Cascade, 2015), 129.

11. This and other quotes of anonymous pastors throughout this chapter come from unpublished interviews with five pastors about their experiences after a suicide in their faith community. The interviews were conducted by Karen Mason and Heather Thornburg.

12. Bryan Chapell, ed., *The Hardest Sermons You'll Ever Have to Preach* (Grand Rapids: Zondervan, 2011), 229.

13. In addition, furthering one's education in suicide prevention will be of immense help in any future pastoral ministry. Resources are listed in appendix C to aid readers in continued instruction in suicide prevention and post suicide care.

14. Paul E. Engle, ed., *The Baker Funeral Handbook* (Grand Rapids: Baker Books, 2017).

15. A surprising and disappointing aspect of the research was the lack of response from several funeral directors contacted to participate in the study. Whether they were too busy or not interested, their contribution to the project is missed.

16. Douglas D. Webster, *Soulcraft: How God Shapes Us Through Relationships* (Downers Grove: InterVarsity, 1999), 215.

17. Roger F. Miller, "Handling the Hard Cases," in Eugene Peterson and Calvin Miller, eds., *Wedding, Funerals and Special Events: The Personal Ministry of Public Occasions*, Leadership Library (Waco: Word, 1987), 131.

18. See Thomas G. Long, *Accompany Them with Singing—The Christian Funeral* (Louisville: Westminster John Knox, 2009), 200.

19. Karen Mason, Monica Geist, and Mollie Clark, "A Developmental Model of Clergy Engagement with Suicide: A Qualitative Study," *OMEGA—Journal of Death and Dying* 79, no. 4 (2019), 347–63.

20. Michael Rogness, "Preaching at the 'Tough' Funerals," *Word & World* 34, no. 1 (Winter 2014): 56.

21. Paul Tautges, *Comfort the Grieving: Ministering God's Grace in Times of Loss* (Grand Rapids: Zondervan, 2014), 15.

22. Mary S. Hulst, *A Little Handbook for Preachers: Ten Practical Ways to a Better Sermon by Sunday* (Downers Grove, IL: InterVarsity Press, 2016), 101–2.

23. Tautges, *Comfort the Grieving*, 60.

24. Larry Peterson, "Spirituality: 'A Month's Mind Mass': Honoring the Departed a Month Later," *Aleteia* (April 27, 2017), www.aleteia.org/2017/04/27/ever-heard-of-a-months-mind-mass-its-making-a-comeback-and-well-it-should.

25. Gerry Moloney and George Wadding, "Celebrating a Life through Liturgy," CatholicIreland.net (November 30, 1999), www.catholicireland.net/ celebrating-a-life-through-liturgy. See Appendix F for a sample suicide funeral liturgy.

26. Andrew J. Weaver and John D. Preston, "The Suicide of a Teenager: A Pastoral Response," *Ministry* 77, no. 9 (September 2005): 8–9.

27. Brian Croft, *Visit the Sick: Ministering God's Grace in Times of Illness* (Grand Rapids: Zondervan, 2014), 56.

28. Croft, *Visit the Sick*, 29.

29. Miller, "Handling the Hard Cases," 125.

CHAPTER 7

1. Sophie Bethune, "Gen Z More Likely to Report Mental Health Concerns: The Latest APA Stress in America Survey Focuses on the Concerns of Americans Ages 15 to 21," *Monitor on Psychology*, vol. 50, no. 1 (January 2019): 20.

2. *Suicide: Facts at a Glance* (2015), accessed April 29, 2020, www.cdc.gov/ violenceprevention/pdf/suicide-datasheet-a.pdf.

3. Centers for Disease Control and Prevention, "National Center for Injury Prevention and Control," Web-based Injury Statistics Query and Reporting System (WISQARS), www.cdc.gov/injury/wisqars.

4. Karen Mason et al., "How Faith Communities Help Build Lives Worth Living" (poster session presented at the Annual Convention of the American Association of Suicidology, Portland, OR, April 25, 2020).

5. James T. Clemons, *Sermons on Suicide* (Louisville: Westminster John Knox, 1989), 8.

6. Get Schooled Tour, "2018/2019 Polling Data," www.getschooledtour. com/2018-2019data/, accessed March 30, 2020.

7. Personal conversation, November 11, 2019.

8. Unpublished quotes from research conducted for Mason et al., "Faith Communities."

9. Unpublished quotes from research conducted for Mason et al., "Faith Communities."

10. Karen Mason, Esther Kim, and W. Blake Martin, "Clergy Use of Suicide Prevention Competencies," *OMEGA—Journal of Death and Dying* (2018), doi. org/10.1177/0030222818777373.

11. Gould et al., "Youth Suicide Risk and Preventive Interventions: A Review of the Past 10 Years," *Journal of the American Academy of Child and Adolescent Psychiatry* 42, no. 4 (2003): 386–405.

12. Visit QPR Institute (www.qprinstitute.com); LivingWorks (www.livingworks. net); the Connect Program (www.theconnectprogram.org); be nice (www. benice.org); and many others listed at "Comparison Table of Suicide

Prevention Gatekeeper Training Programs," SPRC, www.sprc.org/sites/default/files/migrate/library/SPRC_Gatekeeper_matrix_Jul2013update.pdf.

13. Unpublished quote from research conducted for Mason et al., "Faith Communities."

14. You can also get help at their website, www.suicidepreventionlifeline.org.

15. People with this type of health coverage can use www.parityregistry.org to register denials for mental health services. See the Paul Wellstone and Pete Domenici Mental Health Parity and Addiction Equity Act of 2008 at www.cms.gov/CCIIO/Programs-and-Initiatives/Other-Insurance-Protections/mhpaea_factsheet.

16. Unpublished quote from research conducted for Mason et al., "Faith Communities."

17. New Freedom Commission on Mental Health, "Achieving the Promise: Transforming Mental Health Care in America," DHHS pub no SMA-03-3832 (Rockville MD: Department of Health and Human Services, 2003), available at www.sprc.org/resources-programs/achieving-promise-transforming-mental-health-care-america.

18. Karen Mason et al., "Clergy Referral of Suicidal Individuals: A Qualitative Study," *Journal of Pastoral Care & Counseling* 65, no. 3 (2011): 6.

19. Learn more at www.bewelloc.org.

20. Mason et al., "Faith Communities."

21. Karen Mason et al., "Predictors of Clergy's Ability to Fulfill a Suicide Prevention Gatekeeper Role," *Journal of Pastoral Care and Counseling* 70, no. 1 (2016): 34–39.

22. P. Wang, P. Berglund, and R. Kessler, "Patterns and Correlates of Contacting Clergy for Mental Disorders in the United States," *Health Services Research* 38, no. 2 (2003): 647–73.

23. Unpublished quote from research conducted for Mason et al., "Faith Communities."

24. Learn more at www.mentalhealthgateway.org.

25. Learn more at www.remedylive.com and www.soulshopmovement.org.

26. Learn more at www.getschooledtour.com and www.remedylive.com/trendsandteens.

APPENDIX A

1. C. Hassell Bullock, *Psalms: Volume 1: Psalms 1–72* (Grand Rapids: Baker, 2015), 88.

2. Bullock, *Psalms*, 91.

3. Bullock, *Psalms*, 91.

4. Scripture quotations in this sermon are from the New Living Translation.

APPENDIX B

1. The confession and God's absolution of sin is from *The Book Of Common Prayer and Administration of the Sacraments and Other Rites and Ceremonies of the Church: Together with the Psalter or Psalms of David According to the Use of the Episcopal Church* (New York: Seabury Press, 1979) 352–53.
2. Adapted from *Book of Common Prayer*, 337.

APPENDIX C

1. J. Jordan and B. Baugher, *After Suicide Loss: Coping with Your Grief*, 2nd ed. (Newcastle, WA: Caring People Press, 2016).

APPENDIX D

1. Based on Florence Chiu and Chelsea Reed's protocols (in author's possession), 2015.

APPENDIX E

1. All names have been changed.
2. Scripture quotations in this sermon are from the New International Version.

APPENDIX F

1. Episcopal Church, *The Book of Common Prayer and Administration of the Sacraments and other Rites and Ceremonies of the Church: Together with the Psalter or Psalms of David According to the use of the Episcopal Church* (New York: Seabury Press, 1979), 493.
2. *Book of Common Prayer*, 494.
3. *Book of Common Prayer*, 352–53.
4. *Book of Common Prayer*, 360.
5. Adapted from *Book of Common Prayer*, 337.
6. *Book of Common Prayer*, 499.

APPENDIX G

1. Centers for Disease Control and Prevention, "National Center for Injury Prevention and Control," Web-based Injury Statistics Query and Reporting System (WISQARS), cdc.gov/injury/wisqars. The most current facts and statistics can be found at https://suicidology.org/facts-and-statistics.

APPENDIX H

1. For example, http://snorpey.github.io/contrast-distort.

2. This structure draws on Walter Brueggemann, *An Unsettling God: The Heart of the Hebrew Bible* (Minneapolis: Fortress, 2009), 13.

3. A sermon on Psalm 13 is included in Appendix A and can be used as an explanation of lament psalms.

4. Taken from Ian Punnett, *How to Pray When You're Pissed at God: Or Anyone Else for That Matter* (New York: Harmony Books, 2013), 71–73.

5. Punnett, *How to Pray*, 76–77.

6. Edward B. Rogers, Matthew Stanford, and Diana R. Garland, "The Effects of Mental Illness on Families within Faith Communities," *Mental Health, Religion & Culture* 15, no. 3 (2012): 301–13.

7. Philip Yancey and Paul Brand, *In His Image* (Grand Rapids: Zondervan, 1997); Daniel J. Price, *Karl Barth's Anthropology in Light of Modern Thought* (Grand Rapids: Eerdmans, 2002).

8. John F. Kilner, *Dignity and Destiny: Humanity in the Image of God* (Grand Rapids: Eerdmans, 2015), 100.

9. Kilner, *Dignity and Destiny*, 123.

10. William James, "Is Life Worth Living?" in *The Principles of Psychology* (London: Macmillan & Co., 1890), 61.

11. Albert Y. Hsu, *Grieving a Suicide: A Loved One's Search for Comfort, Answers and Hope* (Downers Grove, IL: InterVarsity Press, 2017), 173.

12. Dietrich Bonhoeffer, *Ethics*, ed. Eberhard Bethge (New York: MacMillan, 1962).

13. Droge and Tabor point this out in Arthur J. Droge and James D. Tabor, *A Noble Death: Suicide & Martyrdom Among Christians and Jews in Antiquity* (San Francisco: HarperCollins, 1992), 175.

14. Calvin discussed suicide in his sermons on Saul and his armor bearer as well as on Ahithophel. Jeffrey R. Watt, *Choosing Death: Suicide and Calvinism in Early Modern Geneva* (Kirksville, MO: Truman State University Press, 2001), 67–68.

15. Bonhoeffer, *Ethics*, 123.

16. Bonhoeffer, *Ethics*, 124.

17. Walter Brueggemann, *An Unsettling God: The Heart of the Hebrew Bible* (Minneapolis: Fortress, 2009), 13.

18. Ian Punnett, *How to Pray When You're Pissed at God: Or Anyone Else for That Matter* (New York: Harmony Books, 2013), 71–73.

19. Punnett, *How to Pray*, 74–75.